Grasping Land

SUNY Series in Anthropology and Judaic Studies
Edited by Walter P. Zenner

Grasping Land

*Space and Place
in Contemporary Israeli
Discourse and Experience*

Edited by
Eyal Ben-Ari
and
Yoram Bilu

STATE UNIVERSITY OF NEW YORK PRESS

Published by
State University of New York Press, Albany

©1997 State University of New York

For information, address State University of New York Press,
State University Plaza, Albany, N.Y., 12246

Chapter 4, "Saints' Sanctuaries in Israeli Development Towns" by Eyal Ben-Ari
and Yoram Bilu was previously published in *Urban Anthropology and Studies on
Cultural Systems and World Economic Development* 16(2). Copyright ©1987.
Permission to reprint was generously granted by UAS. Chapter 7, "Re-Making
Place" by Tamar Katriel was previously published in *History and Memory* 5(2)
Copyright ©1993. Permission to reprint was generously granted by Indiana
University Press.

Production by Cathleen Collins
Marketing by Dana Yanulavich

Library of Congress Cataloging in Publication Data

Grasping land : space and place in contemporary Israeli discourse and
     experience / edited by Eyal Ben-Ari and Yoram Bilu.
          p.   cm. — (SUNY series in anthropology and Judaic studies)
     Includes bibliographical references and index.
     ISBN 0-7914-3217-3 (alk. paper). — ISBN 0-7914-3218-1 (pbk. :
alk. paper)
     1. National characteristics, Israeli.   2. Jewish shrines—Israel.
3. Sacred space—Israel.   4. Land use—Israel.   5. Zionism.   I. Ben-
Ari, Eyal, 1953–   II. Bilu, Yoram.   III. Series.
DS113.3.G73   1997
304.2'3'095694—dc20   96-15390
                                                              CIP

10 9 8 7 6 5 4 3 2 1

*This volume is dedicated to the memory
of Lea Shamgar-Handelman*

Contents

vii

Introduction

EYAL BEN-ARI AND YORAM BILU

The Jews as a people, are defined by their religion which is distinctive among the world religions in its territorial focus on *Eretz Yisrael* the [promised] Land of Israel. Yet the people themselves . . . have been de-territorialized through the millennia. Now that they have restored themselves to the primordial territory (or part of it), the question arises: how are they to behave *there?* (Paine 1989:123).

PLACE AND PROBLEMATICS

The chapters in this volume represent attempts to examine processes associated with constructing what has variously been called "The Holy Land," "*Eretz Israel,*" "Zion," "Palestine," or "Israel." More specifically, this book focuses on the ways in which the landscapes of Israel figure in creating and re-creating the identity, presence, and history of groups living there. By landscapes we mean the systems of socially constructed spaces "superimposed" upon and, in effect, constituting the "land" (Jackson 1984:8). Why the focus on space and place, on land and locations? A brief history of our own intellectual interests may explicate the reasons for choosing this theme of inquiry, and set out the implications of the book as a whole and of each contribution found within it.

Our own preoccupation with Israeli spaces and places developed out of a confluence of intellectual and personal interests. Upon completing a Ph.D. thesis on Japanese white-collar communities (written in England), Ben-Ari returned to Israel and felt a need to join his research interests with a commitment to studying 'things Israeli.' One outcome of this commitment has been an ongoing project on social and cultural aspects of the Israeli army (Ben-Ari 1989; Feige and Ben-Ari 1991). Bilu, for his part, had since the beginning of his academic career dealt with aspects of Israeli society, specifically with the folk psychology of healing among Israelis of North African origin (Bilu 1986; Bilu and Abramovich 1985). But he, too, sensed the need to deal with some of the wider issues implied by this work. As a consequence we decided to undertake a joint project on the southern development town of Netivot, which we discuss in more detail below. Soon we began teaching a joint research seminar on the "Sanctification of Space in Israel," and to establish contacts with other scholars who seemed to have intellectual interests similar to or bordering on ours. Later we organized two panels at one of the annual meetings of the Israel Anthropological Association on the same subject. Indeed, we were often as surprised at the intense curiosity people showed in our project, as we were at the large number of scholars—based in such fields as sociology, political science, history, literature, folklore, or Jewish thought—who were dealing with space and place in Israel.

Between 1986 and 1989 we carried out fieldwork in Netivot: the gravesite of a renowned Jewish Moroccan rabbi called Rabbi Israel Abu-Hatzeira (diminutive—Baba Sali), which is a major center of activity for the thriving cults of saint worship among North African Jews in Israel (Ben-Ami 1984; Weingrod 1990). Our initial aims were to document and analyze the development of this holy site and to compare it to the rise of similar places in Israel (Bilu and Ben-Ari, 1992; Ben-Ari and Bilu, chap. 3 of this volume). Yet, as we carried out fieldwork, we gradually became aware of a phenomenon we had only been dimly conscious of before. People, and at times the same people, talked about Netivot and what they associated with it in different, often contrasting voices. For instance, we often found that people would speak about the town in "traditional" North African terms as the locus of a saint's tomb bearing special powers, while at other times they would characterize it as being the heart of "superstitionland," a setting for "primitive" beliefs and practices. Other informants discussed Netivot in terms of the sacred geography of holy places in *Eretz Israel* (the Land of Israel), while at the same time evoking images of the development town as the product of the Zionist initiative of developing and settling Israel's southern desert.

While such representations are obviously related to how the "reputational content" (Suttles 1984) of Netivot is promoted or besmirched, their import seems to go beyond the local. We found that people inside and outside the town used Netivot or the sacred site as mediums for talking about or evoking images of themselves and Israel. Through discussing this specific place, and its attendant qualities, people were constantly advancing or denigrating certain visions of what Israel is like and what it should be like. To give two examples, the characterization of the town as the "Bnei Berak of the Negev" (Bnei Berak being a city heavily populated by ultrareligious Jews) or of the gravesite as the "Southern Wailing Wall" is a vehicle for simultaneously commenting about growing religiosity in Israel, about a greater respect for religious pluralism (at least in its 'ethnic' guise), about a positive valuation of these trends, and about Netivot being an exemplar of this whole process.

Our increased awareness of these points led to more general questions: Are discussions about and criticisms of Israel through talk about land and locations not a pervasive quality of Israeli society? Could a focus on discourses of space and place provide fruitful entry points for analyses of wider cultural processes unfolding in this country? During the initial stages of our project we attempted to answer these questions by drawing upon the vast literature written about Judaism, the Israeli-Arab conflict, and especially Zionism. Here, however, we increasingly found that what was needed was a kind of "defamiliarization" with some of the assumptions and analytical approaches at the base of these works.

According to much of this 'received' intellectual wisdom, the centrality of land and of place is part and parcel of the "traditional"—or what is perceived by many Zionists to be the pre-Zionist—Jewish ethos. The best-known examples brought to confirm this view are the plethora of prayers that emphasize the close connection between the "people of Israel" and the "Land of Israel." Yet this linkage is also said to be evident in the preeminence of people and places in such sources of Jewish thought as the Bible, the Talmud (commentaries and codes of law), fables and popular lore, the Midrash (exegeses of the Scriptures), and the Kabbalah (the mystical tradition in Judaism), as well as works of poetry, philosophy, and interpretation of the Middle Ages (Schweid 1979). Within these sources, it is argued, *Eretz Israel* (the Land of Israel) has repeatedly figured as a place to long for, to make pilgrimage to, or to die and be buried in.

The preoccupation with space has also taken pride of place in portrayals of the Israeli-Arab and Israeli-Palestinian conflicts. These struggles have very often been depicted as competition over places, locations, and land. Thus, not surprisingly, most analyses carried out by political scientists, political sociologists, or experts in international relations have focused on issues of resources and territoriality. A good example is Kimmerling's important work (1982, 1983), which highlights the variety of patterns of control over territory. Within Israel this approach (heavily clothed in neo-Marxist jargon) has been at the heart of Hasson's efforts (1981) to map and analyze how spatial inequalities are related to disparities of political, social, and economic resources.

Capping and reinforcing these diverse emphases has been a very wide scholarly consensus about the pivotal role of the land in Zionism (Schweid 1979). To summarize somewhat crudely, one central role of Zionism has been establishing a national homeland—a Jewish state with all of its territorial and political qualities—for the Jewish people. Yet as we continued our readings we found that the way in which this 'role' has been discussed in more recent studies seemed to offer a more complex, critical approach to the questions we had formulated. As Liebman and Don-Yehiya (1983:3–4) put it:

> The primacy Zionist-socialism gave to agricultural labor stemmed from the bond between man and nature and the redemption of the nation and its homeland, which found their most forceful symbolization in *working the land*. This was the antithesis of the "exilic" way of life. The return to nature was appropriate to a people returning to its own land. . . . A recurrent metaphor in the Zionist-socialist literature was the plant that returns to the soil of the homeland, strikes roots and blossoms anew.

What we found interesting in Liebman and Don-Yehiya's work were their insights into the essentially metaphorical nature and the fundamentally contested quality of various discourses about land. Realizing this point, we continued to ask ourselves whether a change of theoretical focus was not called for. Should we not begin by questioning the very assumption of the centrality of land and place in various Jewish and Jewish Israeli discourses? Could we not benefit from an approach that problematizes the manner by which such concepts as site and space, or "Israel" and the "Holy Land" are used for a variety of ends?

Recently a number of studies have attempted to provide a sustained answer to these questions. Let us briefly cite three such instances, two by other scholars and the third our own. The first example is the work carried out by Katriel and Shenhar (1991) on the discourse of "Tower and Stockade" (*Homa U-Migdal*). As they show, Israel, like many newly established nation-states, has been the site of ongoing efforts to invent and legitimate "new" traditions; that is, sets of cultural forms and practices that provide, inter alia, storified versions of past events that stand as models for collective action (Katriel and Shenhar 1991:376; see also Shamgar-Handelman and Handelman 1986). In this respect, acts of settlement, including but not exclusively those of the "Tower and Stockade" variety, and the rhetoric of place attending them, have been at the heart of Israel's nation-building ethos. As Katriel and Shenhar show, within the parameters of this kind of discourse cultural members portray—and in this way come to regard—themselves as participating in the making of history. Such specific acts as establishing a new kibbutz or a development town are characterized as part of a collective effort to "fix" a link to the land. In this way the rhetoric of place and the rhetoric of action become so intimately intertwined in the discourse of Zionism that "establishing settlements" and "being active agents" come to mean the same thing (Katriel and Shenhar 1991). Indeed, we would further argue that this is as true of the early Zionists (Cohen 1977) as it is of such contemporaries as *Gush Emunim* (Aran 1991), Jerusalem's Teddy Kollek, and (in a curious way) Baba Baruch (Baba Sali's heir) in Netivot. In all these cases the emphasis is on "making" or "creating" Israel on two analytically distinct levels: through transforming the country's actual landscape—by building, assembling, and creating "facts"—and through actualizing one of the Israeli Jewish culture's "key scenarios" (Ortner 1973; Katriel and Shenhar 1991:376).

Our second example is the work carried out by Hannan Hever (1987, 1989), who has dealt with the cultural and political implications of literary work produced in Hebrew by Israeli Arabs such as Anton Shammas. Included in a range of examples that Hever provides is a fascinating story by Emile Habibi about street and place-names in Haifa (a city in the north of Israel that was until 1948 heavily populated by Arabs). The power of the story lies in making "us" (Israeli Jews) question the taken-for-granted geographical appellations that are part of our "common" public knowledge (for example, we refer not to Halsa but to Kiriyat Shemona [a development town], not to Malcha but to Manachat [a Jerusalem neighborhood], and no longer to the Masmiya intersection [of highways] but to the Mesubin intersection). Habibi does this through juxtaposing the 'new' Hebrew and the 'old' Arab names. But because this is done by someone who lives among us— in Israel and at the present time—and in a book written in our language and published by one of our leading publishing houses, the effect is jarring.

By sharpening our awareness of the uneasiness that such works evoke in many Israeli Jews, and especially among members of Israel's literary establishment, Hever has shown how these works of prose and poetry question political assumptions underlying Israeli public discourse: the view of Hebrew literature as a Jewish national literature, and through that the unstated assumption about the link between language and territory (Hever 1987:73). Arabs writing in Hebrew—and critics like Hever—can be seen as contributing to a process of linguistic deterritorialization. They challenge the assumed coincidence of the Hebrew language, its Jewish subject matter, and its "natural" location within the geopolitical boundaries of Israel.

The third instance we would like to cite relates to the way place has found new ways of expression within the past decade or so. Since the late 1970s Israel has witnessed a renaissance of gatherings for *shira-betzibur* (sing-alongs). At these assemblies, which are held throughout the country, well-known songs out of a core body of a few hundred pieces are sung to the accompaniment of small bands or accordion or piano players. Many of these occasions are broadcast on Israeli radio and television. Shokeid (1988:104) discusses his reactions to these programs (in a book devoted ironically to *yordim*, Israelis who have left Israel only to dote upon those very things they have left). He notes something that may be characteristic of many Israeli

Jews in general. For him, the programs evoked a "nostalgia for a different Israel than that of my own urban upbringing. It was Israel as depicted on posters, untainted by the harsh realities of mounting economic, political, and social problems." What is significant for us in this context is that these programs are almost always broadcast from kibbutzim or from studios that have been arranged to represent rural scenery, to represent agricultural settlements. This is mirrored in the contents and origins of the songs, most of which were written during, and depict, the period when the Israeli ethos of pioneering was most closely associated with rural settlements.

Within this kind of depiction, we would argue, rural localities are seen as a sort of repository of the past, of ideals and of "tradition." The portrayal of past or peripheral places thus serves to remind many Israelis of how things used to be and of how they should be. This Israeli nostalgia 'boom,' however, clouds the relationship between the local and the national (see Kelly 1986). It places sing-alongs within particular or specific localities but then decontextualizes them in the service of more general emphases on how folk songs represent notions of the Israeli people. To put this somewhat coarsely, for television viewers or radio listeners it matters less that the program takes place in specific places like Beit Alpha, Yagur, or Negba (all kibbutzim) than that these places represent a more generalized notion of what kind of place a kibbutz is.

RUPTURED CULTURES

By raising such issues, this volume extends and develops recent social scientific inquiries into notions of space and place. Recent studies in anthropology and related disciplines well underline the contested—essentially labile and political—nature of spatial identities (Cohen 1986; McDonogh 1991; Bendix 1992). According to this set of approaches, such identities are no longer conceptualized as a given but rather as an assortment of typifications and images that are constantly negotiated and struggled over (Cooke 1990; Watts 1992). The thrust of such studies has been to question the distinctiveness of societies, nations, and cultures as based on some kind of unproblematic division of space; to interrogate the "fact" that they occupy naturally discontinuous spaces. Indeed, it is "so taken for granted that each country embodies its own distinctive culture and society that the terms 'society' and 'culture' are routinely simply appended to the names of nation-states, as when a tourist visits India to understand 'Indian culture' and 'Indian society'" (Gupta and Ferguson 1992:7). Thus to take off from Gupta and Ferguson's evocative formulation, the aim of this volume is to expand current discussions about "the rupture of independent states and autonomous cultures." We do so by recognizing that space and place are central organizing principles in all complex societies, but also by framing our principal task as one of making problematical the very "naturalness" of such principles. Two kinds of naturalisms are challenged in this respect (Malkki 1992): the first is the anthropological convention of taking the association of a culturally unitary group (the "tribe" or "people") and "its" territory as natural; the second naturalism is the national practice of taking the association of citizens and states and their territories as natural (see Handler 1988; Wright 1985).

This problematization does not only entail (as is the current fashion in anthropology) a matter of producing new kinds of ethnographic texts. An introduction of more sophisticated self-criticism and a greater openness to more flexible methodologies and literary possibilities in ethnographic writing does not imply shirking an analysis of the world out there. To do so would, to put this by way of caricature, lead to a 'navel' anthropology. As Strathern (1987:279) puts it,

> We must, as anthropologists, monitor ourselves. But the world is not entirely composed of anthropologists. Whether we like to or not, our ethnographic subjects continue to play an externalizing role in the judgements of others. This is a political fact with which our communications—not least among ourselves—must deal.

To reiterate, we argue not for a simple concern with new modes of textual experimentation and the creation of spaces for the voices of our various others: "the politics of otherness is not reducible to a politics of representation" (Gupta and Ferguson 1992:17). Rather, we identify a need to address through our work the extratextual roots of the issues we have singled out for analysis.

Along the lines we have just outlined, the chapters presented in this volume suggest a shift of focus from strictly political, geographical, or ideological emphases to an exploration of dimensions hitherto relatively little discussed in writings about Israel. More specifically we propose to go beyond the analysis of specific areas or locations, and ask questions about the manner by which settlement and settlements, sites and territory, figure in different discourses within and about Israel. Our assumption is that the salience of phenomena associated with space is "seized upon" by a variety of groups, commentators, and thinkers in order to promote or denigrate certain visions they have of this society.

At the risk of overstressing disciplinary differences, let us state clearly that our approach is anthropological rather than historical or sociological. We mean by this—following Lofgren (1987:77)—that our level of generalization does not primarily concern the distribution of cultural forms over space and time. Our aim is to generalize about the cultural processes that produce variations in form. This assertion implies (1) that atypical cases have analytical value beyond their place in the search for frequencies; and (2) that the prime analytical focus is on such phenomena as categories of classification, on bases of identity, or on 'imaginings of community' (Anderson 1983).

Thus, this volume attempts to make a more general point regarding the anthropology of Israel. Anthropological discussions of this society, like similar studies carried out in other complex societies (Lofgren 1989), have long been dominated by analyses placed at the level of villages and neighborhoods, of communities and subcultures, or of 'ethnic' and 'minority' groups. Only rarely have anthropological inquiries focused on a grander scale to ask questions about the wider processes that keep parts of this society together or separate them. Indeed, for many decades the anthropology of Israel was heavily influenced by the British tradition of community studies, which was guided by the assumption that a picture of the total society could be created by the addition and juxtaposition of series of local studies (Lofgren 1987:75). Once such example is Deshen's attempt (1982) to create a typology of urban settlements on the basis of ethnographic case studies published in the previous decade.

Since the early 1980s, however, an increasing number of scholars have begun to tackle such issues as the root metaphors that stand at the base of Israeli culture (Katriel 1986; Dolev-Gandelman 1987), the central narratives that figure in the construction of collective meanings (Bruner and Gorfain 1984; Schwartz et al. 1986), and the conceptions of "peoplehood" that underlie various views of what being Israeli entails (Goldberg 1985; Dominguez 1989). These studies all proceed from the realization that a fuller understanding of Israel and 'things Israeli' necessitates making problematical commonplace, everyday cultural notions and conceptions. The chapters presented here, and which follow from these studies, attempt to problematize the taken-for-granted realities of Israeli space and place. It is in this spirit that we turn to the chapters.

A word about the arrangement of the chapters. In general, we have intended the sequence to represent a set of wider analytical movements. By beginning with a motion from cases located outside Israel (Levy and Goldberg) to a case dealing with Israel's periphery (Ben-Ari and Bilu) we underscore the importance of border regions and border-crossings in laying bare the fiction of cultures as discrete phenomena. Next, by relocating to the mainstream or center of Israeli Jewish society (Handelman and Shamgar-Handelman, Ben-David, and Katriel), we offer an analysis of the very assumptions upon which much of contemporary research has proceeded. The next two chapters lead out again to both the most conflictual issue at the heart of contested spaces in Israel (Rabinowitz) and finally to the most general deconstruction of the Israeli Jewish conception of space (Gurevitch). In this manner we hope to underscore how the questioning of the received wisdom (both academic and popular) about boundaries and places is at the heart of more obvious transnational phenomena such as pilgrimages, as it is the analytical examination of the seemingly most stable of concepts, Israel as *the* place of the Jewish and Palestinian peoples. The final piece (Boyarin), situated as it were outside the geographical, cultural, and academic boundaries of Israel, serves to further challenge us as editors and to raise further questions for readers.

THE CHAPTERS

The first chapter is André Levy's "To Morocco and Back: Tourism and Pilgrimage among Moroccan-Born Israelis." During most of Israel's history, many Israeli Jews have been barred from countries from which they originated. In the past few years, however, as relations with some Arab states have thawed and as Eastern European countries have opened up, many Israelis have begun to visit their birthplaces. This chapter is an analysis of one such voyage, a search for identity in a place geographically—and in a sense also temporally—distant. It is based on fieldwork carried out when the author accompanied a group of Moroccan-born Israelis on what can be described as a part pilgrimic voyage and part tourist excursion back to their land of birth. When the group left Israel, these people thought of Morocco as an integral part, in a sense as the 'real' part, of their identity. But what Levy found was a paradox: people discovered their Israeli-ness in Morocco. They had, as it were, to go back in time (to their previous 'selves') and away in space (to contemporary Jews and Muslims in Morocco) to discover how Israeli they had become.

In this respect Levy's contribution raises a number of points that merit mention. The first has to do with the complexity inherent in constructing Israeli identities. By carefully showing the variety of arenas in which the Israelis interact with Muslims in Morocco, he shows how the identities of each group shift with each context. For example, in the cemetery, Jews take a subordinate position vis-à-vis the king, while he himself (in their eyes) takes an inferior position in relation to Jewish saints. In the marketplace, however, as an outcome of their greater purchasing power—and, in a subtle way, as a consequence of Israel's military power—Israelis can invert their older (i.e., preimmigration) status of junior partner. At the same time, these relations are saturated with a deep-seated ambivalence: the Israeli Jews are at one and the same time sure and unsure of themselves, threatened and threatening. In this portrayal, then, Israeli identity is no longer static (or even a set of fixed "entities"), but something that constantly shifts and moves, open to negotiation and full of contradictions.

Levy's analysis—and this is the second point—poses another question mark in regard to discussions of Israeli society—specifically, the unquestioned assumption at the base of many studies that there is an isomorphism between the geopolitical boundaries of the state and its social and cultural limits (Kimmerling 1989). Levy's contribution should thus be seen alongside Shokeid's research (1988) on *yordim* in the sense of arguing for a reconceptualization of Israeli culture. This culture—without assuming too much about its unitary nature—could thus better be understood, we would propose, as a set of negotiated symbols and meanings that cross and travel across national boundaries. In this processual view, gone are the older theoretical concerns with system boundaries (Murphy 1990:333). To put this by way of example, just as it is possible to gain a richer appreciation of the variety of experiences entailed in being Israeli through visiting their hangouts in New York, so it may be possible to learn something about Israeli-ness in contemporary Morocco.

The next chapter, "Gravesites and Memorials of Libyan Jews: Alternative Versions of the Sacralization of Space in Judaism" is by Harvey Goldberg. The case Goldberg focuses on involves the Jewish cemetery in Tripoli over which the contemporary Libyan authorities decided, a few years ago, to build a road. In response, a group of Libyan Jews resolved to build commemorative plaques honoring the graveyard both in Italy (Rome) and in Israel. By concentrating on the experience of one (rather unique) individual, Goldberg shows how people can—in contrast to many of the assumptions upon which modern states are predicated—hold to a set of nonexclusive national identities. He does this through showing how this individual has created a set of metaphors in which Israel is his 'fatherland,' while Italy and Libya are his 'motherlands.' In this way he seems both to accommodate and to question the very notion (basic to Zionism) of the exclusivity of Israeli identity.

In setting up the memorial plaques the Libyan Jews seem to link—to prefigure a theme we return to shortly—their autobiographical, personal action to history. Yet this action bears wider significance, for it raises the issue of the interrelationship between Israel and the Jewish diaspora. As Breckenridge and Appadurai (1989:i) note, diasporas are movements of peoples and experiences that leave trails of collective memories about other places and other times, and in this way create new maps of desire and attachment.

> Diasporas, like pilgrimages, military campaigns and diseases, are indifferent to the idiosyncracies of nation-states and often flow through their cracks and exploit their vulnerabilities. They are thus a testimony to the inherent fragility of the links between people, polity and territory and to the negotiability of the relationship between people and place (Breckenridge and Appadurai 1989:i).

In this regard, Goldberg's chapter suggests something Israeli Jews do not readily admit. If we realize that the Jews he writes of have *chosen* to settle in Rome after their banishment, and that they long for Libya as well as Israel, the notions of 'home' and of 'belonging' are no longer the preserve of Israel. He raises, in their words, the possibility that for many aspects of Jewish attachment Israel may not be necessary at all.

The third contribution is our own composition, "Saints' Sanctuaries in Israeli Development Towns: On a Mechanism of Urban Transformation." In this chapter we examine the reemergence of sacred sites of Jewish saints in a number of Israeli development towns. In focusing on these towns our chapter highlights a type of urban settlement that is often viewed by Israelis with a mixture of condescension, mild disdain, and paternalistic concern (Goldberg 1984:7). We maintain that the appearance of these saints' sanctuaries is rooted in North African 'folk' religiosity and reflects a strengthening of attachment of people to "their" places. This phenomenon is related to what may be termed an internal Israeli cultural debate centering on its identity as a 'Middle Eastern' society. On one level, the continued existence and personal relevance of saints' cults bespeak of a persisting affinity between the beliefs and practices of North African Jews in Israel and similar tenets and rites among our Islamic neighbors (Gellner 1969; Geertz 1968). This similarity has led Cohen (1983:123–24) to characterize saint worship as part of a larger process by which Israel is undergoing "demodernization."

> The re-emergence of saint cults can be interpreted as a sign of symbolic 'diasporization' of Israel: the country . . . loses much of its precedence and special status as the Holy Land and universal center, and is seen increasingly as just another state, though governed by Jews. The spiritual life of North African Jews is consequently re-assimilated to that which has characterized its diaspora past.

The use of such terms as "demodernization" and "diasporization" is indicative of the distress many Ashkenazi intellectuals like Cohen feel in face of the regeneration of saints' cults. Indeed, this cultural elite, placed as it is at a cultural and ethnic distance from these phenomena, has reacted to them with a compound of contempt and wonder, and dread and fascination (Shohat 1992). But could these reactions, we would ask, have to do with the perceived "Arab" nature of saints' cults and of this version of Jewish folk religiosity? Are such responses indicative of the fear that Israel is becoming "just another" Middle Eastern country?

These questions bring us to the next suggestion: while elegant, Cohen's thesis is still too simple. The strengthening of saint worship does not appear to be a unidimensional or unidirectional process of diasporization. Such practices should also be understood as part of the "Israelization" of the Jewish diaspora. In focusing their attention on soliciting contributions from a variety of Jewish communities (in Israel and outside of it), the people who have set up saints' tombs follow paths well trodden by many of the country's Zionist leaders. In seeking to change Israel's landscape by erecting various tombs and synagogues for the saints, such people act in accord with the Zionist ethos. According to this view, then, have these 'saints' entrepreneurs not adopted many of the assumptions of wider Israeli public culture to simply become people like "us"?

The fourth chapter, written by Don Handelman and Lea Shamgar-Handelman, is entitled "The Presence of Absence: The Memorialism of National Death in Israel." Their contribution is about the relationships between the presence or absence of the body of the dead and the visual representation of death on the surface of the land. They single out three different landscapes of national sacrifice for analysis: military cemeteries, military memorials and monuments, and the Holocaust Memorial (in Jerusalem). In more general terms their contribution focuses on the manner by which death is appropriated by the Israeli state for the purpose of creating collective memories within its territory. To use Boyarin's terms (1991b), they show how problematic it is for the state to map history onto territory.

We find that this chapter represents one of a very few sustained and systematic anthropological attempts in Israel to discuss the way in which a geopolitical space is transformed into a nationwide cultural space, a space of national sharing. What is of significance in this respect is the place of death, especially military death, in the construction of national sharing. While a long line of scholars have intuited the central place of the military and military action in legitimating the Israeli state, few studies have attempted to go beyond polemical declarations to show just how this is effected. The authors demonstrate that implicated in military death and sacrifice are a number of elements that resonate with—that is, make sense and stir the emotions of—Israeli Jews. At one and the same time, we find in military deaths a contrast to the Holocaust and the 'exilic' way of life it represents, and in military memorialization a stress on uniquely 'Israeli' style and values (e.g., absence of large amounts or a stress on uniformity and equality). Thus the authenticity of the military graves—reinforced by the presence of the body—is one way in which the state appeals to various unquestioned beliefs and emotions among Israeli Jews (for another, still rather exceptional example, see Rubin 1984–85).

This is no mean point, for it leads us to the question of the place of landscapes—particular arrangements of features such as buildings or gardens—in the creation of a national sharing. The force of landscapes lies, the authors suggest, in their ability both to embody (i.e., give concrete form to) concepts and to serve as a means for triggering emotions and sentiments. Handelman and Shamgar-Handelman's analysis thus suggests the importance of the nondiscursive, the sensuous, or the experiential in the creation of a national cultural space. This point is related to an issue hitherto largely ignored by the recent spate of excellent studies dealing with the logic and root metaphors of Israeli culture. These studies have tended to neglect the experiential and performative. What is suggested by the chapter written by Handelman and Shamgar-Handelman is the possibility of linking the powerful tools developed in regard to the analysis of performance and experience (by such people as Turner 1985) with discourse analysis. Such a linkage may enrich both. We thus may be able to employ theoretical concepts to understand the power of landscapes and such performances as pilgrimages or hikes, and to uncover the rich layers of meaning found in public discourse. This stress on the experiential leads us, in turn, to the next contribution.

Orit Ben-David's "*Tiyul* (Hike) as an Act of Consecration of Space" discusses hikes organized by the Society for the Protection of Nature in Israel. Ben-David shows that these hikes can be understood as combining two aspects: the ritualistic and the taxonomic. The ritualistic aspect of the hikes is evident in their contemporary expression of valued actions found in earlier versions of Zionism: on actualization (*hagshama*) of a link to the land. Thus she suggests that for many Israelis hikes are a means for 'marking' territory and for declaring ownership of the land. In other words, hikes, like similar rituals found the world over, are means for effecting a legitimate connection between people and land.

But Ben-David is not content with this aspect of the hikes, adding a series of rather intriguing suggestions about their taxonomic aspect. Through the hikes, she argues, the land is not expropriated, as a simple political reading of Israel would have it, from some enemy but rather from society. The redemption of the land (*geulat ha-aretz*), a central tenet of Zionism, is not a redemption from the hands of another people but, according to this version of Israeli-ness, from the unrestrained use of civilization. If it is indeed true that the *tiyul* is a means of returning the land from "culture" to "nature," then today's Zionism, while ostensibly using 'old' jargon and symbols, actually presents a radical departure from that of the past. Ben-David does not state so explicitly, but we would suggest that her analysis shows how certain groups in contemporary Israel are motivated by ideas found in any 'normal' Western society. By this we mean the simple, if hardly acknowledged, fact of Israeli groups like the Greens in Europe, which deal with environmental issues and attempt to re-create romantic versions of 'natural' places (Cotgrove 1976). We realize that such a reading flies in the face of many intellectual stereotypes of Israel, but we do think it important to recognize the cultural implications of Israel as 'just' another consumer or postconsumer society

(Birenbaum-Carmeli 1994). It may be ironic (and this is our point, not Ben-David's) that *at times* Israelis are so sure of themselves, so sure of their ownership of the land, that they can turn to the protection and conservation of nature.

"Remaking Place: Cultural Production in Israeli Pioneer Settlement Museums" is the title of Tamar Katriel's chapter. The word "remaking" captures attempts in contemporary Israel to advance certain versions of history by creating anew, by reconstructing 'old' places. The case she discusses involves the plethora of museums now being built to commemorate and to celebrate the country's socialist-Zionist past and the values associated with this past. As she shows, the construction of museums should be seen in the context of history-making practices that inevitably construct selective interpretations of the past.

For many years British and American anthropologies were overwhelmingly preoccupied with the study of peoples placed outside their countries' geopolitical boundaries. Israeli anthropologists, by contrast, have studied their own society almost to the exclusion of others. But the objects they have studied have been—like those of their British and American counterparts—esoteric, exotic 'others': new immigrants, ethnic groups (read Jews from Arabic-speaking lands), or minorities (Arabs or Druze, for example). Katriel's study, like Ben-David's, however, deals with a different group—with "us," the mainly Ashkenazi middle class. In focusing our attention on the largest but as yet little-studied category of 'regular' Israelis, she prefigures, we think, a major scholarly effort that will characterized Israeli anthropology and the anthropology of Israel in the coming few years.

An analysis of museums raises the question, being asked increasingly in anthropological circles, about the relationship between the disciplines of anthropology and folklore, and organized and institutionalized power. By carefully examining how one such museum is organized, Katriel shows its power to engender certain experiences among visitors. These experiences—often containing a set of unstated and unexamined messages—are important because it is through them that the organizers of the museum try to establish their claims to truth. The picture that emerges is, as Herzfeld (1987:13) suggests in regard to modern museums, that of a highly regulated and organized folklorism that creates images of spontaneity and naivete in order to base its claim about the importance of the exhibited material. In this sense Katriel's contribution shows how a cultural analysis can be linked to political economy: to the interests behind discourses and the construction of experiences. The objectifications of space and place in museums are not only about 'symbolic' collective identities; they are simultaneously semiotic and political (Dominguez 1989).

Of no less importance are the contents of what is being represented in the museum. This point is related to the variety of 'preserved others' displayed. Let us highlight one point in this regard: the portrayal of Arabs in the museums. The depiction of these people is, as Katriel shows, basically ambivalent: they are shown as primitive and native, yet closest to nature and its workings and thus to be respected; they are anachronistic and autochthonous, yet only by understanding and emulating them can Israeli Jews find a way to connect to the land. This portrayal thus leads us to the penultimate chapter.

Dan Rabinowitz has entitled his contribution "In and Out of Territory." While the empirical case chosen for study is of a mixed (i.e., Jewish-Arab) town that lies next to a larger Arab city (Nazareth), the analytical focus is on the metaphors and constructs that Arabs use in conceptualizing the territory of these settlements. Rabinowitz's interest lies in examining the socially constructed means individuals employ in order to conceptualize the space associated with their identity as members of a certain nation. Following earlier analyses (Pahl 1975), Rabinowitz looks at the town not only for an understanding of its urban dynamics, but no less importantly, as an arena for understanding the overall society and the complexity of the social forces operating within and without it. Here again the picture is far from unitary. Rooted in a profound ambivalence to the state, Arabs living in Natzeret Il-lit are at once participants in and outsiders to Israel. Like other Arabs in Israel they seem to be unable to decide whether Israel represents homeland or exile (Hever 1987:50). Ironically, they seem similar to Israeli Jews who have emigrated to America to become citizens of that country, only to turn out to be "permanently temporary." They wait for things to work out, and seek uneasy alliances with their present situation in the hope for some change in the future in which they will somehow belong more to their place of residence.

Being aware of the situatedness of each viewpoint of Israel—in this case, the pictures depicted by Israeli Arabs—provides an antidote to some of the older, more totalizing images of Israeli society (Eisenstadt 1967). Rabinowitz underscores the fact that like any society or culture Israel ceases to be a unitary phenomenon. As the Arabs within (and without) show us, it cannot be apprehended from any one angle, nor by any one viewing instrument. At best we can only capture partial Israeli worlds.

This brings us to the final chapter, a discussion by Zali Gurevitch of "The Double Site of Israel." Gurevitch takes off from a struggle over place— *Hamakom*. Yet this is not a struggle between "us" Israelis and others, be they Palestinians, Arabs, Europeans, or diaspora Jews. It is, rather, a struggle within us. Thus in talking about *Hamakom—the* place—he does not explore the significance of specific points in the Land of Israel but examines the place as it figures in different versions of Jewish and Israeli identities. He shows that there is something that is not-fixed, not final—perhaps never fixed or final—in the definition of place in Jewish and Israeli conceptions. Gurevitch has written a *midrash*, an interpretation. In the tradition of the *midrash*, the study is a way of interrogating, of asking things of place. We find this kind of interrogation to be of special significance because by breaking many of the codes of accepted writings, it serves to effect the distancing that is so essential to any analysis of one's own society and culture. In this sense Israeli anthropology must—like the anthropology of mainland Europe (Lofgren 1987:75 –76)—devise techniques not so much for getting *into* a new culture, but for getting *out of* its all too familiar surroundings.

Yet Gurevitch's contribution bears wider import: it necessitates, we propose, a different way of thinking about methodology. Specifically, we refer to issues related to what have been termed in anthropological circles "good entrances" to the field. Older traditions of simply picking a specific community, a cultural scene, or even a set of cultural texts need to be supported by more flexible combinations of sources, sites, and strategies that can serve to link local processes to national ones. This does not imply the abandonment of methodological rigor nor relinquishment of criteria by which to appraise scholarly work. It does mean, as Gurevitch's piece suggests, a greater openness to hitherto little explored avenues and ways of writing and research.

AND THE ANTHROPOLOGY OF ISRAEL?

We began this introduction with a short history of our joint project in order to bring us to the problematics of the book as a whole and to the issues raised by each chapter. It may now be appropriate to suggest something about the relationship between this volume and what may be termed its specific historical situatedness. Any cultural critique must tackle two interrelated tasks: (1) exploring the ways in which social reality is represented by various 'cultural' mechanisms, and the manner through which these mechanisms form part of the reproduction *and* production of social relations; and (2) accounting for the relationship between the position of the authors in a concrete sociohistorical situation and their work. This attempt at self-critique—partial though it may be—is at one and the same time a precondition for, and a limit on the validity of any 'findings' (see editorial foreword to Theory and Criticism 1991). Thus, we think it fruitful to offer a number of speculations about the historical moment in which we write and its relation to our scholarly engagement with place and space. It is also for this reason that we invited Jonathan Boyarin's "Response from New York" as the volume's postscript.

We would suggest that this connection between our scholarly focus and present historical circumstances is related to a set of processes that Israel has been undergoing in the past two-and-a-half decades. For a variety of (political, social, demographic, and economic) reasons, since 1967 Israel has been the site of steady changes in what could be termed the prevailing public attitudes and sentiments (see Aronoff 1989; Horowitz and Lissak 1989; Lustick 1988). Some of the more important of these changes (and the list could be expanded) include a greater acceptance of the Jewish diaspora and the concomitant openness to *Jewish* 'ethnic pluralism'; a certain enhancement of religious sentiments and a related strengthening of nationalistic feelings; a changed attitude toward the Holocaust and a greater willingness to search for continuities with past Jewish identities; the eruption of the Intifada (the Palestinian uprising), the increased militancy of Israeli Arabs, and the unease this has wrought among many Israeli Jews; and, following Israel's debacle in Lebanon, the decreased legitimacy of such institutions as the army. Closely related to all of these, as Dominguez (1990:13) notes, has been the weakening of the centralized state as *the* agent of social transformation affecting housing, language, health, technology, production, dress, and childrearing.

However, the breakdown of the political and cultural hegemony of Labor-Zionism and its associated political bodies seems to be of no less importance. This breakdown has not spelled the disappearance of values and sentiments associated with this group. What does seem to be happening in Israel is that competing worldviews and assertions of Israeli identity and peoplehood are finding greater public expression. As Paine (1989; see also Aronoff 1984) suggests, Israel today is the site of an ongoing and at times violent competition over 'tradition,' that is, a set of meaningful and worthwhile guidelines for people's lives. It is at the interstices of the aforementioned trends and the new—or, perhaps more aptly, renewed—'competition' over tradition that a number of cultural critiques have appeared. Two examples of this pattern are the new journal entitled *Theory and Criticism* and Ram's (1993) reader comprising critical perspectives on Israeli society. The specific aim of both forums is to provide a platform for critical discussion by intellectuals and academics from a variety of disciplines (see also Handelman 1994).

Yet the development of these critiques in Israel cannot be understood apart from changes in the wider (perhaps worldwide) intellectual atmosphere. A number of developments within the human sciences in general, and within anthropology in particular, bear import in this regard. Marcus and Fischer (1986:8) call this a postcolonial or postmodern period, a moment of a crisis of representation; one of its main features is the loosening of the hold of both specific totalizing visions and a general paradigmatic style of organizing research. In regard to anthropology, Jackson (1989) has termed this period one of an anxiety on the part of scholars about the status of anthropological knowledge and methods. It is our suggestion that this crisis or anxiety and the attempts to deal with it have seeped into the human and social scientific disciplines dealing with and situated within Israeli society. The steady stream of publications and studies coming out of Israel since the beginning of the 1980s attest to this. It would have been hard to envisage the impact of a book like Grossman's *Yellow Wind* (1987) even fifteen years ago.

Within academia some people have dismissed these intellectual developments as mere 'fashions' soon to be superseded by other approaches, or as 'attention grabbers' used by (mainly younger) social scientists to establish their academic positions. We believe that there is something more to them; that parts of Israeli anthropology, and Israeli social science and the humanities in general, are undergoing a fruitful self-examination. This process of self-reflection couples a critique of scholarly—in our case anthropological—practice, with a more astute inspection of our 'conventional' objects and subjects of study. Yet the question still remains: What is the specific contribution anthropology can make to the study of Israeli society and culture within this emergent process of cultural critique? While we may sound unabashedly 'traditional' or 'conventional' in our approach, we would maintain that one of anthropology's continuing strong points is its emphasis on empirical work—on the analysis of how concepts and sentiments, feelings and perceptions are embodied *in action*. The strength of ethnography and of ethnographic criticism lies in their enduring respect for context and the recognition of the ambiguity and complexity of any situation (Marcus and Fischer 1986:159). Thus we believe that it is not enough to focus only on discourse in order to get at this complexity and ambiguity. Alternative forms of anthropological practice—which have been coming into vogue during the past decade—may be theoretically liberating but they should not come at the expense of empirical ethnographic work. Thus the chapters in this volume should both caution us and exemplify the need to ground our work in the reality of our subjects. To put this by way of example, a critique of the claims of truth by Labor-Zionism must be founded on the analysis of specific and actual practices such as the arrangement of museums. We realize, following Myers (1988:622–23), that our practices may continue, to an extent, to appropriate into our frameworks those whom we study. But this appropriation is now held in a tension that is more than just our translation of them by giving priority to local political purposes. Thus Rabinowitz, in his chapter, is careful to link the perceptions of Arabs in Natzeret Illit to the power relations and combination of interests that characterize the town.

Furthermore, the stress on openness and the pluralism of perspectives now in fashion in anthropology should not blind us to the "topography"—the broad contours or configurations—of possibilities within which the experiences of space and place in Israel take place. Let us single out two issues in this regard. Paine (1989:128) rightly observes that there is more than one "time" and more than one "place" that is Israel, among Jews living there today. What our volume tries to do is to map out some of the *limits* of the pluralism entailed by such an observation. For example, the chapters in this volume are populated by a limited field of 'others' through which Israeli Jewish identity is constructed: diaspora Jews, native Arabs, Zionist pioneers, Moroccan Muslims and Jews, and (maybe) European "Greens." While these 'others' change at the same time that self-definitions of Israeli Jews change, they nevertheless encompass the broad possibilities within which "Israeli-ness" is defined. As Handelman and Shamgar-Handelman caution (1990:221), we must be wary of an all-too-neat emphasis on the 'invention' of Israeli tradition or traditions. We miss continuities and limits on invention without recognition of the elements of enduring ontological coordinates—that is, the logics of the world and the way human beings within their historical worlds are constituted (Kapferer 1988:19)—in the way Israeli Jews conceptualize themselves, their history, and their tradition. To reiterate, a stress on mutability and change does not imply that 'anything goes.'

By writing and publishing about space and place we are also, of course, participating in the public discussion now taking place in Israel. Perhaps this is a modest aim, but what we can contribute, we believe, is a certain opening, a questioning of current trends. And that perhaps is not such a bad thing.

> You always have to travel, not settle down, like we thought
> when we were young.
> Only travel assures a perspective, a discount for those who
> pay in advance.
> (Zach 1988)

ACKNOWLEDGMENTS

We would like to thank S. Kaplan and P. Lubell for comments on an earlier draft of this introduction and Z. Gurevitch for suggesting the title of the volume. We also gratefully acknowledge the financial and administrative support of the Shaine Center (the Department of Sociology and Anthropology) and the Harry S. Truman Research institute for the Advancement of Peace of the Hebrew University during various stages of this project.

REFERENCES

Anderson, Benedict. 1983. *Imagined Communities: Reflections on the Origin and Spread of Nationalism.* London: New Left Books.

Aran, Gideon. 1991. Jewish Zionist Fundamentalism: "The Bloc of the Faithful" in Israel (Gush Emunim). In *Fundamentalism Observed*, American Academy of Arts and Sciences. Chicago: University of Chicago Press.

Aronoff, Myron J. 1984. Political Polarization: Contradictory Interpretations of Israeli Reality. In *Cross-Currents in Israeli Culture and Politics*, Myron J. Aronoff, ed., 1–23. New Brunswick, N.J.: Transaction.

———. 1989. *Israeli Visions and Divisions: Cultural Change and Political Conflict.* New Brunswick, N.J.: Transaction.

Asad, Talal. 1990. Ethnography, Literature, and Politics: Some Readings and Uses of Salman Rushdies's *The Satanic Verses. Cultural Anthropology* 5(3):239–69.

Ben-Ami, Issachar. 1984. *Folk Veneration of Saints Among the Jews of Morocco.* Jerusalem: Magnes. (Hebrew)

Ben-Ari, Eyal. 1989. Masks and Soldiering: The Israeli Army and the Palestinian Uprising. *Cultural Anthropology* 4(4):372–89.

Ben-Ari, Eyal, and Yoram Bilu. 1987. Saints' Sanctuaries in Israeli Development Towns: On a Mechanism of Urban Transformation. *Urban Anthropology* 16(2):243–72.

Bendix, Regina. 1992. National Sentiment in the Enactment and Discourse of Swiss Political Ritual. *American Ethnologist* 19(4):768–90.

Bilu, Yoram. 1986. Dreams and the Wishes of the Saint. In *Judaism Viewed From Within and From Without*, Harvey Goldberg, ed., 285–313. New York: State University of New York Press.

Bilu, Yoram, and Henry Abramovitch. 1985. In Search of the Saddiq: Visitational Dreams among Moroccan Jews in Israel. *Psychiatry* 48: 83–92.

Bilu, Yoram, and Eyal Ben-Ari. 1992. The Making of Modern Saints: Manufactured Charisma and the Abu-Hatseiras of Israel. *American Ethnologist* 19(4):672–87.

Birenbaum-Carmeli, Daphna. 1994. *A Good Place in the Middle: A Residential Area as a Means of Constructing Class Identity.* Ph.D. dissertation submitted to the Department of Sociology and Anthropology, Hebrew University of Jerusalem.

Boyarin, Jonathan. 1991a. *Space, Time and the Politics of Memory.* Center for Studies of Social Change, Ms.

———. 1991b. An Inquiry into Inquiries and a Representation of Representations. *Sociological Forum* 6(2):387–95.

Breckenridge, Carol A., and Arjun Appadurai. 1989. Editors' Comment: On Moving Targets. *Public Culture* 2(1):i–iv.

Bruner, Edward M., and Phyllis Gorfain. 1984. Dialogic Narration and the Paradoxes of Masada. In *Text, Play and Story*, Edward M. Bruner and Stuart Plattner, eds., 56–79. Washington, D.C.: American Ethnological Society.

Bruner, Jerome. 1986. *Actual Minds, Possible Worlds.* Cambridge, Mass.: Harvard University Press.

Cohen, Anthony (ed.). 1986. *Symbolizing Boundaries.* Manchester: Manchester University Press.

Cohen, Erik. 1977. The City in Zionist Ideology. *The Jerusalem Quarterly* 4:126–44.

———. 1983. Ethnicity and Legitimation in Contemporary Israel. *The Jerusalem Quarterly* 28:111–24.

Connerton, Paul. 1989. *How Societies Remember.* Cambridge: Cambridge University Press.

Cooke, Phillip. 1990. *Back to the Future.* London: Allen and Unwin.

Cotgrove, Steven. 1976. Environmentalism and Utopia. *Sociological Review* 24(1):23–42.

Deshen, Shlomo. 1982. Social Organization and Politics in Israeli Urban Quarters. *The Jerusalem Quarterly* 22:21–37.

Dolev-Gandelman, Tsili. 1987. The Symbolic Inscription of Zionist Ideology in the Space of Eretz Israel: Why the Native Israeli Is Called *Tsabar.* In *Judaism Viewed from Within and Without*, Harvey E. Goldberg, ed., 257–84. Albany: State University of New York Press.

Dominguez, Virginia R. 1989. *People as Subject, People as Object: Selfhood and Peoplehood in Contemporary Israel.* Madison: University of Wisconsin Press.

———. 1990. The Politics of Heritage in Contemporary Israel. *American Ethnological Monograph Series*, No. 2:130–47.

Eisenstadt, Shmuel N. 1967. *Israeli Society: Background, Development, Problems.* New York: Basic.

Feige, Michael, and Eyal Ben-Ari. 1991. Card Games and an Israeli Army Unit: An Interpretive Case Study. *Armed Forces and Society* 17(3):429–48.

Geertz, Clifford. 1968. *Islam Observed.* New Haven: Yale University Press.

Gellner, Ernest. 1969. *Saints of the Atlas.* Chicago: University of Chicago Press.

Goldberg, Harvey E. 1984. *Greentown's Youth: Disadvantaged Youth in a Development Town in Israel.* Assen: Van Gorcum.

———. 1985. Historical and Cultural Dimensions of Ethnic Phenomena in Israel. In *Studies in Israeli Ethnicity: After the Ingathering*, Alex Weingrod, ed., 179–200. New York: Gordon and Breach.

Grossman, David. 1987. *Yellow Wind.* Hakkibutz Hameuchad. (Hebrew)

Gupta, Akhil, and James Furgeson. 1992. Beyond "Culture": Space, Identity and the Politics of Difference. *Cultural Anthropology* 7(1):6–23.

Handelman, Don. 1994. Contradictions Between Citizenship and National-
    ity: Their Consequences for Ethnicity and Inequality in Israel. *Inter-
    national Journal of Politics, Culture and Society* 7(3):441–59.
Handelman, Don, and Lea Shamgar-Handelman. 1990. Shaping Time: The
    Choice of the National Emblem of Israel. In *Culture Through Time:
    Anthropological Approaches*, Emiko Ohnuki-Tierney, ed., 193–226.
    Stanford: Stanford University Press.
Handler, Richard. 1988. *Nationalism and the Politics of Culture in Quebec.*
    Madison: University of Wisconsin Press.
Hasson, Shlomo. 1981. Social and Spatial Conflicts: The Settlement Process
    in Israel During the 1950s and the 1960s. *L'espace Geographique*
    3:169–79.
Herzfeld, Michael. 1987. *Anthropology Through the Looking-Glass: Criti-
    cal Ethnography in the Margins of Europe.* Cambridge: Cambridge
    University Press.
Hever, Hannan. 1987. Hebrew in an Israeli Arab Hand: Six Miniatures on
    Anton Shammas's Arabesques. *Critical Inquiry* 7:47–76.
———. 1989. Hitting at Achilles' Heel. *Alpaim* 1:186–93. (Hebrew)
Horowitz, Dan, and Moshe Lissak. 1989. *Trouble in Utopia: The Overbur-
    dened Polity of Israel.* Albany: State University of New York Press.
Jackson, John B. 1984. *Discovering the Vernacular Landscape.* New Haven:
    Yale University Press.
Jackson, Michael. 1989. *Paths Toward a Clearing: Radical Empiricism and
    Ethnographic Inquiry.* Bloomington: Indiana University Press.
Kapferer, Bruce. 1988. *Legends of People, Myths of State: Violence, Intol-
    erance, and Political Culture in Sri Lanka and Australia.* Washington,
    D.C.: Smithsonian Institution Press.
Katriel, Tamar. 1986. *Talking Straight: Dugri Speech in Israeli Sabra Cul-
    ture.* Cambridge: Cambridge University Press.
Katriel, Tamar, and Aliza Shenhar. 1991. Tower and Stockade: Dialogic Nar-
    ration in Israeli Settlement Ethos. *Quarterly Journal of Speech*
    76(4):359–80.
Kelly, William 1986: Rationalization and Nostalgia: Cultural Dynamics of
    New Middle-Class Japan. *American Ethnologist* 13, 603–14.
Kimmerling, Baruch. 1982. Change and Continuity in Zionist Territorial
    Orientations and Politics. *Comparative Politics* 14(2):191–210.
———. 1983. *Zionism and Territory: The Socio-Territorial Dimensions of
    Zionist Politics.* Berkeley: University of California Institute of Inter-
    national Relations.
———. 1989. Boundaries and Frontiers of the Israeli Control System. In *The
    Israeli State and Society*, Baruch Kimmerling, ed., 265–84. Albany:
    State University of New York Press.

Liebman, Charles S., and Eliezer Don-Yehiya. 1983. *Civil Religion in Israel: Traditional Judaism and Political Culture in the Jewish State.* Berkeley: University of California Press.

Lofgren, Orvar. 1987. Deconstructing Swedishness: Culture and Class in Modern Sweden. In *Anthropology at Home*, Anthony Jackson, ed., 74–93. London: Tavistock.

———. 1989. Anthropologizing America. *American Ethnologist* 16(2):366–74.

Lustick, Ian S. 1988. *For the Land and the Lord: Jewish Fundamentalism in Israel.* New York: Council on Foreign Relations.

Malkki, Lisa. 1992. National Geographic: The Rooting of Peoples and the Territorialization of National Identity Among Scholars and Refugees. *Cultural Anthropology* 7(1):24–43.

Marcus, George E., and Michael M. J. Fischer. 1986. *Anthropology as Cultural Critique: An Experimental Moment in the Human Sciences.* Chicago: University of Chicago Press.

McDonogh, Gary. 1991. Discourse of the City: Policy and Response in Post-Transitional Barcelona. *City and Society* 5(1):40–63.

Murphy, Robert F. 1990. The Dialectics of Deeds and Words: Or Anti-the-Antis (and the Anti-Antis). *Cultural Anthropology* 5(3):331–37.

Myers, Fred R. 1988. Locating Ethnographic Practice: Romance, Reality, and Politics in the Outback. *American Ethnologist* 15(4):609–24.

Ortner, Sherry B. 1973. On Key Symbols. *American Anthropologist* 75:1338–46.

Pahl, Robert E. 1975. *Whose City? And Further Essays on Urban Society.* Harmondsworth: Penguin.

Paine, Robert. 1989. Israel: Jewish Identity and Competition over 'Tradition.' In *History and Ethnicity*, Elizabeth Tonkin, Maryon McDonald, and Malcolm Chapman, eds., 121–36. ASA Monographs 27. London: Routledge.

Ram, Uri (ed.). 1993. *Israeli Society: Critical Perspectives.* Tel-Aviv: Breirot Publishers. (Hebrew)

Rubin, Nissan. 1984–85. Unofficial Rites in an Army Unit. *Social Forces* 6(3–4):795–809.

Schwartz, Barry, Yael Zerubavel, and Bernice Barnett. 1986. The Recovery of Masada: A Study in Collective Memory. *The Sociological Quarterly* 27(2):147–64.

Schweid, Eliezer. 1979. *Homeland and a Land of Promise.* Tel Aviv: Am Oved. (Hebrew)

Shamgar-Handelman, Lea, and Don Handelman. 1986. Holiday Celebrations in Israeli Kindergartens: Relationships between Representations of Collectivity and Family in the Nation-State. In *The Frailty* of Authority, Myron J. Aronoff, ed., 71 –103. New Brunswick, N.J.: Transaction.

Shohat, Ella. 1992. Rethinking Jews and Muslims: Quincentennial Reflections. Middle East Report 178(22:5):25–29.

Shokeid, Moshe. 1988. Children of Circumstances: Israeli Immigrants in New York. Ithaca: Cornell University Press.

Stoller, Paul. 1989. The Taste of Ethnographic Things: The Senses in Anthropology. Philadelphia: University of Pennsylvania Press.

Strathern, Marilyn. 1987. Out of Context: The Persuasive Fictions of Anthropology. Current Anthropology 28(3):251–81.

Suttles, Gerald S. 1984. The Cumulative Texture of Local Urban Culture. American Journal of Sociology 90(2):283–304.

Theory and Criticism. 1991. Theory and Criticism: An Israeli Forum, Summer. (Hebrew)

Turner, Victor. 1985. On the Edge of the Bush: Anthropology as Experience. Tucson: University of New Mexico Press.

Watts, Michael J. 1992. Space for Everything (A Commentary). Cultural Anthropology 7(1):115–29.

Weingrod, Alex. 1979. Recent Trends in Israeli Ethnicity. Ethnic and Racial Studies 2:55–65.

———. 1990. The Saint of Beersheba. Albany: State University of New York Press.

Wright, Patrick. 1985. On Living in an Old Country: The National Past in Contemporary Britain. London: Verso.

Zach, Natan. 1988. Lost Continent. In A Feeling of Place, by Nissim Kalderon. Hakibbutz Hameuchad. (Hebrew)

1

To Morocco and Back

Tourism and Pilgrimage among
Moroccan-Born Israelis

ANDRÉ LEVY

EDITORS' COMMENTS

This chapter is André Levy's "To Morocco and Back: Tourism and Pilgrimage among Moroccan-Born Israelis." Its focus is on a trend that has been developing in the past few years: the pilgrimages of Israeli Jews back to their or their parents' homelands in Eastern Europe and North Africa. Levy's chapter is an analysis of one such voyage, which is in a deep sense a search for identity in the old home country of Morocco. It is based on fieldwork carried out when the author accompanied a group of Moroccan-born Israelis on what can be described as a part pilgrimic voyage and part tourist excursion back to their land of birth. When the group left Israel, these people thought of Morocco as an integral part—in a sense, as the 'real' part—of their identity. But what Levy found was a paradox: people discovered their Israeli-ness in Morocco.

Over the past several years, organized tour groups of Moroccan-born Israelis have been traveling back to their native land. These tours back to 'childhood districts' are part of the ethnic revival in Israel, and can also be seen as part of the emergence of a worldwide trend toward a "new ethnicity."[1] The emergence of this kind of ethnicity raises an important set of questions related to ethnocultural continuity and change in complex industrialized societies: Does the trend toward ethnic renewal express a nostalgic yearning for

25

a (remembered and imagined) 'better past' and "good old tradition"? Or, does it represent, following Gans (1979), a further stage in the acculturation and assimilation of ethnic minorities into the larger society?

This chapter, dealing with these issues in the context of Israelis' travel to Morocco, centers on two main modes of travel—tourism and pilgrimage—and on their relation to ethnicity. The chapter poses two fundamental questions: How do the 'touristic' and 'pilgrimic' experiences (upon which we elaborate later) influence the modes of selection, presentation, and interpretation of travelers' ethnic identities? What are the implications of the selection, presentation, and interpretation of the travelers' ethnic identities for an understanding of the 'new ethnicity' in the contemporary Israeli context?

This analysis of the ethnic identities draws its basic assumptions from the situational approach to ethnicity. This approach attempted to overcome "the problem of reification of the concept of ethnic group that follows from its identification with an objectively defined, shared, uniform cultural inventory or with common normative patterns of behavior that are assumed to be consistently adhered to" (Okamura 1981:452). Following Okamura, we may distinguish between the 'objective' and 'subjective' points of view of analysis, that is, the structural features of the setting that provide the overall framework of social relations, and the situation in which actors may pursue different courses of action, according to their understanding of their personal circumstances within the overall framework.

As I demonstrate later, the 'objective' aspect of social structure is not always relevant to the trip. Because travel removes people from their familiar social surroundings and relations, the subjective aspects of lived experience tend to become more significant. The travelers are concerned with the comprehension and interpretation of 'objective' structural frameworks in which they operate and which influence their selection of ethnic identities. The 'pilgrimic' and 'touristic' frames of interpretation constructed by the travelers themselves are the prime ways for their accounting for 'what they are doing' and for regulating their conduct. These frameworks prescribe appropriate behavior when, for example, the Israelis visit saints' tombs or shop in the *suqs* (markets) of Morocco. Such frameworks are predicated on certain assumptions about the settings and boundaries within which the specifics of interests and power relationships come to the fore. It is within these frameworks that the Israelis play their roles and present their identities in each situation.

ETHNICITY IN CONTEXT: MOROCCAN JEWS IN ISRAEL

Until the recent Jewish exodus from the former Soviet Union, Moroccan Jews and their descendants comprised the largest Jewish ethnic group in Israel. Most of them had immigrated to the new country during the 1950s and early 1960s, pulled by the vision of the recently established Jewish state (which many of them interpreted in religious idioms) and pushed by the growing nationalistic sentiments in Morocco following independence and the departure of the French (Stillman 1991). Following this massive wave of *aliya* (immigration to Israel), the impressive Jewish presence in Morocco, which had preceded Islam by one millennium at least (Hirschberg 1981), has dwindled to several thousand (Schmelz and DellaPergola 1988).

While Jewish life under Muslim rule in Morocco had its ebbs and flows, the extent of the symbiotic relations established between Moroccan Jews and their Arab and Berber neighbors over the course of their lengthy coexistence could hardly be met elsewhere. As *Dhimi* (protégés of the Islamic community), the Jews had their legitimate niche, humble and inferior as it has been, within the Islamic society (Bat-Ye'or 1985). As merchants, peddlers, and craftsmen, they played a vital role in the economy of rural Morocco and constituted an integral part of its occupational system (Shokeid 1982). Unlike the Jewish communities of Eastern Europe, which were separated and alienated from their non-Jewish neighbors in most spheres of life, in the Maghreb the Jews had adopted various aspects of the local culture and lifestyle (Sharot 1976).

Following the establishment of the French Protectorate in 1912, however, the distinctively religious character of the Jewish communities and the traditional ways of life they shared with the Muslims were massively corroded (Stillman 1991). A current of internal migration, started already at the end of the nineteenth century, had swept the Jews in the hinterland, as many of them moved to Casablanca and other coastal towns, attracted by the new opportunities that French technology and industrialization had created (Chouraqui 1973). This process of rapid transition that undermined the traditional structure and cohesiveness of the communities was still under way when Moroccan Jews started to leave for Israel, and no doubt contributed to their predicaments of homecoming (Deshen and Shokeid 1974).

Beyond the situational vulnerability of the newcomers caught between tradition and modernity (Bensimon-Donath 1968; de Nesry 1958), a host of harsh circumstances in the new country exacerbated their absorption process and made it particularly agonizing. Lack of resources in the young country flooded by immigrants that almost tripled its population in less than one decade, led to large-scale housing shortages and unemployment and relegated many of the Moroccan newcomers to the bottom of the socioeconomic ladder (Horowitz and Lissak 1989). In the name of the Zionist vision of dispersing the population, blooming the desert, and defending the borders, many of them were settled in hastily erected development towns and *moshavim* (semicooperative villages), located in the unattractive periphery, where economic opportunities were particularly bleak (Aronoff 1973; Cohen 1970; Hasson 1981).

These difficulties were augmented by the ethnocentric and condescending attitudes of the absorbing mainstream, mostly Ashkenazi (of European extraction) and secular. In line with the ideal of melting pot integration, strong pressures were exerted on the newcomers to divest themselves of their cultural heritage and traditional values and become "new Israelis" (Bar-Yosef 1966; Eisenstadt 1954). This process of imposed "desocialization and resocialization" was abortive but painful. It nursed a strong sense of acrimony and deprivation on the part of the Moroccan newcomers. At the same time, it stigmatized them as hot-tempered, primitive, and more problematic than other immigrants in the eyes of the Ashkenazim.

From the vantage point of the late 1980s, with the modest but systematic improvement in the socioeconomic status of many Moroccan Jews and the rise of some to power positions in the sociopolitical structure, many of the adversities of the post-*aliya* years were attenuated though not entirely removed. As the years passed, a sense of belongingness and "Israeli-ness" was gradually acquired, even in the most peripheral development towns; but this Israeli identity was strongly informed by the ethnocultural heritage of the Maghreb as well as by the collective "Moroccan experience" in Israel. The amalgamation of deep Jewish traditional sentiments, nationalistic attitudes, and animosity toward the socialist-Zionist secular establishment of the traumatic 1950s had far-reaching consequences in the political arena. More than any other ethnic group in Israel, Moroccan Jews were responsible for the political turnover that brought the right-wing Likud Party to power in 1977, after three decades of socialist hegemony.

Being part and parcel of present-day Israel, Moroccan Jews' role in shaping the sociocultural face of Israeli society cannot be overstated. Yet the scars of the past still haunt them. Israelis of Moroccan origin are overrepresented in the lower socioeconomic strata and on various indexes of social pathology.

One cardinal cultural characteristic of the Jewish traditional society in Morocco that was carried over to Israel has been the folk veneration of saints (*tsaddiqim*). Since hagiolatric sentiments have shaped most of the tours of Moroccan Israelis to their native land into quasi-pilgrimages, this cultural tradition and its vicissitudes in Israel should be reviewed in brief.

While the belief in *tsaddiqim*, based on classical Jewish sources, has not been unique to Moroccan Jews, no other Jewish group has cultivated hagiolatric practices as they did (Ben-Ami 1984). Given the distinctive Maghrebi style of these practices, it seems clear that they were influenced by indigenous *maraboutism* (veneration of holy men endowed with supernatural power), which in scope and profundity has no equivalent in any other Muslim society (Eickelman 1976; Geertz 1968; Gellner 1969). The Jewish saints were charismatic rabbis, distinguished by their erudition and piety. They were believed to possess a special spiritual force, the manifestation of which is similar to the Muslim *baraka* (Rabinow 1975; Westermarck 1926). This force, ordinarily revealed only after the holy man's death (Stillman 1982), could be utilized for the benefit of his adherents. Consequently, the tombs of the saints, scattered all over the country, became the focus of their cults.

While it appears that every Jewish community had at least one patron saint of its own (Ben-Ami 1984; Goldberg 1983), the reputation of most of these local *tsaddiqim* was quite circumscribed. Some of them, however, have acquired popularity and followings that exceeded local or even regional boundaries. Sainted figures like Rabbi Amram Ben-Diwan, Rabbi David u-Moshe, Rabbi Chaim Pinto, Rabbi Ya'acov Abu-Hatsera, and Rabbi David Dra Halevi have been venerated in all the traditional segments of Moroccan Jewry. Some of the saints were well known historical figures, coming from cherished families of pious sages (like the Abu-Hatseras and the Pintos), while many others, devoid of any historical identification, appear to be legendary figures.

The main event in the veneration of each saint was the collective pilgrimage (*ziyara* in Arabic) to his tomb on the anniversary of his death and the *hillulah* (celebration) there. The *hillulah* was a multivocal event that combined deep spirituality and ecstatic devotion with flesh-and-blood concern and a picnic-like atmosphere. In the case of a popular saint, many thousands of pilgrims would gather around his tomb for several days, feasting on slaughtered cattle, drinking arak, dancing and chanting, praying and lighting candles. The *hillulot* of the ahistorical saints were conducted as a rule on *Lag Ba'Omer* (the thirty-third day after Passover), the assumed death anniversary of talmudic luminary Rabbi Shim'on Bar-Yohai. As the putative author of the *Holy Zohar (The Book of Splendor)*, the most important text in Jewish mysticism, Rabbi Shim'on was deemed *primus inter pares* in the Jewish Moroccan pantheon of saints.

While the *hillulot* loomed high in the annual life cycle of Moroccan Jews, highlighting and reinforcing Jewish solidarity, the presence of the saint was strongly felt in daily routine as well. By and large, the *tsaddiq* was a basic given in the Maghrebi social reality, a central idiom for articulating a wide range of experiences. One major cluster of such experiences was the miraculous intercession of the saint on behalf of a Jewish devotee threatened by a Muslim perpetrator. While this central theme attests to the existence of tension and conflicts in Jewish Muslim relations, it should be noted that the saint, as a symbolic idiom common to both groups, could also serve as a mitigating bridge between them.

The massive immigration of the 1950s put the continuity of hagiolatric traditions among the Moroccan newcomers in jeopardy. This threat was created by the fact that the saints' sanctuaries had been left behind, remote and inaccessible, as well as by the traumatic encounter with the modern secular cosmology of mainstream Israeli society with its hegemonic and homogenizing melting pot ideology. Indeed, the cultural shock felt by the newcomers, amplified by cultural supression on the part of the absorbing agencies, contributed to the general diminution and decentralization of the *hillulot* in the first years after *aliya* (Ben-Ami 1984; Deshen 1977). But this cultural attenuation process was thwarted and even reversed in the 1970s and 1980s, when Moroccan Jews became more integrated into the Israeli society and started to regain their self-confidence and sense of identity (Ben-Ari and Bilu 1987). In proudly asserting their distinctive cultural heritage, the idiom of the saint was an indispensable resource (Weingrod 1990). As a result, Moroccan Jews have become the major carriers of the revival of hagiolatric practices in present-day Israel. They have "annexed" old-time native sanctuaries, created new traditions of *hillulot* around recently deceased sages, and even "transformed" saints from Morocco through visitational dreams (Bilu 1987).

The question whether this hagiolatric revival represents a deepening ethnic distinctiveness and a "symbolic diasporization of Israel" (Cohen 1983a) or a more profound integration into Israeli society (Gans 1979) need not concern us here. But it will reverberate in the discussion of the tours to Morocco, to which we now turn.

THE TOUR

A fairly prudent estimate suggests that, over the past twelve years, about two thousand Israelis have visited Morocco in organized 'tour' groups each year.[2] In the spring of 1987, I joined one such group as participant-observer and after our return to Israel, I held about forty interviews with most of the twenty-eight tour participants, as well as with members of other groups.

Like most of the trips, we began our journey shortly before *Lag Ba-'Omer*, the death anniversary of Rabbi Shim'on Bar-Yohai. The itinerary we followed was highly standardized, and included the following: after two days in Spain, awaiting the *laissez passer*, we proceeded to travel along the southeast coast of Spain toward Algeciras, sailed to Ceuta, and then took a bus to Tangiers, Morocco. The fourth and fifth days included Tangiers, Larache, Ouezzane (tomb of the saint Rabbi Amram Ben-Diwan), and Fes, while the fifth involved Fes (the tomb of female saint Lala Soliqa), Meknes, Ifrane, Sefrou, and return to Fes. The sixth day was comprised of a visit to Fes, Salé

(Rabbi Raphael Ankawa's tomb), Rabat, and Casablanca. After spending the Sabbath in Casablanca, we left on Saturday night for the tomb of Rabbi Yihya Lakhdar in Benhamad, to celebrate the great *hillulah* of Lag Ba-'Omer. On the eighth day, we traveled south to Marrakech (tomb of Rabbi Raphael Ha-Cohen) and on the next (ninth) day, we continued touring Marrakech before continuing south to Ourika (Rabbi Shlomo Belkhanes's tomb). We then traveled a great distance to Agadir, on the Atlantic Ocean. On the tenth day, we traveled through southwest Morocco, heading north along the Atlantic Coast: to Agadir, Essawira (Mogador—to Rabbi Chaim Pinto's tomb), Azemmour (the tomb of Rabbi Abraham Mul-Nes), and, finally, Casablanca, where we dispersed. After ten free days, we reassembled to return to Israel via Casablanca. We crossed into Spain by way of Ceuta and, after a two-day stay in Torremolinos, returned to Israel. Some participants traveled to France before returning home.

In tours such as these the Israeli travel agent sends along an Israeli escort, who usually does not have any formal training. He is generally someone who succeeded in recruiting several participants on condition that he act as group escort; he receives a free ticket. The Moroccan Tourist Bureau assigns a local guide, who serves as mediator between the travelers and the local population (see Cohen 1985).

From interviews I learned that the decision to travel was usually made in family gatherings: one person would raise the suggestion and two to four people would decide to join her or him. Sometimes other friends joined, or acquaintances would come along. Few people came alone. The ages of the participants ranged from the late thirties to the early sixties; in the group I joined four participants were over seventy.

This was the first time most of the participants had left Israel since their arrival from Morocco. For all of them the tour represented their first encounter with the region where they had spent their childhood and adolescence. Moreover, the tour took place after two to three decades during which they were certain that they would never see their native land again.

For the participants, the reason for traveling was never defined as pleasure. No one, not even the few who had traveled to Morocco once or twice before, claimed that the trip was for the purpose of relaxation. Most people expressed very profound reasons for their travel, such as the desire to visit the tombs of parents or other family members. One person claimed he was traveling with a marble tombstone from Israel to place on his father's grave, while others considered bringing their parents' bones back to Israel. Still others linked their visit to the desire to complete business left unfinished as a results of their hasty departure from Morocco. One participant planned to bring back an aged father who was not allowed to come on *aliya* (emigration) to Israel with his children when a selection policy (during the 1950s) was in force; another planned to bring to Israel a sister who "became en-snared by the charms of a Muslim suitor" and had married him.

A number of core elements of the Jewish-Maghrebi experience in Israel surfaced during the course of the trip. The itinerary itself was a kind of en-capsulation of Jewish history: "exile" to Spain, "expulsion from Spain" to Morocco, a sojourn in Morocco, followed by return to the Land of Israel. Confirmation of this theme was expressed over the course of the trip. For example, when the lights of the Malaga airport first came into view, the im-mediate association in the minds of the travelers was of their immigration to Israel. "There's Haifa! There's Haifa!" one of them exclaimed; her neighbor reiterated, "When we came on *aliya* (to Israel), we clapped our hands and said, 'There's Haifa! There's Haifa!' " Someone said in Arabic, "N'amlu kif 'amlu jadudna di harzu mil'Maser" ("Let us do as our forefathers did when they left Egypt"). The clearest expression of reliving the Jewish experience was enunciated by the guide who, while we were moving along the south-eastern coast of Spain, stated that we were traveling along the route taken by our forefathers when they were expelled from that country.

TOURISM AND PILGRIMAGE: A CONTRAST OF JOURNEYS

The first question posed focuses on the link between different motifs of ex-perience that surfaced during the trip and the nature of presentation of ethnic identity. Yet in order to analyze the effect of different thematic structures—'touristic' and 'pilgrimic'—on the presentation of ethnic identity in the course of the journey, it is wise to briefly review their constituent characteristics.

Before the publication of Dean MacCannell's work on tourism (1973, 1976), social science researchers tended to adopt the popular view, regard-ing it as a superficial phenomenon not worthy of serious study (Cohen 1983b). MacCannell, however, revealed aspects and levels of tourist behav-ior that cast it in a very different light. His main claim was that modern tourism is a continuation of pilgrimage and bears 'deep' meanings similar to those of traditional pilgrimages (see also Graburn 1977). Indeed, in a Durkheimian vein, MacCannell saw tourism as a modern substitute for tra-ditional religion: "Sightseeing is a form of ritual respect to the society. . . . Tourism absorbs some of the social functions of religion in the modern world" (MacCannell 1973:13). Society thus worships itself when it sight-sees. Cohen (1981) has termed this kind of analysis, which compares tourism to traditional pilgrimages, the "convergence" approach. Other scholars, however, take the opposing view and emphasize the "divergence" of the two phenomena. They see tourism as a degraded product of modernity, a popu-lar mass phenomenon made possible by a combination of advanced and in-expensive transportation and an increase in leisure time. According to these scholars (Boorstin 1972; Fussell 1979), tourism is devoid of any deep spiritual or cultural significance. The tourist is but a "deviant" from the serious traveler of the past, who embarked on such journeys as the "grand tour."

Cohen has attempted to account for the differences between the two approaches by showing that scholars have focused on different aspects of tourism. Whereas "divergence" approach advocates concentrate on the level of explicit behaviors, their opponents focus on the implicit deeper level of meaning. Cohen (1979) goes on to suggest a typology of tourism, by presenting a structural model that combines analysis of tourism and pilgrimage. He suggests two dimensions for examining such phenomena: the depth of the experience of the tourist/pilgrim and the distance of the tourist/pilgrim from the center of his or her society.

Building on Eliade's model of the "center," Cohen suggests that the 'ideal' (and perhaps empirically nonexistent) pilgrim undergoes a deep experience during pilgrimage; this pilgrim travels to the religious-spiritual center of his society. While he has physically and geographically traveled far from his quotidian territory, this physical distance is actually an approach toward the meaningful center of his society. Traveling a great distance is designed both to free the pilgrim from the chains of routine, day-to-day existence, and to create in him a sense of spirituality.

In contrast to the pilgrim, Cohen enumerates several types of tourist experiences. In general, the deeper the tourist experience, the closer the tourist comes to the center of the society he his visiting. Thus, for example, a man who goes to a hotel in his town to relax does not have a deep experience, just as he does not distance himself at all from the center of values of his own society. By contrast, a Westerner who chooses to spend a long period in a Buddhist monastery eventually makes this "other" center into his own "elective center" (Cohen, Ben-Yehuda, and Aviad 1987).

ZIYARAS: A CONTINUATION OF A CULTURAL FRAMEWORK

One of the main reasons given by the travelers for their trip was their desire to visit the tombs of the *tsaddiqim* in Morocco. As mentioned before, the group as a whole visited seven such major sites. In addition, the pilgrims visited several minor places (both in terms of the emphasis placed on these graves in the tour and in the consciousness of Moroccan immigrants), such as the tomb of the "Angel" Raphael Bardugo in Meknes. As individuals, the travelers also visited many other graves during the free days, such as the tomb of Rabbi Raphael Ha-Cohen near Marrakech, Rabbi David Ben Baruch in Taroudant, and Rabbi Eliyahu in Casablanca. I would suggest (and this is a conservative estimate) that each traveler visited at least ten tombs of *tsaddiqim*.

The centrality of the *tsaddiqim* for the tour was reflected in other ways as well. In Israel, the material published by the travel agencies constantly emphasizes the names of the main sacred sites to be visited. The tombs are thus actually milestones marking the journey, and the occasional disputes and quarrels among the travelers over the itinerary were in fact struggles over the issue of which *tsaddiqim* would be visited. These struggles reflected the fact that the members originated from different areas in Morocco. As mentioned before, each community had its own patron saint.

In the course of the journey, the travelers manipulated the saints to suit their own needs. The Israeli escort, for example, used the saints to suppress complaints and dissatisfaction. He bombarded the travelers with many names of *tsaddiqim* we were to visit in order to divert attention from the poor organization of the tour (for which he bore responsibility). One of the voyagers employed the *tsaddiq* in a dispute with an elderly couple. He invoked the *tsaddiq*'s help when he felt he could not confront the couple directly. "No *tsaddiq* will help them. When they see a *tsaddiq* they'll see nothing but darkness; all this thanks to the *tsaddiq* Raphael, besides whom my grandfather lies buried," he intoned, with suppressed anger. These few examples illustrate the constant use of the cultural idiom of saints throughout the tour. The best proof of the centrality of pilgrimage was, of course, the planning of the tour so that people would arrive on *Lag Ba-'Omer* at the central *hillulah* (celebration) in honor of Rabbi Yihya Lakhdar in Benahmed (near Casablanca).

The influence of the pilgrimic framework on the travelers was remarkable. Even the very few people who declared that they could not identify with this religious practice would not violate the appropriate rules of conduct when visiting the tombs of the saints.

In the pilgrimic framework, certain features of Moroccan Jewish ethnic identity are expressed with great vitality. The cemetery is the meeting place of the pilgrims with three types of symbols and representatives of Morocco: the symbols of the king, the Muslims, and the Moroccan Jews.

The King in the Shrines

On the institutional level, the presence of the Maghreb royalty can be seen everywhere. The portraits of the king and his heir-apparent stare from every wall in the cemeteries and in the shrines of the *tsaddiqim*. The king sends his official emissaries to bless the pilgrims to the *hillulah*, and his protection is clearly visible, as he (or, more accurately, his representatives) sends soldiers to guard the sites where the *hillulah* ceremonies take place. To the external observer it seems that nothing has changed: the Israelis—ex-inhabitants of Morocco—accept the rule of patronage just as they did in the past. In the framework of the *ziyara*, they act as if they had never left Morocco. The king remains an object of veneration even after the long separation. The homage paid the king is an indication of the deep imprint of the patron–client relationship on the Moroccan experience (Deshen 1989; Meyers 1982; Rosen 1972; Shokeid 1982). This pattern seems to continue almost unchanged.[3]

An interesting attitude, comparing the king to the *tsaddiq*, was clearly expressed on the way to the tomb of Rabbi mram Ben-Diwan in Wazzan by the Israeli escort in his request: "Ululate in honor of *Mulai* Hassan, ululate in honor of *Sidna* (our master), ululate in honor of Rabbi Amram!" It is not clear whom he meant by "*Sidna*" (our master)—the king, the *tsaddiq*, or perhaps both together. Similarly, people often had their pictures taken next to the tombs of the *tsaddiqim* and next to posters bearing the king's portrait, which were placed near these tombs.

The concept of patronage also applies to the role of the *tsaddiq*. The *tsaddiq*, like the king, has the power to protect the Jews in a world that is politically chaotic and unpredictable, where the greatest certainty is uncertainty. The king himself is the descendant of a holy Muslim lineage and is thus a kind of "saint," even if not for the Jews (Bowen 1988; Combs-Schilling 1989). The behavior of several of the Israelis in the mausoleum of Muhammed V, the father of the present king, can easily be understood in light of the parallelism of king and *tsaddiq*. For example, some women spread their hands to the sides and kissed them as they entered the sepulchre, as they would at least a *tsaddiq*'s tomb. Moreover, their behavior did not surprise, in the least, the others who did not do so.

Despite all these venerative gestures, it is clear that the *tsaddiq* is perceived by the Jews as more authoritative and superior to the king. By the very fact of his inferiority to the *tsaddiq*, the king is expected to attend the *ziyara*. He (or his representatives) does not come to express 'symbolic' participation (in the political sense); rather, he takes the actual power of the saint for granted, and this supernatural power compels the king to pay homage to the *tsaddiq*. Thus, for the Israelis, the king pays respect not to the participants at the *hillulah*, but to the *tsaddiq*.

Israelis and Muslims in the Cemetery

The pilgrimic aspect of the tour does not take place in a contextual vacuum. The indigenous Moroccans who are aware of the practices associated with the pilgrimage—a vital force (though with certain differences) among Muslims as well (Eickelman 1976; Geertz 1968; Gellner 1969, 1981; Rabinow, 1975)—are intricately woven into these rites. For example, the pilgrims required the assistance of Muslim Moroccans in finding the way to the *tsaddiqim*. Indeed, the pilgrims did not succeed, not even once during the course of the trip, in finding their way to the holy sites by themselves. The need, or rather the necessity, to employ Muslim assistance in performing a Jewish religious practice thus worked to emphasize the Israelis' separation and estrangement from Morocco, and to remind the pilgrims of their past dependence on Muslim good will. At the same time, this increased the Jews' suspicion of the Muslims. For example, they accused the Muslim guide of being responsible for the great delay in arrival at the tomb of Rabbi Yihya Lakhdar, claiming that he deviated from the route in order to visit his parents' home in nearby Settat. The fact that the Israeli guide, who claimed to "know Morocco by heart and have no need of a map," gave the directions made no difference. Furthermore, it was the Muslims who provided the services that made the *ziyara* possible: they maintain the cemeteries, whitewash the tombs, get rid of the weeds, and sell candles. It appears that the high ambivalence characteristic of the Jewish-Muslim relations in the past is also typical of the attitude of the Israelis on the tour toward the Moroccans. Their dependence on the latter created a special atmosphere of fear and suspicion interwoven with manifestations of intimacy and gratitude.

Jews in the Cemetery

The Israelis' attitude toward the Jews still living in Morocco is also complex and ambivalent. This ambivalence was noted when they encountered local Jews, primarily workers of the communal burial societies, in the cemeteries visited on the tour. In conversations that evolved, the issue of the Moroccan Jews' reluctance to make *aliya* was raised time and again. Raising this issue reflected, on the one hand, a genuine concern of the visitors for their brethren in exile who were presumably living under politically unstable and therefore potentially hazardous conditions. On the other hand, the Jews who chose not to leave Morocco presented for the Israelis a sort of 'hypothetical situation' of what would have happened had they not come on *aliya* to Israel. In a word, they appeared to see in those Jews the image of their own past lives. In this framework, the energy they invested in exhorting the locals to immigrate to Israel appeared as a covert attempt to justify their own *aliya*.

The lack of desire of the local Jews to immigrate to Israel is a fact difficult for the Israelis to accept, for it puts into question their own decision to come to Israel and renders the option of remaining in Morocco tangible. So unsettling was the provocation posed by this position that many of the Israelis were led to suggest that any Jew remaining in Morocco must be either mentally unbalanced or physically unhealthy. In this vein, they treated Jews they encountered in the cemeteries as marginal, odd people.

TOURISM IN MOROCCO

The touristic framework of the trip found ample expression during the free days in Casablanca. As long as the trip was conducted within an organized framework, the pilgrimic elements predominated. During the final ten days, when the travelers were on their own, contact with Muslims was greater, as most of the shopping in the *suqs* (markets) took place then. During those days, the travelers did not remain inside the 'ecological bubble' (Cohen 1972) that regulated their contact with their surroundings. The division into smaller groups and the lack of a bus to serve as a physical 'ecological bubble' compelled the travelers to interact more intimately with the Moroccan environment. The encounter, within the touristic framework, took place between Israelis and Muslims, as well as between the Israelis and Jewish family members who had remained in Morocco.

Muslims in the Suq

In contrast to the cultural continuity in attitudes toward king and Muslims in the pilgrimic frame, in the touristic frame the attitudes toward the Muslim surroundings were marked by a certain 'reversal.' The use of the word 'reversal' here is deliberate: the relationships between Jews and Muslims, as perceived by the Israelis, are not only different, but inverted: "Then (in the past), you called him (the Muslim) '*sidi*' (sir). Now, it is the reverse—he calls you '*sidi*'; the Arab calls the Jew '*sidi*'!" The symbolic reversal of the patron–client relationship between Israelis and Muslims is context-dependent. It takes place in a different framework than that of the encounter with symbols of the king. Whereas the latter appear in cemeteries, alongside tombs of *tsaddiqim* and in the context of the *ziyara*, the most significant and frequent encounter with Muslims generally takes place in the touristic-economic arena of the *suq*. The informant's description of the reversal of relations concerned precisely this context. He boasted of the new situation, as an expression of his power and courage in entering and shopping in a certain *suq* in Casablanca that Jews were previously forbidden to enter.

Another expression of the reversal of relations was made in regard to the prostitutes in Morocco. In the past, it was extremely dangerous for Jews to meet with Muslim prostitutes. It would have been considered a manifestation of forbidden symbolic use of Muslim 'property.' The Jews, whose social function could metaphorically be compared to that of women, could certainly not meet prostitutes in public.[4] On the tour, however, one could demonstrate self-confidence vis-à-vis the Muslims and consort in public with a Muslim whore. The symbolic reversal in power relations inherent in the use of whores was clear to the tourists, who consorted with the whores and tended to defiantly emphasize this in the presence of Muslims.

The emphasis on the reversal of relations between the tourists and the Muslims helped the travelers hide the fear they felt in the course of their journey. As long as they were within the shelter of the bus, their fear was not concealed as there was no need to do so. But when the tourists were exposed to the direct contact with the Muslims in the touristic frame—in the *suq*, the cafes, and the souvenir shops—the tourists employed the tactics of 'reversal of relations,' emphasizing elements that would present a facade of superiority and wealth.

Israeli Tourists—Moroccan Jews

The fear experienced by the tourists in Morocco would seem to contradict the manifestations of superiority and reversal of relations. In the past, Jews were largely unaware of the fears and anxieties to which they were subject in living together with Muslims. They resembled, or so it seemed to the tourists, the Jews living in Casablanca today. But now the tourists were phenomenologically in a different position: they could sense their own fears as well as those of the Jews living in Morocco—fears whose very existence was denied by the latter. Thus, a young girl who occasionally visits her parents in Casablanca recounted that each time she travels to Morocco, fears arise in her heart, and that her parents were astounded by such feelings. She added that she became aware of the fear only after her immigration to Israel.

The Israelis' ambivalence toward the Jews they met in Morocco resulted from a feeling of superiority toward people who appeared to relinquish their personal honor for the sake of economically more comfortable lives. In their behavior toward the Jews, the tourists emphasized the nationalist components of their identity. This strategy was employed when no benefits or interests were involved in their relations. When the tourists needed accommodation in Jewish houses or other similar benefits, they displayed the 'Jewish-Maghrebi' side of their identity, emphasizing the common elements between them and native Moroccan Jews. Some went even further, laying aside their national honor (which was expressed on other occasions) and accepting their hosts' claims that life in Israel was incomparably worse than life in Morocco. They agreed to take part in painting a picture of Israel as a land of robberies and murders, rapists and drug addicts. Within the tour group, however, the same tourists condemned the Jews' decision to remain in Morocco.

THE JOURNEY'S DEEP STRUCTURE: PILGRIMIC AND TOURISTIC EXPERIENCE

As we have seen, the pilgrimic frame tends to evince cultural continuity in the attitudes of the travelers toward the Muslims and the king. The primary explanation for this striking continuity is the existence of organized pilgrimages as cultural forms rooted in past tradition; that is, the pilgrimage is a well known and articulated cultural phenomenon. This is particularly apparent in the Israelis' attitude toward the king. In contrast, the touristic frame is particularly marked by a reversal of traditional Jewish-Muslim relations and is especially conspicuous in the realm of power relations. As we saw, while pilgrimage imposes a certain presentation of identity, in the touristic frame conscious manipulative use is made of the Jewish-Maghrebi past to serve various interests.

These facts raise the following questions: Why do such contradictory trends exist? Why is the presentation of ethnic identity in the pilgrimic frame characterized by preservation of traditional patterns, whereas in the tourist frame it is marked by change? These questions focus our attention on the differing deep structures of tourism and pilgrimage. A systematic exposition of these two deep structures may help us understand the contradictory patterns of presentation of ethnic identity.

The territory of pilgrimage is primarily a sacred one, whereas the touristic arena is the profane sphere of financial activity and the quotidian. The tombs of the *tsaddiqim* are sites sacred not only to the Jews; they are revered or at least guarded and respected by Muslims as well. In spite of many differences, this cultural idiom is common to both Jews and Muslims in the Maghreb. The "extremely Jewish" nature of the *tsaddiqim* (Goldberg 1983)—their location in Jewish cemeteries or their protection of the Jews against decrees—limits Muslim access to the cemetery. For the latter, the tombs are not *terra incognita*, as Schroeter (1990) has claimed, but rather an *ex-territory*. Most Muslims would refrain from entering the cemetery, while paying due to its sacredness. The relative exclusion of Muslims (though not of their symbolic representatives) from the cemeteries gave greater opportunity for expressions of Jewish sentiments and presentation of particularistic ethnic identity. Whereas in the markets many of the travelers bargained as if they were fully Moroccan, in the cemetery they could give expression to their particular religious identity. When the Israeli escort once exited the cemetery at Salé wearing a *kipa* (skullcap), everyone was frightened and demanded that he remove it. The *kipa*, they explained, may be worn only within the precincts of the cemetery. This was also the only safe territory outside the tour bus, where Hebrew could be spoken.[5]

The delimitation of the cemetery by clearly marked borders (even in a physical sense, by a fence or wall around it) provides a relatively secure and comfortable feeling. Their comfort in manifesting their Jewish identity there highlights, paradoxically, the Israelis' strong sense of personal insecurity in Morocco. Here, the past feelings of insecurity and uncertainty resurface.

The pilgrims approach the tombs of the *tsaddiqim* out of a basic desire to 'receive.' They come to receive the *tsaddiq*'s grace; they visit the site to enjoy the benefits of his religious charisma and power. This orientation, of receiving grace, of subordination, of recognition of the patron's superiority, runs, to a great extent, along the lines of Jewish-Muslim relations in the past. In those ties as well as in pilgrimage, 'taking' was seen as illegitimate. Although there is a certain element of mutuality or reciprocity in the "pilgrimic contract"—protection in return for faith—this mutuality is not built on a relationship of equality. Rather, this cultural pattern reinforces patron–client relationships. Of course, I do not claim that subordination to the *tsaddiq* and subordination to the Muslims were of equal weight and value, but rather that the underlying theme of 'receiving' in pilgrimage results from an orientation of subordination.

Unlike pilgrimage, which is delimited by clear boundaries preventing unmediated contact with Muslims, the touristic frame, by its very nature, exposes Israelis to the possibility of open contact with them. The nature of the contact gave rise to a situation in which Israelis enlisted the larger political context to express positions of power, capitalizing on the image of Israel held by many Moroccans as a strong, aggressive state.

In the touristic frame, power relations are the name of the game. The financial situation in such contexts is one of a priori inequality (Sutton 1967). The tourists possess the economic means and resources that are of interest to the hosts. For the Israelis, such a situation gives them an advantage: they can afford to *take* of the finest of Morocco. As owners of wealth, they may *take* whatever their heart desires. The economic strength of the Israeli shekel, compared to the Moroccan dirham, further emphasized these aspects, for the Israelis could buy whatever was available at, what were for them, extremely low prices.

Economic relations between hosts and their guests involve a basic distrust, inherent in the nature of the tourism (van den Berghe 1980). The short-range nature of the relationship arouses suspicions of cheating. The hosts are suspicious of such things as counterfeit money or thefts from stores, while the guests are wary of price gouging or flawed merchandise. The suspicions of deception heighten mutual distrust and may make displays of force all the more necessary.

The power relations that arise from the touristic situation are not devoid of specific cultural characteristics. In the Moroccan markets power relationships are negotiated through a kind of game of simulated friendship. The travelers use elements of pseudofriendship in order to advance their economic interests and to reduce prices. Like the locals, they, too, are aware of the knowledge needed and of the appropriate conduct involved in Maghrebi bargaining. But their display of elements of their postethnic identity as Moroccans is one the whole unsuccessful, for the vendors, too, play the game of pseudofriendship (and for the same economic reasons). Thus, they try to maneuver the Israelis into a position that precludes bargaining—the tourists will not be cheated, for they are brothers from the old days. But the nature of the game is clear to all. The tourists know that the vendors relate to the Israeli aspect of their identity; the vendors use Hebrew words learned through their contact with Israeli tourists. Some play cassettes of a popular Israeli singer in order to attract the shoppers in the *suq*. They thus display the relevance of the tourists' Israeli identity.

The two frameworks chosen for analysis, the touristic and pilgrimic, represent the two extreme types of travel experience. Yet two other intermediate types of experience took place during the trip to Morocco: visits to houses in which travelers previously lived, and visits to parents' tombs (or those of other family members). With respect to the attitude toward Muslim surroundings, the former is closer to the tourist end of the spectrum of experience by Cohen's (1979) typology, as there is a great measure of contact with Muslims. The element of change is prominent in the areas visited, because the ongoing life of Morocco has resulted in visible changes in the neighborhoods and houses in which the travelers grew up. But there is a certain pilgrimic element in this visit. It is a kind of pilgrimage to a center that no longer exists, to a minor sanctuary that, as it turns out, has been destroyed. "It's no longer my house. Our house—'*allah yrakhamo*' ('May God have mercy on it')." Thus spoke one of the women who visited her house and found an office building erected on its foundations.

In contrast to changes in former dwellings, most family tombs have not been damaged. The experience of this kind of visit is closer to that of a visit to saints' tombs. Even if the graves are somewhat damaged, this is the result of the effects of time and nature weathering the tombs. And, as this damage is not man-made, it is accepted with forgiveness. Furthermore, the attitude is that the graves can always be repaired and renovated. It is possible and permissible (from the authorities' point of view) to renovate the graves damaged by corrosion. For the Muslim workers of the cemeteries, this was a source of employment. Like the saints' tombs, the family tombs are in Jewish territory and under Jewish control. They are a foothold, a symbolic marker on Moroccan soil, and the preservation of this marker is both possible and legitimate even today.

CONCLUSION: THE ETHNIC SIGNIFICANCE
OF THE TRIP TO MOROCCO

While I have focused in this chapter on the social and experiential organization of the trip itself, I have not considered its long-range effects: How did this journey affect the group of travelers? The focus on the situational aspect of ethnic identity limits the ability to analyze the implications of the experience for Israeli society, since we cannot examine the daily life of the members of the traveling group after its return to Israel from such a trip.

On the surface, the trip to Morocco seems to be an expression of nostalgia for a better past. The travelers expressed a deep desire to return to the old days. This supports Cohen's arguments about 'symbolic diasporization' of Israeli society (Cohen 1983a). Moroccan immigrants who travel to visit their native land are 'exiled' from Israel; their behavior lends metaphorical and concrete support to Cohen's claims. But a closer look at our case reveals that things are not so simple. The travelers, it is true, are very aware and constantly preoccupied with aspects of their ethnic identity. They are intensely obsessed with questions that have to do with segregation and particularism. But the answers they give themselves are 'Israeli' ones. For example, the symbolic reversal of the 'exilic stage,' as expressed by the undertaking of the trip to Morocco, to an *'aliya* stage,' as expressed by the travelers in their cries, "There's Haifa! There's Haifa" when they saw the lights of the port, is an indication of their complex relation to Israel. The trip does not express a return to the past. The reversal of terms emphasizes the "Israeli-ness" of their feelings toward Morocco. In identifying the shores of North Africa as the shore of Haifa, they impose the Israeli reality on the Moroccan one.

The central definition of ethnicity—the relationship to the past, to common history—acquires a meaning through the trip. Studies of ethnicity, in spite of their emphasis on the dynamic and manipulative use of ethnic identity, tend to assume a stable relation to a common past, both real and imagined. Yet, as this analysis shows, the trip demonstrated the dynamic elements found within this relation as well. Claims put forward by researchers such as E. Cohen about 'symbolic regression' or 'symbolic diasporization' assume the existence of a static diaspora, a well-defined past toward which one regresses.

The material I collected, however, clearly indicates that sentiments toward an idealized past, with which the Israelis came to Morocco, gradually dissipated along the way, with the growing awareness that present-day Morocco is not "theirs" anymore. I believe that the feelings of loss and alienation that this awareness entailed were compensated by emphasized use of "Israeli" idioms of power and affluence by the tourists. In light of these findings, I would suggest the need to rethink the diasporization assumption. We could argue that the travelers left to search for their Maghrebi roots, and thus manifested a trend toward segregation. But we could equally, and perhaps more forcibly, argue that in Morocco they found the roots of their Israeli identity.

ACKNOWLEDGMENTS

This chapter is based on part on an M.A. thesis presented to the Department of Sociology and Anthropology of the Hebrew University in Jerusalem. I would like to thank the Shaine Center for Research in the Social Sciences, the Jerusalem Center for the Study of Anthropology, and the Research Scholarship Project for the Study of Oriental Jewry for their assistance in the realization of this project. My deepfelt thanks to Professor Yoram Bilu and Professor Harvey Goldberg for their help and devoted guidance. I would like also to express my gratitude to Professor Eyal Ben-Ari for his help.

NOTES

1. See, e.g., Bennett 1975; Colburn and Pozzetta 1979; and Gans 1979.

2. The semilegitimate nature of the tours to Morocco (no formal diplomatic relations exist between the two states) and the frequent crises between Israel and her Arab neighbors made exact figures unavailable. Since 1989 even non-Moroccan-born Israelis can visit Morocco, although in organized tours only.

3. No doubt, the king had something to gain politically from his liberal approach toward the Israelis. However, an elaboration of the Moroccan perspective is beyond the scope of this chapter. For detailed analysis of the underlying reasons for King Hassan's moderate approach to the Israeli-Arab conflict, see Tessler (1988).

4. On this, Rosen writes: "Nor is the Jew entirely like that other category of person whose status and power always carries an edge of the problematic for Moroccan men: Moroccan women. Like women, the Jews are at once admired, feared, coddled, abused, treasured, expended, and only half seen. Jewish men are often explicitly linked to women: confronted by a strong man Jews are seen to be as 'frightened as women.' . . . To kill a Jew is to kill someone so inherently weak as to appear little more than a coward oneself. Yet, like women, the Jews are often treated with caution since some of them— particularly the learned men and old women—are said by many to possess spiritual and magical powers both positive and dangerous" (Rosen 1984:159–60).

5. Needless to say, the general reluctance of the participants to wear a *kipa* and to speak Hebrew outside the exclusively Jewish cemeteries was also related to the profound sense of insecurity that they felt in an Arab territory. These fears were not foundless in light of terrorist attacks on Israeli tourists abroad.

REFERENCES

Aronoff, M. J. 1973. "Development Towns in Israel." In M. Curtis and M. S. Cherrtoff, eds., *Israel: Social Structure and Change.* New Brunswick, N.J.: Transaction, 27–46.

Bar-Yosef, R. 1966. "Desocialization and Resocialization." *International Immigration Review*, 2, 27–43.

Bat-Ye'or (pseud.). 1985. *The Dhimmi: Jews and Christians under Islam.* Rutherford: Faileigh Dickson University Press.

Ben-Ami, I. 1984. *Saint Veneration Among the Jews in Morocco.* Jerusalem: Magnes. (Hebrew)

Ben-Ari, E., and Y. Bilu, 1987. Saint Sanctuaries in Israeli Development Towns: On a Mechanism of Urban Transformation. *Urban Anthropology*, 16(2), 243–272.

Bennett, J. W. (ed.). 1975. *The New Ethnicity: Perspectives from Ethnology.* Proceedings of the American Ethnological Society, 1973. St. Paul: West.

Bensimon-Donath, D. 1968. *Evolution du judaïsm marocain sous le protectorat francais, 1912–1956.* Paris: La Haye, Mouton.

Bilu, Y. 1987. "Dreams and the Wishes of the Saint." In H. E. Goldberg, ed., *Judaism Viewed from Within and from Without.* Albany: State University of New York Press, 285 –313.

Boorstin, D. J. 1972. *The Image: A Guide to Pseudo-Events in American Expedition.* New York: Atheneum.

Bowen, D. L. 1988. "Congruent Spheres of Religious Authority: National and Local Levels of Charismatic Leadership." *The Maghreb Review*, 13(1), 32–41.

Chouraqui, N. A. 1973. *Between East and West: A History of the Jews in North Africa.* Philadelphia: Jewish Publication Society of America.

Cohen, E. 1970. "Development Towns: The Social Dynamics of 'Planted' Urban Communities in Israel." In S. N. Eisenstadt, ed., *Integration and Development in Israel.* Jerusalem: Israel University Press.

———. 1972. "Toward a Sociology of International Tourism." *Social Research*, 39(1), 164–82.

———. 1979. "Phenomenology of Tourist Experience." *Sociology*, 13, 197–201.

———. 1981. *Pilgrimage and Tourism: Convergence and Divergence.* Draft.

———. 1983a. "Ethnicity and Legitimation in Contemporary Israel." *The Jerusalem Quarterly*, 28, 111–24.

———. 1983b. *The Sociology of Tourism.* Jerusalem: The Hebrew University.

———. 1985. "The Tourist Guide: The Origins, Structure and Dynamics of a Role." *Annals of Tourism Research*, 12, 5 –29.

Cohen, E., N. Ben-Yehuda, and J. Aviad. 1987. "Recentering the World: The Quest for 'Elective' Centers in a Secularized Universe." *The Sociological Review*, 35, 320–46.

Colburn, D. R., and G. E. Pozzetta (eds.). 1979. *America and the New Ethnicity.* New York: Kenniket.

Combs-Schilling, M. E. 1989. *Sacred Performances: Islam, Sexuality, and Sacrifice.* New York: Columbia University Press.

de Nesry, C. 1958. *Les Israélites marocains a l'heure du choix.* Tangier: Edition Internationales.

Deshen, S. 1977. *"The Hillulot of Tunisian Immigrants."* In M. Shokeid and S. Deshen, *The Generation of Transition: Continuity and Change among North African Immigrants in Israel.* Jerusalem: Ben-Zvi, 110–21. (Hebrew)

———. 1989. *The Mellah Society: Jewish Community Life in Sherifian Morocco.* Chicago: University of Chicago Press.

Deshen, S., and M. Shokeid. 1974. *The Predicament of Homecoming: Cultural and Social Life of North African Immigrants in Israel.* Ithaca: Cornell University Press.

Eickelman, D. F. 1976. *Moroccan Islam: Tradition and Society in a Pilgrimage Center.* Austin: University of Texas Press.

Eisenstadt, S. N. 1954. *The Absorption of Immigrants.* London: Routledge and Kegan Paul.

Fussell, P. 1979. "The Stationary Tourist." *Harper's Magazine,* 258(1547), 31–38.

Gans, H. J. 1979. "Symbolic Ethnicity: The Future of Ethnic Groups and Cultures in America." *Ethnic and Racial Studies,* 2(1), 1–19.

Geertz, C. 1968. *Islam Observed: Religious Development in Morocco and Indonesia.* New Haven: Yale University Press.

Gellner, E. 1969. *Saints of the Atlas.* Chicago: University of Chicago Press.

———. 1981. "Saints and Their Descendants." *Muslim Society.* Cambridge: Cambridge University Press.

Goldberg, H. E. 1983. "The Mellahs of Southern Morocco: Report of a Survey." *The Maghreb Review,* 8(3–4), 61–69.

Graburn, N. H. H. 1977. "Tourism: The Sacred Journey." In V. L. Smith, ed., *Hosts and Guests: The Anthropology of Tourism.* Philadelphia: University of Pennsylvania Press, 17 –31.

Hasson, S. 1981. "Social and Spatial Conflicts: The Settlement Process in Israel During the 1950s and 1960s." *L'Espace Geographique,* 3, 169–79.

Hirschberg, H. L. 1981. *A History of the Jews of North Africa.* Leiden: E. J. Brill.

Horowitz, D., and M. Lissak. 1989. *Trouble in Utopia: The Overburdened Polity of Israel.* Albany: State University of New York Press.

MacCannell, D. 1973. "Staged Authenticity: Arrangements of Social Space in Tourist Settings." *American Journal of Sociology,* 79, 589–603.

———. 1976. *The Tourist: A New Theory of the Leisure Class.* New York: Schocken.

Meyers, A. R. 1982. "Patronage and Protection: The Status of Jews in Pre-colonial Morocco." In S. Deshen and W. P. Zenner, eds., *Jewish Societies in the Middle East.* Washington, D.C.: University Press of America, 85–104.

Okamura, J. Y. 1981. "Situational Ethnicity." *Ethnic and Racial Studies*, 4(4), 452–65.

Rabinow, P. 1975. *Symbolic Domination: Cultural Form and Historical Change in Morocco.* Chicago: University of Chicago Press.

Rosen, L. 1972. "Muslim-Jewish Relations in a Moroccan City." *International Journal of Middle East Studies*, 3, 435 –49.

———. 1984. *Bargaining for Reality: The Construction of Social Relations in a Muslim Community.* Chicago: University of Chicago Press.

Schmelz, O. U., and S. Della Pergola. 1988. "World Jewish Population, 1986." *American Jewish Book*, 88, 433–41.

Schroeter, D. 1990. "Trade as a Mediator in Muslim-Jewish Relations: South Morocco in the Nineteenth Century." In: M. R. Cohen and A. L. Udovitch, eds., *Jews Among Arabs: Contacts and Boundaries.* Princeton, N.J.: Darwin, 113–40.

Sharot, S. 1976. *Judaism: A Sociology.* New York: David and Charles.

Shokeid, M. 1982. "Jewish Existence in a Berber Environment." In S. Deshen and W. P. Zenner, eds., *Jewish Societies in the Middle East.* Washington, D.C.: University Press of America, 105–22.

Stillman, N. A. 1982. "Tsaddiq and Marabut in Morocco." In I. Ben-Ami, ed., *The Sepharadi and Oriental Jewish Heritage.* Jerusalem: Magnes, 489–500.

———. 1991. *The Jews of Arab Lands in Modern Times.* Philadelphia: The Jewish Publication Society.

Sutton, W. A. 1967. "Travel and Understanding: Notes on the Social Structure of Touring." *International Journal of Comparative Sociology*, 8(2), 218–23.

Tessler, M. 1988. "Moroccan-Israeli Relations and the Reasons for Moroccans' Receptivity to Contact With Israel." *The Jerusalem Journal of International Relations*, 10(2), 76–108.

van den Berghe, P. 1980. "Tourism as Ethnic Relations: A Case Study of Cuzco, Peru." *Ethnic and Racial Studies*, 3(4), 375–79.

Weingrod, A. 1990. *The Saint of Beersheba.* Albany: State University of New York Press.

Westermarck, E. 1926. *Ritual and Belief in Morocco.* London: Macmillan.

2

Gravesites and Memorials of Libyan Jews

Alternative Versions
of the Sacralization
of Space in Judaism

HARVEY E. GOLDBERG

EDITORS' COMMENTS

This chapter, "Gravesites and Memorials of Libyan Jews: Alternative Versions of the Sacralization of Space in Judaism," is by Harvey Goldberg. The case Goldberg focuses on involves the Jewish cemetery in Tripoli over which the contemporary Libyan authorities decided, a few years ago, to build a road. In response, a group of Libyan Jews resolved to build commemorative plaques honoring the graveyard both in Italy (Rome) and in Israel. Goldberg concentrates on the experience of one individual in order to show how people can—in contrast to many of the assumptions upon which modern states are predicated—hold to a set of nonexclusive national identities. He does this through showing how this individual has created a set of metaphors in which Libya is his motherland, while Italy and Israel are his fatherlands. In this way he seems both to accommodate and to question the very notion (basic to Zionism) of the exclusivity of Israeli identity.

    The patterns of sanctification of time and of space in Jewish culture are ancient. Their form, content, degree of salience, and interrelationship have varied under different historical circumstances (Davies 1982). An emphasis on time was probably highlighted by the long diaspora existence during which Jews did not control the territories within which they lived (Zerubavel 1981:105). Heschel's (1951) characterization of Jewish ritual as architecture in time is an apt expression of that emphasis. At the same time, the sanctification of space was never totally submerged in Jewish consciousness (Boyarin 1991:18–19). Both synagogues and cemeteries were ever-present physical and territorial expressions of sanctity.

The emergence of modern Jewish nationalism, of course, brought notions of spatial sanctity to the fore. The tangibility and concreteness of territory make it a natural candidate for conflict. This is obviously the case when territory is the basis of important social and strategic resources, but also may be seen in the struggle for control of symbolic dimensions of territory (Kimmerling 1983). Observers of North African life have pointed to cases in which both Jews and Muslims venerate the same saint's shrine, seeing in this an indicator of symbiosis. It is less often noted that such shrines may also be sites of contestation of the religious identity of the saint (Shinar 1980). In the European world, the recent controversy over the convent in Auschwitz (Bartoszewski 1990) provides another example of the intertwining of spiritual debate with a sense of place.

Sites of death, and those memorializing the dead, are thus both concrete and, at the same time, open to considerable symbolic reworking. They take on different meanings not only across different traditions, but within a given tradition. A study comparing two Jewish cemeteries in a Midwestern city in the United States shows how distinctive conceptions of Judaism are inscribed in each (Gradwohl and Gradwohl 1988). Similarly, in Israel today, the enhanced attachment to land that is a correlate of national sovereignty does not obliterate alternate readings of territorial sanctity. Important diaspora communities continue to exist, side by side with a Jewish state. They, and the individuals who comprise them, formulate variant views of Judaism, and construct appropriate symbols locating their lives in Jewish space.

In the present chapter we follow a complex set of developments involving the memorialization of gravesites among the Jews of Libya. Our discussion revolves around the symbolic and political program of one individual. Not only do his actions and views exhibit an outlook that differs from simple nationalism, but his approach is dynamic and evolved over time. We thus explore the ideology of one Libyan Jew, named Raffaello, whose concerns with the graves of his family and ancestors is one element of an elaborate worldview linking, among other things, both memory and plans for the future. Understanding this worldview will also provide the opportunity to reflect upon diverse currents of meaning in the symbolism of gravesites within Jewish and Israeli culture at large.

GRAVESITES IN JEWISH CULTURE

Graves and gravesites have always been important in Jewish culture. One biblical prototype is the story of Abraham's purchase of a grave plot for Sarah (Genesis 23). This personal act also is a claim to the land on the part of Abraham's descendants. Similar symbolism links the patriarchs with the Exodus. Joseph, viceroy of Egypt, commands that his remains be brought back to Canaan (Genesis 50:25). Generations later, in the midst of the drama and the hurried exodus from Egypt, Moses is careful to heed this request (Exodus 13:19).

The attachment to the Land of Israel through the idiom of burial continued to receive expression in Jewish tradition. Graves clearly mark the past, but they also point to the future. The ancient cemetery on the slopes of the Mount of Olives, which figures in messianic imagery (Zechariah 14), is but one example of the link between death and the hope for eventual personal and collective redemption.

The orientation to ultimate redemption in the Land of Israel did not prevent Jews throughout the Diaspora from valorizing attachments to their local communities. Writing of the Muslim Middle Ages, Goitein claims that the Muslim, Christian, and Jewish communities each formed a nation, *umma*, in itself, but in every country they shared a homeland, *watan*, in common. Both concepts were of highest practical and emotional significance (1971:274). This sense of homeland, designated *balad* (rather than *watan*), characterized North African Jews up to the present. Moreover, it was expressed through their particular religious idiom and concretized in their religious places. Jews from the Jebel Gharian in Libya, transplanted to Israel during the mass immigration of the late 1940s (Goldberg 1972), still retained thoughts of their homeland. When they asked me, in 1964, if I, as an American, could visit the region of their birth, I replied in the affirmative. If you go there, they said, "tell us about the synagogue and the cemetery. That is all we care about."

DISPLACEMENT FROM GRAVESITES:
THE CASE OF THE JEWS OF LIBYA

When the above conversation took place, about four thousand Jews lived in Libya, having chosen to remain in that land while the majority of the Jews emigrated during the years 1949–51. Many of those remaining had believed that Jews could continue to find a place for themselves in the context of an independent Libya. In 1967, during the Six-Day War between Israel and her Arab neighbors, the Jews in Tripoli felt themselves in mortal danger, and a number were attacked and murdered. After the war was over, the Jews were allowed, and in fact encouraged, to leave by the Libyan government. Most went directly to Rome and began the process of liquidating their assets in the country that had been their home for centuries. In September 1969, Mu'ammar Qaddafi seized power, and in the spring of the following year, two decrees were issued by Libya's Revolutionary Command Council. One banished the Italians from the country and nationalized their property; the other confiscated all the property of the Jews, whatever their nationality (De Felice 1985).

One of the Jews leaving Libya after the events of 1967 was Raffaello Fellah. Raffaello was born in1935. He retains the early memory of a military parade in his native Tripoli, which demonstrated the might of German armor and discipline. Only later did he learn that this political and military power had been turned brutally against his own people. At the end of 1942, the Axis forces were driven from Tripolitania by the British Eighth Army. In November 1945 a riot broke out among the Arabs of Tripoli and the neighboring villages, as a result of which over 130 Jews were killed (De Felice 1985; Goldberg 1990). Raffaello's father was murdered during this pogrom.[1] He consciously states that the memory of his father, and his mothers loyalty to that memory, are among the main motivating factors shaping his economic, communal, and political activities.

Raffaello and his family were among the four thousand Jews who remained in independent Libya after 1952. Utilizing his inheritance, he became an active businessman, working along with Arab partners as required by Libyan law. When the 1967 War broke out, the situation of the Jews became untenable. Along with most Libyan Jews, Raffaello moved to and settled in Rome, where he now lives.[2] He immediately became active in organizing a new refugee group and laid the groundwork for claims against the Libyan government. While always a man of action, Raffaello also has been keen to press the cultural side of his economic plans and political convictions. His project concerning the Jewish cemetery in Tripoli is an example. I continue the story in his own words, interspersed with my queries:[3]

R: There existed an Italian town plan to build a road leading from the port and continuing across the Jewish cemetery. The plan, drawn up about 1930, called for a beautiful road, passing along the sea. During the Italian period, however, the plan was never implemented. It would have involved destroying or removing some graves and tombstones.

There was a story, I never was sure of the details, about a high-ranking army officer or engineer. He wanted to move ahead with the project despite the fact that it was a cemetery. This Italian official was on a horse, supervising workers to begin moving tombstones. He shouted orders not to hesitate, despite the protests that the Jews had voiced. At that moment, the horse jumped. He fell off and was badly injured.

H: People take this as a true story?[4]

R: The story stayed in people's memory. The town plan remained, but it was never implemented, even under Balbo,[5] when Tripoli was a much larger city. I don't know whether it was out of consideration for the Jews, or a matter of budget, but the fact is that plan was never carried out.

Later there was an attempt to revive the plan, in the 1950s. The mayor of Tripoli was Taher Qaramanli, a descendant of the dynasty that once ruled all of Tripolitania. The road was important for the expansion of the town and the continuation of the coastal road. Qaramanli stated that so long as I am mayor, the Jewish cemetery will not be touched. Instead, he ordered to look into a modified project.

About 1973 we heard that work was proceeding that would destroy the Jewish cemetery. I decided that the Association of Libyan Jews should write a letter to the Libyan government, and try to have a meeting with the Libyan ambassador here in Rome. We explained how important the question of the dead, and of the cemetery, is for Jews. We stated that we were willing to purchase the land. Our letter also said that if it is absolutely necessary to go through the cemetery, we would like the right to remove the remains, under the supervision of rabbinic authority, and that we would bear the costs.

Raffaello described the details of his proposal, his initial correspondence with the Libyan government, and his meeting with the Libyan foreign minister in Rome. Then he continued:

R: In the meantime we heard rumors that work near the cemetery was beginning. There were still about fifty Jews there. Just a few months before, one Jew had died and was buried in the cemetery. His wife and son are two of the six or eight Jews still in Libya today.

In any event, we heard that the bulldozer had already been through the cemetery tract. They bulldozed all of the graves without realizing that we bury our dead deep in the ground, different from the Muslim practice. That meant that removal of the remains was a big operation. Therefore, they used a bulldozer just to level off the land. Either they crushed the marble or put some of the pieces aside.

H: How do you know these details?

R: By a stroke of luck. We have to bless an unknown Italian who had the courage to take pictures of the operation. A certain Jew gave them to me without disclosing the identity of the Italian. He was worried that he might be recognized, but deserves thanks for his bravery. Taking those pictures could have been dangerous.

Raffaello did everything he could to stop the building of the road. He attempted to influence the contractor, a Muslim from Crete. Raffaello met in
Rome with a relative of the contractor who was also a partner in the project. When all these efforts to protect the actual cemetery came to naught, he
began to think in a new direction.

R: The cemetery was important to all the Jews. That is the reason I decided to make a monument here in Rome, dedicated to all the Jews buried
in Libya. I commissioned Eddie Levy, from Tripoli, to design it, along with
an Italian architect, working under the supervision of Bruno Zevi.[6] I tried to
develop an idea of great significance, and had sand brought from the Libyan
shore, with the help of my [former, Arab] partner. The steel represents the
bulldozer, the violence that brought the cemetery to its end. I was pleased
with the work.

H: Where is the monument located?

R: In the Jewish cemetery in Rome. When it was ready, we organized a
ceremony with the Union of Italian Jewish Communities. I gave Abe Karlikow, from the American Jewish Committee,[7] the honor of unveiling the
monument, and Professor Zevi gave an address on the design. I spoke about
the communal and political implications of the initiative.

Given the pressures of daily life, it is easy to forget that you belong to a
people, including my own Libyan community. But I said to myself that I cannot abandon the memory of centuries of people who had died there, including my father. Something had to be done to memorialize the community and
to remind people of their past in Libya. I received many positive reactions
and messages of approval. Until today, close to Rosh Hashanah, many
Libyan Jews visit the monument and recite Kaddish there along with a
memorial prayer.

The monument to Libyan Jewry, in the Rome cemetery, is one of the ac-
complishments with which Raffaello is especially gratified. But it is not the
final resting place for the memories of his parents, nor of his concerns. He
has worked at developing, in cooperation with the Jewish National Fund, a
memorial forest in Israel for the Jews of Libya, urging Libyan Jews to purchase trees commemorating relatives buried in North Africa. Recently, in the
wake of the new political processes in the Middle East after 1991, he has met
with Colonel Qaddafi in an attempt to create cultural links between Libyan
Jews and their country of origin.

RAFFAELLO'S VIEWS

On one occasion I pressed Raffaello to explain how he claims to be strongly
attached to Italy, Libya, and Israel:

H: When you first arrived in Rome from Libya, you began working to have Libyan Jews recognized as Italians. At the same time you went back to Libya to deal with your affairs there, and wanted to be seen as part of Libyan society. Some people might see that as contradictory. You are trying to have your cake and eat it too! In addition, you are committed to Israel. How do you view these matters?

R: In a very, very comfortable way, for two reasons. The first is the special conditions in which the Jew always is found. Those conditions are created by others, not by the Jews themselves. Jews are always interested in participating in the societies in which they live, except for the question of religion. It is only the prejudice of others that paints them a different color. If people portray us in this manner, why should we not demand our rights according to their definitions?

H: You see your various loyalties as morally and legally defensible?

R: Yes, we can claim rights both as Libyans and Italians; we have credit in both societies. In Italy, our rights were recognized by Italian law, which stated that we must be considered Italian. We simply applied for the application of the law.

H: But how do you see yourself in relation to the different national societies with which you are engaged?

R: The Jews always have had a concept of internationality with regard to citizenship. We do not claim that we are Libyan because we are ready to die for Libya. We are Libyan because our motherland is Libya. That is a fact. Even if she is a prostitute, she's still our mother. We are linked by love and nostalgia, and that cannot change.

H: So there's a difference between a motherland and a fatherland?

R: They are completely different. The concept of motherland concerns sentiment. Fatherland has to do with rights, that to which you are entitled.

H: You are saying that Libya is your motherland, but not your fatherland? Can you envision Italy as a fatherland?

R: In some ways it is; it is a bridge to our fatherland. Italy has treated us well. It has symbolically accepted responsibility for having discriminated against us under the fascist regime, and genuinely has tried to alleviate that feeling of guilt in many ways. Most important is the warm acceptance of Jews in its midst, including the Jews of Libya.

But from my point of view the fatherland of the Jews can only be Israel. However, Jews, like other people, must have the right to choose which they love more, the motherland or fatherland. That choice may entail obligations. If tomorrow it is necessary to fight for Italy, because we have chosen to live here and become Italian, we all have to do our duty.

Even with an attachment to a fatherland, Jews can also have deep attachments to their motherland, a deep commitment of love that might be mixed with bitterness, with discrimination and other difficult moments. Such suffering is sometimes shared with other local citizens who feel the love of their motherland. As I said, even if she is bad, she always is your mother.

The concept of motherland is particularly appropriate for Jews because of our special history. Every Jew, no matter where he comes from, has a story full of events, of discrimination, of circumstances that forced us to change our countries. There are Jews who have been immigrants two or three times during their lives. The concept is particularly valid for us, but may be applicable to other groups as well.

H: You suggest that there are different bases for national commitments?

R: Where is it written that you cannot have two loyalties? In one case you have your legal obligations and it's important to fulfill them. The other kind of attachment is linked to your will, your freedom to choose. If I am Italian, or French, and want to volunteer to fight for Israel, I should have the right to do so.

H: You describe a world where people will have the inclination to split their commitments in different lands. How would that work out in your case?

R: In the world of tomorrow, in which I believe, I would have a way of expressing, my—shall we say—Libyanity. I would be able to contribute my best efforts to the country that gave me my father and my mother, and my roots. I could act out of loyalty to that sense of motherland, unhindered by a piece of paper that determines my citizenship. I could contribute to Libya in one way, to Italy in another, and to Israel in a third, without any complexes.

The three countries in which Raffaello would like a tangible expression of his parents' memory are also three countries in which he is actively involved in business and communal affairs. He believes that the processes of unification in Europe vindicate his views on the paring down of nationalism. While very much a man of the current world, at times I think of Raffaello in terms of the popular healers among Moroccan Jews, who have been the subject of research by Bilu (1993:55). Bilu found that many of these healers lost parents at an early age, and that their attempts to heal the ills of their patients through a demonologically based symbol system may stem from their own need to mend a shattered world. Raffaello, who tragically lost his father when young, would also like to join together disparate worlds, in very concrete and practical terms.

Along with a deep personal meaning, there also are ideological and cultural aspects of Raffaello's interwoven attachments to three different countries. The relation of Israel to the Diaspora is one of the knotty issues in Zionist thought (and a problem that explicitly concerns Raffaello). One extreme position totally separates the new state of Israel from the Jewish past in the Diaspora. More generally, classic Zionism implied the negation of life in exile (*galut*), and assumed that immigration to Israel entailed an abandoning of behavior patterns and values that characterized Jewish life abroad. From this point of view, the migration to Palestine (later Israel) of the Middle Eastern Jews did not fit the classic Zionist formula because their ties to Israel usually did not grow out of a formal ideology.

It has been noted that the immigration of the Oriental Jews into Palestine did not imply a break with their traditional social and cultural structures (Eisenstadt 1950:201–202). From this perspective, the move to Israel was no different from Jews moving to Palestine from other areas in the Ottoman Empire in the pre-Zionist era. The meaning of territorial attachment as an expression of modern nationalism was not fully appreciated by the Middle Easterners, according to this line of analysis. This mode of thought also assumed that Jews from the Middle East would have to learn the full meaning of contemporary nationalism.

Classic Zionism, however, also has its critics, and some aspects of the ideology prove to be problematic as the number of Israelis taking up permanent residence in other countries grows (Shokeid 1988). While most Zionist theories reflected the work of Central and Eastern European thinkers, Israeli society today is constituted, in roughly equal proportions, by both Jews of European and Middle Eastern provenance. Perhaps the more traditional stance, that attachment to the land is a central but not exclusive value and mark of Judaism and Jewishness, held unreflectively by many Jews from the Middle East, will prove to be of enduring power as an Israeli diaspora becomes a lasting reality.

Raffaello's simultaneous valuation of the Diaspora and of Israel thus reflects that of other Middle Eastern Jews. His views, however, are not just a recent systematic expression of conventional traditionality. They may also reflect the specific Libyan Arab milieu that he experienced, in which notions of nationality were slowly emerging, but also were challenged by competing ideologies. In Libya, as in other Arab countries, the national identity of individual states was by no means a self-evident reality.

Libya, the first North African country to gain formal independence, was probably the Maghreb country least characterized by widespread nationalistic conceptions and sentiments at the time. Various observers have commented that nationalism developed in Libya *after* independence, which came about in part because of a special combination of Big Power politics, rather than having been a factor that fueled an independence movement. Thus, the nation-state was not a taken-for-granted entity in Libyan society, and the direct exposure to Nasser's brand of pan-Arab nationalism in the 1950s and 1960s further put the importance of a specific Libyan identity in question.

Analysts of Qaddafi's regime in Libya have pointed to various ways in which his ideology struggles with notions of the national state that are viewed as natural in the West (Davis 1987). Raffaello (with both Italian and Arabic as mother tongues) was forced to formulate his combination of Libyan and Jewish identities while many Muslim Libyans were still making sense of their own national existence.

In exploring Raffaello's worldview, a question occurred to me that I first suppressed, but then decided to try:

H: I hope you won t mind my saying this, but I think that there is one thing that you and Mr. Qaddafi have in common. You both want the world to pay attention to Libya!

R: That's true. We both are international in mentality. I want to bring my share of history to the global arena. If you do not recognize me, I have to impose on you my right to have a hearing. If my history is not deemed important, I must make it compelling enough to attract attention. I cannot wait until you discover me; I'm not that type. I demand attention because I would feel guilty if I were to leave the evaluation of my past to others. Then, I would have to wait until they think it is the right moment. My duty is to do what is possible, now.

DISCUSSION

We have explored the ideas concerning the national identification of one Jewish man from Libya, now living in Italy, and how he has sought to express those ideas in the symbolism of gravesites. The three correlated resting places of the Jews of Libya, in North Africa, in Italy, and in Israel, correspond to countries in which Raffaello has material interests. While this symbolism has clearly been shaped to reinforce Raffaello's political program, it has been done so in a way that draws upon ancient Jewish cultural associations and resonates with the sentiments of other contemporary Jews, both of Middle Eastern and European provenance.

Raffaello is not learned in rabbinic sources, but his memorial project in Rome, providing a surrogate burial site, is congruent with rabbinic sensibilities. Jewish tradition is characterized by a complex set of attitudes toward grave markers. The most prominent of Jews, Moses, was buried, according to biblical narrative, in a manner such that no human being knows his grave's location (Deuteronomy 34:6). In ancient Jewish sources, one of the main legal motivations for placing a marker on a grave is that priests (*kohanim*), who become ritually defiled by contact with a grave, would be able to avoid them. The sources also recognize the role of a grave marker (*tziyyun*) to memorialize those who have passed on, but this is not obligatory. One source states that a marker should *not* be placed on the graves of the righteous, because their words are their memorial. Maimonides' medieval code cites this last source.[8]

Commentators from the late Middle Ages and early modern period acknowledge these strictures, but also point to the fact that visiting the graves of relatives and of sainted righteous people has become a well established practice. Rabbi Aaron Berakhiah ben Moses of seventeenth-century Modena, whose book on death and mourning became an authoritative work, surveys the various viewpoints and indicates that the practice of visiting the graves of the righteous is particularly entrenched in North Africa.[9]

His book also includes appropriate prayers to be cited on such occasions, further legitimizing those customs. In light of this overall historical trend, Raffaello s initiatives, while innovative, do not challenge the limits of tradition. In fact, the establishment of a physical marker far from the original gravesites highlights their memorial function over the importance of any physical link to the grave and its contents.

One eschatological belief, stemming from a talmudic source[10] and prevalent in Diaspora communities, claims that, at the end of days, all those bodies buried in the diaspora will find their way to the soil of the Land of Israel. Within traditional Jewish concepts, the diaspora periphery and the center in The Land coexisted comfortably, each filling its allotted notch. The centrality of the Land of Israel did not negate the diaspora. Space was sacralized, but not in an exclusive mode.

Zionist ideology proclaimed the importance of return to the Land in the here and now, and extreme versions of Zionism denied all value to Jewish existence outside its borders. Ancient Jewish symbols were reworked to fit nationalist collective identity. These symbols, however, once selected, have their own logic and power, which sometimes stand in dialogic relationship to the intents of their users.

Israel does not possess a tomb of the unknown soldier. Rather, one day a year, the society commemorates those soldiers whose place of burial is unknown. This is the seventh day of the Hebrew month of Adar (in late winter), which, according to the Talmud, basing itself on the narrative in Deuteronomy, was the day on which Moses died.[11] The phraseology depicting the day (*shemaqom qevuratam lo noda`*) makes this connection explicit. At tombs of unknown soldiers, place is identified and sacralized; the person remains anonymous. On the seventh of Adar, people are known and memorialized— and sanctified space remains a desirable, but not absolutely essential, aspect of remembrance. Burial space can be, as it were, anonymous. Whether consciously or not, this aspect of contemporary Israeli symbolism retains a certain reserve over the total and unconditional sanctification of territory, an attitude that has been characteristic of Judaism throughout the ages.

Both Raffaello and the creators of modern Israeli symbols have drawn upon Jewish tradition regarding the sacralization of space. They have pushed the received symbols in different directions, but there still remains a family resemblance among these diverse expressions. Correspondingly, they point to different, but overlapping, perspectives on the Jewish future.

ACKNOWLEDGMENT

Some of the data presented in this chapter were gathered with the aid of a grant from the Lucius N. Littauer Foundation. An earlier version was read at the 89th annual meeting of the American Anthropological Association, New Orleans, December 2, 1990.

NOTES

1. A picture of Raffaello's father is found in Patai and Rosow's pictorial history (1980:122).

2. Many of the Libyan Jews who first moved to Rome immigrated to Israel about a year later.

3. The following quotes are taken from recorded conversations between Raffaello and myself during the summer of 1989.

4. There are several popular legends about the Jewish cemetery being saved, in 1903, from destruction as a result of a flash flood in the nearby wadi (Zuaretz 1960:415). A somewhat related incident concerns a conflict between Jews and Muslims over the identity of a grave uncovered during excavations at the beginning of Italian rule in Tripoli (Goldberg 1996).

5. One of the most active governors of Italian Libya, who governed from 1934 to 1940 (Segrè 1987). He tried to limit the impact of the racial laws enacted in Italy on the Jews in Libya (De Felice 1985:143–74).

6. Eddy Levy, more than ten years younger than Raffaello, was born in Tripoli and traveled to Rome to study architecture; shortly thereafter, the 1967 War began. Bruno Zevi is a well known professor of architecture in Italy.

7. Abe Karlikow was a representative of the American Jewish Committee who worked with the Jewish community in Libya in the period before Libyan independence. The community hoped to ensure that the constitution of the new state would protect the rights of minorities (De Felice 1985:239 and *passim*). Raffaello met Karlikow in Europe in the early 1970s.

8. See the Mishnah, Tractate *Sheqalim*, 1:1 and 2:5, and the comments of the Jerusalem Talmud on the latter passage. See Maimonides, *Yad Ha-ḥaz-aqah*, the Book of Judges (*Shoftim*), Laws of Mourning (*Evel*): 4:4.

9. Aaron Berakhiah ben Moses of Modena (1896:44a–45a).

10. Babylonian Talmud, Tractate *Ketubbot* 111a.
11. See the Babylonian Talmud, Tractate *Qiddushin* 38a.

REFERENCES

Aaron Berakhiah ben Moses of Modena. 1896 [1626]. *Ma'avar Yabboq.* Vilna: Ram. (Hebrew)

Bartoszewski, W. T. 1990. *The Convent at Auschwitz.* London: Bowerdean.

Bilu, Y. 1993. *Without Bounds: The Life and Death of Rabbi Yáacov Wazana.* Jerusalem: Magnes Press. (Hebrew)

Boyarin, J. 1991. Jewish Ethnography and the Question of the Book. *Anthropological Quarterly* 64:14–29.

Davies, W. D. 1982. *The Territorial Dimension of Judaism.* Berkeley: University of California Press.

Davis, J. 1987. *Libyan Politics: Tribe and Revolution.* Berkeley: University of California Press.

De Felice, R. 1985. *Jews in an Arab Land: Libya, 1835–1970.* Austin: University of Texas Press.

Eisenstadt, S. N. 1950. The Oriental Jews in Palestine. *Jewish Social Studies* 12:199–222.

Goitein, S. D. 1971. *A Mediterranean Society: The Jewish Communities of the Arab World as Portrayed in the Documents of the Cairo Geniza,* vol. 2, *The Community.* Berkeley: University of California Press.

Goldberg, H. E. 1972. *Cave-dwellers and Citrus-growers: A Jewish Community in Libya and Israel.* Cambridge: Cambridge University Press.

———. 1990. *Jewish Life in Muslim Libya: Rivals and Relatives.* Chicago: University of Chicago Press.

Goldberg, H. E. 1996. The *Maskil* and the *Mequbbal*: Mordecai Ha-Cohen and the Grave of Rabbi Shimon Lavi in Tripoli. In *Sephardi and Middle Eastern Jewries: History and Culture in the Modern Era,* H. E. Goldberg, ed., 168–90. Bloomington: Indiana University Press.

Gradwohl, D. M., and H. R. Gradwohl. 1988. That Is the Pillar of Rachel's Grave Unto This Day: An Ethnoarcheological Comparison of Two Jewish Cemeteries in Lincoln, Nebraska. In *Persistence and Flexibility: Anthropological Perspectives on the American Jewish Experience,* W. P. Zenner, ed., 223–59. Albany: State University of New York Press.

Heschel, A. J. 1951. *The Sabbath: Its Meaning for Modern Man.* New York: Farrar, Straus and Young.

Kimmerling, B. 1983. *Zionism and Territory: The Socio-territorial Dimension of Zionist Politics.* Berkeley: University of California, Institute of International Studies.

Patai, R., and E. Rosow. 1980. *The Vanished Worlds of Jewry*. New York: Macmillan.

Segrè, C. G. 1987. *Italo Balbo: A Fascist Life*. Berkeley: University of California Press.

Shinar, P. 1980. La recherche relative aux rapports judéo-musulmans dans le Maghreb contemporain. In *Les relations entre Juifs et Musulmans en Afrique du Nord, XIXe-XXe siècles.*, J.-L. Miège, ed., 1–31. Paris: Centre National de la Recherche Scientifique.

Shokeid, M. 1988. *Children of Circumstances: Israeli Emigrants in New York*. Ithaca: Cornell University Press.

Zerubavel, E. 1981. *Hidden Rhythms: Schedules and Calendars in Social Life*. Chicago: University of Chicago Press.

Zuaretz, F. et al. eds. 1960. *Yahadut Luv* [Libyan Jewry]. Tel Aviv: Va`ad Qehillot Luv be-Yisrael.

3

Saints' Sanctuaries in Israeli Development Towns

On a Mechanism of Urban Transformation

EYAL BEN-ARI AND YORAM BILU

EDITORS' COMMENTS

This contribution is the editors' own composition, "Saints' Sanctuaries in Israeli Development Towns: On a Mechanism of Urban Transformation." This chapter examines the reemergence of sacred sites of Jewish saints in a number of Israeli development towns. The basic argument is that the appearance of these saints' sanctuaries is rooted in North African 'folk' religiosity and reflects a strengthening of attachment of people to "their" places. The central argument is that by constructing such sites, people in development towns come to terms with their peripherality in Israel. This phenomenon is related to what may be termed an internal Israeli cultural debate centering on its identity as a 'Middle Eastern' society: on the extent to which Israel shares with its Arab neighbors a set of cultural concepts and guidelines by which public life is carried out.

Since the early 1970s a number of Israeli development towns have been sties of a largely unnoticed but nevertheless constant urban transformation. This transformation (which has occurred in such places as Beit She'an, Safed, Hatzor-Haglilit, Kiriyat Gat, and Ofakim) has been the outcome of the establishment of new sacred sites of Jewish saints.[1] Typically the sanctification of such sites, which serve as pilgrimage centers and healing shrines, has been effected either through a translocation of a saint from Morocco or through the discovery or renewal of a sacred place in the locality on the basis of folk beliefs and local traditions. While these patterns of sanctification of space are usually the outcome of the spontaneous initiative of individuals, they nevertheless have a number of notable consequences for the transformation of the physical and social environment of the development towns where they occur.

These consequences are especially notable against a background of what are taken to be the main social and cultural characteristics of these towns. These "planted" communities (Cohen 1970) were founded during the 1950s and early 1960s in Israel's urban periphery (Matras 1973) and now encompass between one-fifth and one-sixth of the country's population.[2] These towns have been characterized (especially in regard to the initial phases of their development) in some of the following terms: lacking in social consolidation (Spiegel 1966:180–81); lacking a sense of community-wide identification and responsibility (Berler 1970:144; Aronoff 1973:39); marked by unamicable relations among people (Altman and Rosenbaum 1973:323); having relatively little civic identification and citizen participation (Kramer 1973:49); and dependent on outside government and public bodies (Marx 1975, 1976).

Yet despite such negative portrayals, the establishment of saints' shrines has brought about a measure of change in many of what are taken to be the major parameters of urban transformation. Spatially, the changes have been circumscribed to such matters as the erection of new facilities around the sites (e.g., synagogues, abattoirs, covered compartments for lighting candles, public bathrooms, improvised parking lots, signboards, and areas for visitors). Socially, the effects of the new holy sites have been in the mobilization of locally based kith and kin in and around such activities as escorting visitors, ritual slaughtering, preparing refreshments, and cleaning the surroundings. While some of this aid is proffered throughout the whole year in order to help maintain the site, most of it is given before and during the *hillula*, the annual celebration commemorating the death anniversary of the patron saint. In more successful cases, these *hillulot* may become the foci of mass pilgrimages, the number of pilgrims far exceeding the population of the local community. A less tangible, but no less important effect of the erection of the sites has been the development of a greater sense of localism in terms of attachment to place and an assertion of civic pride. Finally, the image of the communities within which the sites are located has grown in importance as these settlements have sometimes gained recognition by national leaders, and more often by municipal officials, religious figures, and pilgrims from all over the country.

The social science literature on Israel's development towns normally does not include suitable conceptual tools for dealing with the changes wrought by the construction of saintly sites. The earlier studies found within this literature contain thorough analyses of the planning devices that determined the placement and initial development of these towns and of the mechanics of migration that affected their subsequent growth and stagnation. The more recent literature is marked by detailed probes of local politics and its influence on the dynamics of these urban settlements. While these types of analyses furnish an excellent background for an examination of the case at hand, they do not seem to fit its peculiarities. An examination of the establishment of these new sites thus necessitates an analysis of a relatively unexplored mechanism of urban transformation that is of central importance for understanding these settlements: the sanctification of space.

Three related analytical issues, or sets of issues, suggest themselves in this regard. The first has to do with the dynamics of the sanctification of urban space. It involves elucidating the ways in which sites are consecrated in the context of a wider map of religious significance, and legitimated and accepted among a group of believers. The second question is related to the social preconditions for the emergence of this process of sanctification. Here we must deal with the "urban peripherality" of the phenomenon, that is, with its emergence in communities marked by a high percentage of Middle Eastern Jews, relatively low status, and a working-class population "locked into" their communities for a number of decades. The third set of questions, clearly a derivative of the two former sets, is about the effects of the sanctification of space. It entails drawing out the specific effects of erecting such sites for the local allocation of resources, the dynamics of communal social networks, and the development of a sense of "home" among the populace of these settlements.

BEGINNINGS: CENTRAL PLANNING
AND HOUSEHOLD MIGRATION

The initial shaping of the spatial and social character of Israel's development towns was effected primarily through the use of one mechanism: the formal policy-making and planning processes undertaken by the country's central government.[3] The use of this mechanism grew out of the special circumstances that Israel faced during the first years of its existence. Until 1948, Israel's Jewish population was concentrated either in one of the three main cities (Jerusalem, Tel Aviv, or Haifa) or in small agricultural settlements. The intermediate-sized towns, like Ramle, Lod, or Tiberias, were either comprised totally of Arabs or had an Arab majority. With the flight of Arabs from the country during the 1948 War, most of these medium-sized towns were left nearly vacant and the need for similar sized Jewish settlements became apparent. It was against this background that the establishment of the development towns throughout the country was begun.

While other countries such as Australia, Brazil, or the former soviet Union have had programs designed to promote the development of frontier areas, Israel stands as an exception in this regard. For in Israel there "has been practically no significant settlement of peripheral areas independent of deliberate, policy-originated and policy-supported settlement" (Matras 1973:3). Israel has not been the scene of a "gold rush," nor of the discovery of any important oil fields or mineral deposits that propelled governments to formulate planning policies for frontier areas. The initial mechanism for the construction of development towns, then, was that of formal decision making, that is, a process that involved the formal proceedings and decrees of a highly centralized government machinery. Through the use of this essentially political mechanism (Cohen 1976:54), the features of these towns (their location, detailed planning and implementation, social makeup, industrial infrastructure, and physical layout) were all controlled and carried out by large and centralized government and public agencies. In this process the country's "urban frontier" was politically organized in terms of super- and subordination: each town was granted some rights over its territory but was at all times subject to the overall regulation of the central government.

At the same time this political organization of space had an explicit collective orientation. For these thirty or so new, or as they came to be known, development towns were seen to be instrumental in achieving four national objectives (Shachar 1971; Comay and Kirschenbaum 1973; Cohen 1977): providing housing and employment for large numbers of immigrants; establishing regional centers that would service their rural hinterlands; dispersing the population from the overconcentrated cores of the main cities; and securing Jewish presence in areas of sparse population for defense purposes.

These, then, were the lines along which the development towns were begun and which determined their initial social character. As Cohen (1970:489) notes, these were essentially "planted" communities:

> The planned character of the new towns as well as the framework of their development—an apparatus of governmental and other public, central institutions—attest to the fact that they are "planted" communities, established by decree for overall social purposes, and have not evolved in accordance with the pressures and demands of local conditions. This means that these communities and their inhabitants are, or at least considered to be, passive objects of manipulation by central agencies.

These "planted," or what Suttles (1972:chap. 4) perhaps more aptly terms "contrived" communities, were artificially created settlements. They were artificial both in that they were set up by large external agencies on the basis of national priorities and in that their establishment was effected despite the lack of existing social institutions and "natural" networks.

An understanding of the beginnings of these towns involves an examination of another transformative mechanism that began to operate almost as soon as people were placed in these towns. This second mechanism (the patterning of migration) is related to the constant movement of people in and out, as well as within, the development towns. If the previous mechanism of planning and policy making was essentially a collective one, this device involved the individual household. Here the determining considerations did not have to do with national priorities. Rather, they involved considerations about the location of the development town in respect to "other resources, productive facilities, or populations linked with the realization of different goals" (Cohen 1976:52). In the case of development towns, this implied accessibility to better accommodations, job opportunities, relatives, higher-status areas, or cultural and educational opportunities.

As we shall see, given the nature of the land and property markets, governed as they are by the forces of exchange and pricing, and given the peculiar characteristics of the populations settled in the development towns, the effects of this mechanism were serious.[4] This is because for many of the new immigrants who arrived in the country the peripheral settlements served as temporary places of abode until they acquired the resources to move to other, more desirable communities. In short, the trend that evolved in most of the development towns was that of a selective in- and outmigration:

> Major difficulties were encountered by these new towns in attracting immigrants from Europe or America, or even veteran and native born Israelis of higher socio-economic status. The turnover rate was high, with immigrants who had improved their socio-economic status after a few years in the development towns generally tending to move towards the older cities on the coastal plain (Ben Zadok and Goldberg 1984:18).

On a national scale what emerged were serious disparities: the peripheral new town steadily came to be characterized by a high ratio of Middle Eastern Jews and by a low socioeconomic status. In other words, they came to be spatial loci within which a relatively distinct socioeconomic and ethnic stratum crystallized (Weintraub and Krauss 1982:377).

The people who remained within the towns tended to have modest occupational aspirations or to require the housing and welfare assistance available to them as residents of such settlements. The towns thus grew to become "residual communities" (Kramer 1973:49), to become "sinks" for the less resourceful immigrants (Spilerman and Habib 1976:805). As Marx (1976) notes, the single word most aptly describing these communities in their initial stages is dependence. Thus, for example, in many towns external agencies tended to exploit internal divisions and to impede the growth of a sense of community identification and responsibility (Aronoff 1973:39). Moreover, the transient nature of many settlements entailed by the high pop-ulation turnover (Altman and Rosenbaum 1973:324) led to the development of indifference in regard to the future of the town and to the obstruction of spontaneous action on the basis of common interests (Berler 1970:144).

It was thus the conjoint operation of these two mechanisms, government direction and selective migration, that determined to a large degree the rather bleak circumstances of the development towns during the first decade or so of their existence. Yet, at the same time, many of these circumstances appear to have been associated with the relative youth, with the earliest stages of development, of the settlements (Matras 1973:13). For alongside these processes new mechanisms that were slowly transforming the urban experiences of these towns began to operate.

CONTINUATION: LOCAL ACTIVISM
AND ATTACHMENT TO THE LOCALITY

From the late 1960s a new mechanism began to bring about changes in the urban environment of many development towns. Centered essentially around the workings of local activism and local government, this mechanism has been described variously as interest articulation, making demands, or political participation. Against the background of the social circumstances of these "planted" communities, however, the effecting of this mechanism should not be taken for granted. Indeed, it is not surprising to learn that many of the inhabitants of these towns were either indifferent to politics or did not believe in the efficacy of their actions (Bernstein 1984:25ff.)

But this was a different period, one in which the new political and civic sentiments that began to emerge after the 1967 War started to pervade many public issues. In very abbreviated terms, these new sentiments (or "the eth-nic issue") grew out of the rising aspirations of the younger elite, and the re-sentment of many second-generation youth of Middle Eastern origins over their predicament (Cohen 1983:120–21).

From the point of view of the "Middle Eastern" majority who resided in the development towns, the implication of these wider trends was the ap-pearance of a combination of a sense of legitimacy in expressing their de-mands, and of a perception of the political efficacy of these expressions. These, however, were not vague or ill-defined perceptions, but ones that were firmly rooted in the changing content of local politics. As Deshen (1982:24) puts it, the local political level developed from the grass roots in these settlements as "a new power arena which was wide open to the new immigrants."

A number of studies have documented the effects of the changing qualities of local politics in development towns. Thus we are told of the emergence of local electoral lists that are independent of the national political parties (Ben-Zadok and Goldberg 1984:23); the strengthening of localism, that is, an affirmation of local interests and a distinction between local and national policy (Ben-Zadok and Goldberg 1984:20); the rise of ethnic representation in local municipal and workers' councils and the increase of influence on decision making (Avineri 1973; Yishai 1984:286); the growth of a greater sense of attachment to the local community (Deshen 1982:28); or, outside the formal arena, the establishment of local newspapers (Caspi 1980:13) and the appearance of protest movements (Hasson 1983:178; Bama'aracha 1985). As Ben-Zadok and Goldberg (1984:27) phrase it, "the stereotype of a 'manipulated subject' does not fit the present new town resident."

It is important to note that while local activism is also an essentially political mechanism, its focus and effects differ from the political devices that figured in the initial shaping of the development towns. While both processes involve formal policy making and the promulgation of ordinances and decrees, the loci of their operations differ. From the point of view of the development towns, while the devices used during their beginnings involved directions coming from above, local activism implies the use of negotiations as the means for accomplishing things. While the national collective priorities figured as the central considerations earlier on, now it is local (albeit still collective) criteria that are taken into account in the decision-making processes.

Alongside this new mechanism, other less tangible processes began to operate within the development towns. These processes (which have to do with the creation of a sense of attachment to the locality) have only been alluded to in the literature on Israel's urban periphery. The general lack of attention to the development of sentiments of belonging to and ties with the local community is related, no doubt, to the way these towns were portrayed in the earlier literature. Indeed, within the earlier studies, the creation of local sentiments was seen to be especially difficult within the context of artificially created locales like the development towns. This is because such settlements, as mentioned earlier, were viewed as having a transient nature, as populated by people with previous attachments elsewhere, and as marked by a general lack of "natural," informal social ties.

Despite this view, for a large part of the permanent population of the development towns, the simple facts of living for a long time in the settlement and of coming into contact with others there were significant for the creation of ties within and with the locality. Thus, a close reading of the literature on the towns reveals a constant, if somewhat subdued, emphasis on some of the following qualities: Soen (1973, 1976–77) underlined the strong relationship between length of residence and presence of kith and kin in the development towns and identification with them; Berler (1970:144) categorized the phenomenon, in somewhat derogatory tones, as ethnic particularism and cited a number of studies that illuminated the link between the continued residence of relatives in the settlements and the strengthening of attachment to them. Deshen (1974) highlighted the development of active neighboring ties centering around religious activities, while Efrat (1977:66) hinted at the creation of what one might call "urban villages" in one town. Goldberg (1984a:15) gives examples of the growth of "home territories" of different groups in a northern settlement.

In brief, what all of this seems to point to is the operation of a process through which attachment or a sense of belonging to the locality is created. As Guest (1984:1) rightly notes, the growth of such sentiments (in older as well as in newer "contrived communities") is related to the interplay of two elements: territorial contiguity and ecological stability. Taken together, these two requirements make possible the "natural" maturation of local ties and the emergence of a sense of sharing a common experience and identity. To quote Guest (1984:16),

> Such simple acts as living for a long time in an area and interacting with nearby others make social claims upon us. . . . We become caught up in webs of social relationships which have no rational basis but are meaningful and important for us.

It is the interplay of the four mechanisms discussed above that formed the background—or more aptly, the preconditions—for the emergence of the processes by which holy sites were established in a number of development towns.

THE ESTABLISHMENT OF HOLY SITES: THE CASE OF RABBI DAVID U-MOSHE

In order to facilitate an exploration of the way holy sites are established it may be helpful to trace the specifics of one case: that of the "House of Rabbi David u-Moshe" in Safed. In later sections, which will deal with the analysis of this case, we shall have occasion to refer to relevant comparative material from other development towns.

In 1973 a forestry worker named Avraham Ben-Haim dedicated a room in his small Safed apartment to a Jewish Moroccan saint, Rabbi David u-Moshe. This saint was one of the most popular saints in Morocco and his *hillulah* would draw thousands of people from all over the Maghreb country to this sanctuary located in the High Atlas Mountains. The dedication itself came after a dream-series in which the Rabbi had appeared and claimed that he had left his tomb and that he wanted a new abode in Avraham's residence. Avraham published these dreams as "announcements to the public," which were circulated among Moroccan synagogues throughout the country. The impact of those announcements was remarkable, and within a few years the new tomb was transformed into a major pilgrimage center that serves as a full-fledged substitute for the original sanctuary. As a consequence, the saint's residence draws to it a constant flow of supplicants all year long. It is by far the most successful of the sacred loci that have been created through individual initiative, and has been designated as an obligatory station in the "saint map" of northern Israel by many North African immigrants.

Having traced the general contours of this case, let us begin to explore it in greater detail. Avraham was a native of a fairly large southern Moroccan village near Marrakech. Despite its remoteness from rabbinical centers, the village was a place where Jewish life could be lived fully and piously. His father was an unsophisticated man who earned his living as a shoemaker, but who did not fail to inculcate in his children from an early age a deep-seated faith in the *tsaddiqim* (holy, pious men). Indeed, Avraham's childhood recollections are replete with memories of visits to the tombs of the local village saints. In addition, Avraham views his Moroccan past with affection and sentiments. He describes life in his native village as characterized by peaceful and harmonious relations both among the Jews and between them and the Muslims, plentiful and uncontaminated natural resources, and a Jewish lifestyle that was marked by strict observance of laws and spirituality. If this is an idyllic view, it is in no small measure the outcome of the strong contrast with the hardships encountered in an Israeli development town.

In his mid-twenties and already married with an infant daughter, Avraham came to Israel in 1954 and was immediately sent to the town of Safed. Life was not easy in the new neighborhood, which had been created according to the model of development towns on the site of a small Jewish settlement. The apartment was tiny and during the first years was devoid of running water and electricity. Avraham found that he had to give up his former occupation of shoemaker and soon began to earn a living as a forest worker, which is one of the lowest-ranked jobs in terms of status and salary.

Since his immigration and settlement in Safed Avraham has lived in Shikun Canaan, as the immigrant housing project is known. Because his parents and most of his siblings settled in the same neighborhood, the extended family has managed to preserve a sense of "togetherness" that was typical of their life in Morocco. Indeed, as the family's married children also tend to find residence nearby, and with the fourth generation (now) being born in the

1980s, an impressive cross-generational stability (not unlike what is found in other development towns) has been established.

In 1972, a year before Rabbi David u-Moshe's first visitation, Avraham's closest brother was killed in a car accident. Avraham's religious faith had never before been so seriously shaken, but it was the *tsaddiq* who put an end to Avraham's prolonged distress. In one of his first oneiric apparitions, he took Avraham to a magnificent garden and picked one of the most beautiful roses that grew there, explaining that in the same way God selects the best people to reside with him. Under the saint's explicit demand, Avraham stopped his mourning and complaints.

The death of his brother undoubtedly created in Avraham a state of emotional turmoil that constituted a "suitable" background for the appearance of the *tsaddiq*. The event that immediately precipitated this appearance, however, was related to his intention to move from his apartment to a bigger place in another neighborhood. This change was prevented at the last moment by Rabbi David u-Moshe's announcement in 1973 that he desired the old apartment as his permanent residence. It is because of his appearance that Avraham and his family have become bound to their place.

Interestingly, a firm decision to change the place of living by moving to a less peripheral town or neighborhood, eventually annulled by a *tsaddiq*, underlies the creation of other sacred sites as well. The town of Beit She'an, for example, has recently been the locus of intense hagiolatric revivals and two sites have been established there in adjacent neighborhoods. In both cases, the precipitating factors underlying the establishment of the new sites were the firm intentions of the future initiators to move to another place. The same pattern was discerned in other sites in the southern development towns of Ofakim and Yeru'ham.

The recurrent precipitating factor well reflects an ambivalence that initiators-to-be (along with many residents of development towns) have felt toward their communities. On the one hand, these are areas that are marked by lack of employment and educational opportunities and by a rather poor public image. On the other hand, many of those people find themselves linked to their locality through various networks of friends and family. In many of these instances, however, the conflict is solved by the *tsaddiq*, who sanctifies the old place of living and impels its inhabitants to stay there.

The revelations of Rabbi David u-Moshe in 1973 marked a dramatic change in Avraham's life. From then on the saint's oneiric messages became his sole guidelines for action. One of these first messages was to write down his dreams and to distribute them in all the Moroccan communities in Israel. In complying with the *tsaddiq*'s command, Avraham transformed his private vision into a public affair, shared and supported by many.

Following the phase in which Avraham's house emerged as the saint's chosen abode, there was a long period of effort aimed at developing the site and securing the economic basis of the *hillula*. Gradually, the apartment and its environs were turned into a shrine complex. While the complex itself is located in the standard, rather unattractive house that is indistinguishable from other apartment blocks in the neighborhood, at its center is situated the saint's room. Placed within it are a marble tablet, which acts as a substitute for the absent gravestone, a donation box and various ritual objects, a bookcase designed as a Holy Ark, an ornamental chair for use in circumcisions, and a narrow bench for praying. These are placed against a colorful (almost eye-dazzling) array of carpets, tapestries, and amulets, which lend the room an aura of ceremoniality.

On the day of the *hillulah* the tiny room becomes the focus of a mass celebration in which some 15,000 to 20,000 people take part. Although the inhabitants of Safed and its hinterland are overrepresented among the celebrants, many pilgrims come on a one-day journey from all over the country. While most of the participants in the *hillulah* are of Moroccan extraction, in recent years groups of Libyan and Tunisian Jews have also participated in the celebration.

Upon reaching the neighborhood, the visitors are channeled into a narrow alley where a small but variegated market spontaneously emerges at the time of the *hillulah*. The commodities that are sold comprise the peculiar mix of sacred and secular that is so typical of pilgrimage sites (Meeker 1979:209). Holy books, oil and candles, and popular portraits of renowned *tsaddiqim* are offered alongside a variety of edibles, garments, and ornaments. Beggars and sellers of blessings (also an indispensable part of the pilgrimage setting) are grouped at the end of the trail near the entrance to the apartment, which has been enlarged and reshaped into an area for servicing the pilgrims. However, since this area too is small, most of the celebrants locate themselves wherever they find an empty space, be it a yard of a neighboring house or a nearby sidewalk.

In the absence of a formally imposed ritual structure, the only act deemed compulsory during the *hillulah* is a visit to the saint's room. From the early hours of the evening until late at night a long line is formed opposite the entrance to the apartment. Some sturdy men, recruited from a group of relatives, neighbors, and friends who voluntarily participate in the organization of the *hillulah*, regulate the massive flow of human traffic.

Inside the *tsaddiq*'s room an atmosphere of fervor and ecstasy prevails. The devotees, particularly women, enter the room displaying gestures of submission. They kiss the marble tablet and the carpeted walls and utter their prayers and wishes with great excitement. Before leaving they place generous sums of money in the donation box. On their way out, the visitors have ample opportunity to survey the rest of the apartment, the modesty of which stands in sharp contrast to the grandeur of the richly decorated room of the *tsaddiq*.

Most of the celebrants conclude their visit to the saint's room by lighting candles in his honor. In other pilgrimages, where the tombs are located in the open, candles are lit very close to the grave. In "Rabbi David u-Moshe's House" a special, covered compartment on the far side of the front yard is used for this purpose. Pilgrims throw candles inside the compartment, which soon becomes a fiery furnace and is the focus of much excited praying and crying. Another place of note are three small booths adjacent to the house, where teams of local volunteers deliver food for free to the celebrants. The food is prepared during the week preceding the *hillulah* by a group of female relatives and neighbors supervised by Avraham's wife.

Toward the late evening the *hillulah* becomes a formidable spectacle of mass celebration. The streets near the house are jammed with parked vehicles. Visitors continue to flow toward the house, pushing their way to the *tsaddiq*'s room. Police from the nearby station are called to control the heavy traffic. The crowded front yard becomes the scene of varied social activities as groups from places throughout the country intermingle, old acquaintances meet again, and new associations are formed. Women whose vows have been granted offer trays of sweets to people; popular singers attract the celebrants with traditional songs in praise of Rabbi David u-Moshe; and local political figures appear to congratulate the pilgrims.

The shift from this climax of mass celebrations to the ending of the *hillulah* is quite abrupt, for by midnight most of the visitors have already left for their homes. Many of the people to be found around the site on the morning following the *hillulah* belong to the core of relatives and friends who help Avraham's family put the place back to its ordinary state. Soon the neighborhood reassumes its shabby provincial character.

Inspired by the positive response to his project, Avraham has sought to maximize its potential by absorbing other saints into it. Rabbi David u-Moshe, Avraham's patron saint, has remained the dominant figure in the site, but the house bearing his name has become in recent years a pantheon of saints as six other *tsaddiqim* successively appeared in Avraham's dreams and expressed their wish to have their *hillulot* celebrated in his place. Well-dispersed throughout the whole year, the seven *hillulot* have strengthened Avraham's' web of associations with the *tsaddiqim*. For, by incorporation of these other saints, Avraham has expanded the one-day temporal marker of holiness into a sacred annual calendar that regulates the rhythm of life course of his family and neighbors.

Clearly Avraham has succeeded in creating a "sacred space" (Eliade 1954) in erecting the house that serves Rabbi David u-Moshe and the six other saints and a "sacred time" in and around the *hillulot* days of these *tsaddiqim*. Yet an understanding of the process of consecration or sanctification (Cohen 1976:57) of space in development towns involves explicating a complex mix of elements: the specific cultural tools through which sanctification is effected, the preconditions for its emergence, and the spatial and social implications for the local community.

SANCTIFICATION: PRECONDITIONS AND MACHINERY

The sanctification of space is always carried out through the symbolic idiom, the traditional "tools" that a specific culture provides. The cultural tools by which the holy sites were consecrated in Israel's development towns are part of the indigenous Moroccan traditions (Jewish as well as Muslim) of maraboutism and hagiolatry (Westermark 1926; Eickelman 1976; Geertz 1968; Gellner 1969).

The presence of saints was a basic given in the culturally constituted reality of Moroccan Jews and Muslims. Indeed, on the basis of recent studies (Ben-Ami 1984; Goldberg 1983) it has become clear that almost all of the Jewish communities had their own patron saints. The high points of veneration of these saints were the collective pilgrimages to their sanctuaries. But what is of importance in regard to these holy men is that they provided one of the central idioms through which people articulated and came to terms with their experiences (Crapanzano 1975:1). Thus, in addition to collective pilgrimages, visits to saints' tombs were often conducted on an individual basis in times of trouble. Devotees lit candles in honor of these holy men, held festive meals for them, and in many cases the relationship with a saint spanned an entire life course. The adherent displayed due respect for "his" saint, visited his tomb on the *hillula*, and expected that the latter would intercede on his behalf whenever he faced any difficulties or problems.

This hagiolatric tradition formed the background for the actions of people like Avraham Ben-Haim in Safed. The specific psychological mechanism through which the holy sites were established is related to the role of visitational dreams. The role of dreams in sustaining and facilitating the innovation of cultural traditions has been documented in a number of societies (Bourguignon 1972; Lanternari 1975; O'Nell 1976; Stephen 1979). In Morocco the role of visitational dreams in discovering and maintaining linkages to saints has long been a feature of both Jewish and Muslim practices. In Avraham's case dreams appear as devices that aided him on numerous occasions: in deciding to stay in Safed, in gaining confidence to negotiate with contractors and municipal officials, or in providing justification for his actions.

Yet the following question still remains.[5] In what way is this kind of sanctification of space related to the peculiarities of development towns? One answer may have to do with the high percentage of Middle Eastern, and especially North African, immigrants in these settlements. This argument would posit that such towns are populated by people who would be predisposed to use these kinds of cultural devices. Yet, surely, such an explanation is at best only partial. While Maghrebi immigrants reside in many different kinds of Israeli settlements, urban as well as rural, the phenomenon of establishing holy sites appears only in development towns. A fuller explanation may thus lie in the way this sanctification fits with the basic conditions (or, more specifically, with a basic predicament) shared by certain residents of development towns.

A brief digression by way of Cyrenaica may help illuminate this point. Meeker (1979:210–11) in a revealing insight shows how the veneration of saints' tombs among the bedouin of Cyrenaica is related to the basic social circumstance of certain men, to what he called their "vulnerable domestic interests." These men were caught in a situation in which they had an interest in the land, but did not possess the suitable political resources for controlling access to it. By positing a fixed link between a man and the land through the form of a saint's tomb these men attempted to usurp a measure of ownership of the land. Through the vehicle of saints' tombs, they thus sought to come to terms with their situation by transposing an essentially precarious political and economic situation into an immutable religious one.

It is a similar process, we contend, which goes on in regard to many of the holy sites recently established in Israel's development towns. It is a process that is most obviously observed in relation to the problematic nature of deciding whether to leave or stay in these peripheral settlements. On the one hand, residents of development towns live in places that are characterized by few employment and cultural opportunities, and by a constant flow of in- and outmigration. They reside in towns that are often viewed by Israelis with a mixture of condescension, mild disdain, and paternalistic concern (Goldberg 1984a:7). Moreover, many of these people (and especially those who are not politically oriented) are vulnerable. They lack the political and economic ability to restructure their living environment.

Yet for these people a move out of the development town (even given that they possess the requisite resources) is not an act that is easily realized. For there are residents who have never left their hometowns since their immigration to Israel. In their case the sentiments of being an integral part of the locality (whether through local activism or through networks of friends and neighbors) are often reinforced by the transgenerational continuity of families in the town: witness the four generations of Avraham's family in Safed.

The establishment of holy sites in Israel's development towns can now be more fully understood. These holy sites were established in towns that were shaped into two opposing directions by the mechanisms that operated during the decades of their existence. The juxtaposition of the "negative" consequences of the earlier devices of planning and selective migration, and the "positive" outcomes of local activism and creation of a sense of belonging created a dilemma for residents of many development towns. This dilemma (whether to leave or to stay and somehow change the town) was resolved for some people through the establishment of holy sites. It was resolved by the transposition of the "real" contradictory situation onto an otherwordly plane, that is, onto a plane in which persons became decisively "fixed" to their local communities.

While the above explanation illuminates the relation between the holy sites and their erection in Israel's urban periphery, it leaves unexplored the specific operations on these sites' space. These operations are related to the movement and establishment of (to create a metaphor) the otherworldly immigrants, the saintly settlers. Three points merit underlining in this regard. The first involves the special potential inherent in the visitational dreams for overcoming the restrictions imposed by a lack of political and economic resources. This kind of dreaming (in ways akin to what Sack [1980:149] calls mythical thinking) makes possible the negation or suspension of spatial distance. This implies that the visitational dreams facilitated the migration of saints between Morocco and Israel without the limitations faced by the thousands of "real" immigrants who made such journeys. It allowed (to put this somewhat crudely) the movement of the holy men without the need to incur the costs of transportation or the difficulties of crossing international borders.

Second, this mechanism of sanctification makes possible a linking between the symbolic space of society and "real" space. This is similar to the way an act of settlement or construction serves such a function in societies all over the world (Tuan 1977:104; Sack 1980:155). Thus, the installment of a saint in a development town serves to do two things: to re-create the special cultural forms of Jewish life in Morocco and to inscribe the holy site on the map of Jewish holy places in Israel.

The third, and perhaps most concrete, point is related to the effects of housing the saintly immigrants on the development towns as built-up systems. Given the limited resources of the innovators at the beginning it was natural that the constructional effects of establishing the sanctuaries were limited to only a partial restructuring of the sites themselves. As Choay (1968:31), in a distinctly continental parlance, puts it,

The acceleration of history reveals the vice inherent in all built-up systems: a permanence and a rigidity which makes it impossible for them to continually transform themselves according to the rhythm set by less rooted systems such as language, technology, clothing or painting. Against this permanent threat, the modern city's own means allow it but one meagre defense: partial restructuring.

Put less abstractly, this means that the expression of the special logic or rhythm of sanctification (e.g., sumptuousness or ceremoniality) was limited more or less to the existing structures and houses. Thus the rich display of the centrality of the saint's abode in Safed was limited to a tiny room in a "regular" residence with only a modest reconstruction of the housefront. This holds true for other places, such as Yeruham, Ofakim, or Beit She'an. In all these places the recently erected saints' shrines are contained in small rooms or huts within their initiators' apartments or yards. This is not to deny that sanctification often takes place on a grand architectural scale. It is rather to underscore the fact that it can find a measure of expression even within the limits of "ordinary" residences and neighborhoods.

CONCLUSION: IMPLICATIONS AND SUGGESTIONS

The establishment of holy sites in Israel's development towns is not limited to the installation of saints in "new" locations. A number of other devices for the sanctification of holy sites have been in operation in Israel's urban periphery. One such vehicle has been the consecration of tombs of local *tsaddiqim* (mainly from the talmudic period), which have been pilgrimage centers from as early as the Middle Ages. Two examples of this process are the Jewish Moroccan appropriation of talmudic sages' tombs in Hatzor Haglilit and Yavneh. In both cases long-existing traditions of holy sites have been "colored" by North African practices.

Aside from "annexing" old-time native pilgrimage sites, new centers have been established around the tombs of contemporary rabbis who were allotted saintly attributes in their lifetimes or, more often, posthumously. The most impressive examples of this trend are the mass pilgrimages to the tomb of Rabbi Haim Houri (a Tunisian rabbi who died in 1957), which is located in the municipal cemetery of Beersheba (Weingrod 1990), and to the tomb of Baba Sali of the venerated Abu Hatsera family in Netivot. Other minor, local-bound *hillulot* following this pattern take place in such places as Ashdod, Ofakim, and Migdal Ha'Emek.

Against this background it appears that sacred sites may well continue to emerge in large communities of traditionally oriented North African Jews. Indeed, these processes (though short of encompassing all such Jews in Israel) are too recurrent to be considered sporadic or episodic. In such places as Beit She'an, Hatzor, and Safed, the traditional pattern of a community with "its" own *tsaddiq* has been reestablished. The messages carried by such actions are as follows: "One should not turn one's face to Morocco when looking for Rabbi David u-Moshe's help; one should go to Safed instead." "Beit She'an is not a place to be disregarded and deserted for it contains a site of utmost sanctity."

These kinds of messages are related in turn to the significance of the *tsaddiq* to the town in which the site has been erected. The appearance of a saint in a development town may contribute to (as well as reflect) a change in the image of the place. As noted before, the *tsaddiq* accords the town an aura of sanctity, through which it is "cathected" with the holy man's divine grace. In this way, the residents' sense of belonging to the locality acquires a wider meaning. The sense of attachment, if you like, is placed within a larger meaning-giving system, within a holy map of pilgrimage sites in Israel.

Yet the growth and implications of these contentions cannot be understood apart from the changing context of ethnic consciousness in Israel. For it is in this context that the legitimacy of a whole range of cultural tools for contending with the difficulties faced by the Middles Eastern immigrants to Israel are anchored. Thus, the installation of saints in new locations should be seen in the context of the tenacious preservation or revival of such sponsored, as well as spontaneous, practices as folk healing, Middle Eastern music and dance (Cohen and Shiloah 1985), ethnic festivals, lecture series, museum exhibits, radio programs dedicated to aspects of Jewish culture in the Muslim world, ethnic journals, or the memorialization of rabbis (Goldberg 1977:170–76).

Contrary to a naive "melting pot" conception, the relative improvement in the socioeconomic conditions of the North African Jews in Israel has facilitated an awareness of their distinctive ethnic identity. The folk veneration of saints and the establishment of their sanctuaries have (along with a whole array of practices outlined above) provided many Middle Eastern Jews in Israel with a set of cultural means to deal with their situation. To underscore this by way of example, by furnishing his community with a viable idiom, Avraham's project has become a cultural resource of considerable importance. The appearance of saints in Israel's urban periphery has thus facilitated a process through which the inhabitants of these areas (once the reluctant or passive victims of arbitrary policies promulgated by the central government) have actively contended with their situation, become more rooted in their localities, and strengthened local patriotic sentiments. As such, the *hillulot* in various sites partake of the nature of "ethnic renewal ceremonies" (Gluckman 1963; Weingrod n.d.)—rites that reflect the growing confidence of an émigré group in being part of the contemporary Israeli scene while, at the same time, indicating a strong sense of ethnic distinctiveness.

A recognition of these trends raises, in turn, a question about the "Middle Eastern" quality of Israel's development towns. In a wide-ranging paper in which he compared the urban experience of Israel with that of the Arab world, Cohen (1979:18) suggested the following: that despite government efforts to the contrary, Israel's development towns have undergone a process of Levantinization, a reversion to the "habitual lethargy" of the Levant. According to Cohen (1979:87) in these towns, the

> customs and life ways to which the inhabitants were accustomed prior to immigration took over, neutralizing in many respects the forces of incorporation emanating from the center of Israeli society. This Levantinization process was probably reinforced by the formation of ethnoclasses of Afro-Asian origin in these towns, itself an unintended consequence of the new town policy.

At first glance, the establishment and activation of new centers for the veneration of saints in some of the country's development towns seems to fit this characterization. Yet, as we have rather relentlessly been stressing, this phenomenon puts in question Cohen's description of a reversion to an "habitual lethargy" that is devoid of potential for innovation and an active contention with the changing circumstances of the towns. By way of conclusion it may perhaps be apt to highlight a number of these innovative and active aspects of the phenomenon under study.

The establishment of saints' tombs should be seen, first of all, as one of a number of alternative mechanisms people and organizations use to change their physical and social environments. Thus we propose that, in dealing with the patterns of transformation of Israel's development towns, different kinds of mechanisms (and mixes of mechanisms) should be taken into account. More specifically, this implies going beyond the stress on the instrumental and political devices—planning, migration, and activism—which have figured as the prime foci of research on Israel's urban periphery, toward an examination of the "cultural" resources that are at people's disposal in order to transform their urban settlements. These kinds of resources, in other words, may be the only viable means through which people such as Avraham in Safed (who belongs to the rank and file in terms of background and political acumen) may have.

In this regard, if the cultural resources that individuals use are remarkably similar to those used in the Levant (or more specifically in the Maghreb) this is because people naturally utilize the social techniques that their tradition bequeaths them. Thus neither the mere existence of these techniques nor their similarity to Moroccan traditions is necessarily a reason for believing that they contribute to a lethargic passivity. As Goldberg (1984b) rightly notes, culture or tradition should not be seen as a monolithic force from the past but as a system of meanings, parts of which are actively utilized by persons in changing social circumstances.

In this regard, however, we would suggest two additional problems for further research.[6] The first has to do with a refinement of our general assertion that there is a relation among saints, shrines, and development towns. Since these towns differ historically in the way they have been subject to the macroforces of planning, migration, and local activism, one may well ask the following question: How are these differences related to variations in the kinds of shrines that are being built, and to the diversity of processes through which they are being sanctified? The second problem involves comparing the establishment of saints' shrines with other mechanisms by which the residents of the development towns have produced symbolic manifestations of themselves and rationalized their continued residence in the settlements. Here the question is how the saintly sanctification of space differs functionally and symbolically from such activities as building synagogues or community centers, congregating in cafes or on neighborhood corners, or the operation of youth clubs or sports organizations.

These contentions and questions should not be misconstrued as an argument for the establishment of saints' tombs as a panacea for all the problems of development towns in Israel. One cannot make the easy assumption that all such difficulties will be solved to the extent that the inhabitants of such settlements become (politically or "culturally") active. For governments and private corporations vary greatly in their ability to take effective action. As Spiegel (1966:184; see also Handelman and Shamgar-Handelman 1978) noted two decades ago, many, if not most, of the problems of these towns are related to the twin factors of population stabilization and the creation of more and better jobs. What we do argue for, however, is a richer appreciation of the means people utilize to come to terms with and change their social and physical circumstances.

ACKNOWLEDGMENTS

Thanks are due to V. Azarya, E. Cohen, H. Goldberg, R. Kahane, A. Seligman, and two anonymous reviewers for comments on earlier drafts of this chapter, and to the Harry S. Truman Research Institute for generously helping us complete it.

NOTES

1. During 1981–82 Yoram Bilu conducted extensive observations and interviews in several sites in Israel where local or Moroccan traditions of saint veneration had been renewed. Most of the material was gathered in two locales in northern Israel: Safed and Beit She'an. In order to render the picture more complete, however, he also conducted research in Hatsor Haglilit, Ofakim, and Kiriyat Gat.

2. No one definition of development towns exists. Following Goldberg (1984a:2), however, we refer to those towns on the country's geographical periphery in Galilee (north) and the Negev (south).

3. A good, if abbreviated, historical overview of the growth of development ment towns in Israel can be found in Goldberg (1984a: chap. 1).

4. For reasons of brevity the main argument in the text will emphasize migration into and out of the development towns. An important parallel mechanism that we leave unanalyzed involves intratown mobility (Don and Hovav 1971–72; Efrat 1977).

5. Greater detail regarding the psychological aspects of this case can be found in Bilu (1986) and Bilu and Abramovich (1985).

6. We are greatly indebted to an anonymous reviewer for aiding us in formulating these questions.

REFERENCES

Altman, E. A., and B. R. Rosenbaum. 1973. Principles of Planning and Zionist Ideology: The Israeli Development Town. *Journal of the American Institute of Planners* 39:316–25.

Aronoff, M. J. 1973. Development Towns in Israel. In *Israel: Social Structure and Change*, M. Curtis and M. S. Chertoff, eds.. New Brunswick, N. J.: Transaction, 27–46.

Avineri, S. 1973. Israel: Two Nations? In *Israel: Social Structure and Change*, M. Curtis and M. S. Chertoff, eds.. New Brunswick, N. J.: Transaction, 281–305.

Bama'aracha. 1985. The "Struggle-85" Movement: Activists in Urban Neighborhoods and in Development Towns. *Bama'aracha* 292:26. (Hebrew)

Ben-Ami, I. 1984. *Folk-Veneration of Saints Among Jews in Morocco*. Jerusalem: Magnes. (Hebrew)

———. 1981. The Folk-Veneration of Saints Among Moroccan Jews; Traditions, Continuity and Change. The Case of the Holy Man, Rabbi David u-Moshe. In *Studies in Judaism and Islam*, S. Morag et al., eds.. Jerusalem: Magnes, 283–345. (Hebrew)

Ben-Zadok, E. 1985. National Planning–The Critical Neglected Link: One Hundred Years of Jewish Settlement in Israel. *International Journal of Middle Eastern Studies* 17:329–45.

Ben-Zadok E., and G. Goldberg. 1984. Voting Patterns of Oriental Jews in Development Towns. *The Jerusalem Quarterly* 32:16–27.

Berler, A. 1970. *New Towns in Israel*. Jerusalem: Israel Universities Press.

Bernstein, D. 1984. Political Participation: New Immigrants and Veteran Parties in Israeli Society. *Plural Societies* 5:13–32.

Bilu, Y. 1986. Dreams and the Wishes of Saint. In *Judaism Viewed From Within and From Without*, Harvey Goldberg ed. New York: New York University Press, 285–313.

Bilu Y., and H. Abramovich. 1985. In Search of the Saddiq: Visitational Dreams Among Moroccan Jews in Israel. *Psychiatry* 48:83–92.

Bourguignon, E. 1972. Dreams and Altered States of Consciousness in Anthropological Research. In *Psychological Anthropology*, F. L. K. Hsu, ed. Cambridge, Mass.: Schenkman 403–34.

Brown, K. D. 1976. *People of Salé*. Manchester: Manchester University Press.

Caspi, D. 1980. *The Growth of Local Newspapers in Israel: Trends and Appraisals*. Bar Ilan University: Institute of Local Government. (Hebrew)

Choay, F. 1968. Urbanism and Semiology. In *Meaning in Architecture*, G. Baird and C. Jenks, eds.. London: Barrie, 27–37.

Cohen, E. 1983. Ethnicity and Legitimation in Contemporary Israel. *The Jerusalem Quarterly* 28:111–24.

———. 1979. Urban Hierarchy, Urban Policy and Urban Social Change in Israel and the Arab World: A Comparative Analysis. In *Contemporary Urbanization and Social Justice*, J. Beuujeu-Garnier and S. Reichman, eds.. Jerusalem: Ministry of Energy and Infrastructure, 70–94.

———. 1977. The City in the Zionist Ideology. *The Jerusalem Quarterly* 4:126–144.

———. 1976. Environmental Orientations: A Multidimensional Approach to Social Ecology. *Current Anthropology* 17(1):49–70.

———. 1970. Development Towns: The Social Dynamics of "Planted" Urban Communities in Israel. In *Integration and Development in Israel*, S. N. Eisenstadt et al., eds.. Jerusalem: Israel Universities Press, 587–617.

Cohen, E., and A. Shiloah. 1985. Major Trends in the Dynamics of Change of Jewish Oriental Ethnic Music in Israel. *Popular Music* 5:199–223.

Comay, Y., and A. Kirschenbaum. 1973. The Israeli New Town: An Experiment at Population Redistribution. *Economic Development and Cultural Change* 22:124–34.

Crapanzano, V. 1975. Saints, Jnun and Dreams: An Essay in Moroccan Ethnopsychology. *Psychiatry* 38:145–59.

Deshen, S. 1982. Social Organization and Politics in Israeli Urban Quarters. *The Jerusalem Quarterly* 22:21–37.

———. 1974. Political Ethnicity and Cultural Ethnicity in Israel During the 1960s. In *Urban Ethnicity*, A. Cohen, ed. London: Tavistock, 281–309.

Don, Y., and H. Hovav. 1971–72. The Measurement of Population Mobil-
    ity: A Case Study of an Israeli Development Town. *Economic Devel-
    opment and Cultural Change* 26:703–21.
Efrat, E. 1977. Residence and Internal Migration in the Immigrant City of
    Ashdod. *Ir-Ve'eizor* 4:61–71. (Hebrew)
Eickelman, D. F. 1976. *Moroccan Islam.* Austin: University of Texas Press.
Elazar, D. J. 1973. Local Government as an Integrating Factor in Israeli So-
    ciety. In *Israel's Social Structure and Change*, M. Curtis and M. S.
    Chertoff, eds.. New Brunswick, N. J.: Transaction, 15–26.
Eliade, M. 1954. *The Myth of the Eternal Return.* New York: Pantheon.
Firey, W. 1947. *Land Use in Central Boston.* Cambridge, Mass.: Harvard
    University Press.
Geertz, C. 1968. *Islam Observed.* New Haven: Yale University Press.
Gellner, E. 1969. *Saints of the Atlas.* Chicago: University of Chicago Press.
Gluckman, M. 1963. *Order and Rebellion in Tribal Africa.* London: Cohen
    and West.
Goldberg, H. 1984a. *Greentown's Youth: Disadvantaged Youth in a Devel-
    opment Town in Israel.* Assen: Van Gorcum.
———. 1984b. Historical and Cultural Aspects of the Phenomenon of Eth-
    nicity. *Megamot* 29(2–3):233–49. (Hebrew)
———. 1983. The Mellahs of Southern Morocco: Report of a Survey. *The
    Maghreb Review* 8(3–4):61–69.
———. 1977. Introduction: Culture and Ethnicity in the Study of Israeli So-
    ciety. *Ethnic Groups* 1:163–86.
Guest, A. M. 1984. Robert Park and the Natural Area: A Sentimental Re-
    view. *Sociology and Social Research* 69(1):1–21.
Handelman, D., and L. Shamgar-Handelman. 1978. Social Planning Prereq-
    uisites for New and Expanded Communities. *Contact* 10(3):86–122.
Hasson, S. 1983. The Emergence of an Urban Social Movement in Israeli So-
    ciety: An Integrated Approach. *International Journal of Urban and
    Regional Research* 7(2):157–74.
———. 1981. Social And Spatial Conflicts: The Settlement Process in Israel
    During the 1950s and the 1960s. *L'Espace Geographique* 3:169–79.
Kramer, R. M. 1973. Urban Community Development in Israel. In *Israel:
    Social Structure and Change*, M. Curtis and M. S. Chertoff, eds. New
    Brunswick, N.J.:Transaction, 47–66.
Lanternari, V. 1975. Dreams as Charismatic Significants: Their Bearing on
    the Rise of New Religious Movements. In *Psychological Anthropol-
    ogy*, T. R. Williams, ed. The Hague: Mouton, 221–35.
Marx, E. 1976. *The Social Context of Violent Behavior.* London: Routledge.
———. 1975. Anthropological Studies in a Centralized State: Max Gluck-
    man and the Bernstein Israel Research Project. *Jewish Journal of So-
    ciology* 17:131–50.

Matras, J. 1973. Israel's New Frontier: The Urban Periphery. In *Israel: Social Structure and Change*, M. Curtis and M. S. Chertoff, eds. New Brunswick, N.J.: Transaction, 3–14.

Meeker, M. E. 1979. *Literature and Violence in North Arabia.* Cambridge: Cambridge University Press.

O'Nell, C. W. 1976. *Dreams, Culture, and the Individual.* New York: Chandler.

Sack, R. D. 1980. *Conceptions of Space in Social Thought: A Geographic Perspective.* London: Macmillan.

Shachar, A. S. 1971. Israel's Development Towns: Evaluation of National Urbanization Policy. *Journal of the American Institute of Planners* 37(6):362–72.

Soen, D. 1976–77. Primary Relations in Poor Urban Neighborhoods and in Development Towns in Israel. *Ir-Ve'eizor* 3:65–73. (Hebrew)

———. 1973. Migdal-Ashquelon: A Social Analysis. In *Cities in Israel*, A. Schachar et al., eds. Jerusalem: Akademon, 600–618. (Hebrew)

Spiegel, E. 1966. *Neue Stadte/New Towns in Israel.* Stuttgart: Karl Kramer.

Spilerman, S., and J. Habib. 1976. Development Towns in Israel: The Role of Community in Creating Ethnic Disparities in labor Force Characteristics. *American Journal of Sociology* 81(4):781–812.

Stephen, M. 1979. Dreams of Change: The Innovative Role of Altered States of Consciousness in Traditional Melanesian Religion. *Oceania* 50:3–22.

Suttles, G. 1972. *The Social Construction of Communities.* Chicago: University of Chicago Press.

Tuan, Y. F. 1977. *Space and Place: The Perspective of Experience.* London: Arnold.

Weingrod, A. 1990. *The Saint of Beersheba.* Albany: State University of New York Press.

Weintraub, D., and V. Kraus. 1982. Spatial Differentiation and Place of Residence: Spatial Dispersion and Composition of Population and Stratification in Israel. *Megamot* 27(4):367–81. (Hebrew)

Westermark, E. 1926. *Ritual and Belief in Morocco.* London: Macmillan.

Yuchtman-Ya'ar, E., S. E. Spiro, and J. Ram. 1978. Reactions to Rehousing: Loss of Community or Frustrated Aspirations? *Urban Studies* 16:113–19.

Yishai, Y. 1984. Responsiveness to Ethnic Demands: The Case of Israel. *Ethnic and Racial Studies* 7(2):283–300.

4

The Presence of Absence
The Memorialism of National Death in Israel
DON HANDELMAN AND
LEA SHAMGAR-HANDELMAN

EDITOR'S COMMENTS

This chapter, written by Don Handelman and Lea Shamgar-Handelman, is entitled "The Presence of Absence: The Memorialism of National Death in Israel." Their contribution centers on the relationships between the presence or absence of the body of the dead and the visual representation of death on the surface of the land. They single out three different landscapes of national sacrifice for analysis: military cemeteries, military memorials and monuments, and the Holocaust Memorial (in Jerusalem). In more general terms, their contribution focuses on the manner by which death is appropriated by the Israeli state for the purpose of creating collective memories within its territory.

A man whose son died in the war
walks up the street
like a woman with a dead fetus in her womb.
"Behind all this, some great happiness is hiding."

(Amichai 1986:96)

Everything visible conceals something visible.

—Rene Magritte

Lea Shamgar-Handelman (1934–95) died on August 4, 1995. The absence of her presence is deeply and sorely felt.

The political existence of modern states is predicated on their control over precisely (indeed, absolutely) bounded territories, their control of access to these territories, and their determination of who has the right to live here (Handelman 1994). Territory is said to belong and to be integral to the state. In the modern era, such spaces are constructed, shaped, and furnished as national landscapes, as territorial contexts molded with meaning and sentiment through the interaction of ideological claims, historicist ethos, and political strategies (Williams and Smith 1983:504; Cosgrove 1984:13). Those people (usually citizens) who identify with the ideological tenets and historicist visions of the state often feel themselves to have special affinities with its national landscapes. They may well see themselves as emerging (naturally, historically, mythically) from the land and belonging to it, just as this belongs to the state. Issues of ownership and belonging are especially acute when national territory is contested space, where peoples in conflict compete to constitute landscapes that substantiate and that harmonize with their own claims to affinity with the land. The validation of political claims to land in the modern era is obsessed with the creation of reality—indeed, with the substantive reality of national presence that is perceived as singularly and uniquely engendered for/by a particular people and state, and whose presence must be made visible and empowered by material presence.[1] In the romanticism of the modern state, territorial borders are boundaries of being within which national landscapes are threaded with collective memory.

The territory of the State of Israel is contested space that Israeli Jews shape with meaning and emotion in ongoing ways, to constitute landscapes that resonate with and are unified by their claims of ownership and belonging.[2] Of central importance to the production of these claims is the placement of death—that is, death in general, but especially that which is understood to have national import. The placement and commemoration of national death have been central to the molding of holistic collective memory and identity in numerous states of the modern era (Shamgar-Handelman 1986; Mosse 1979; Ben-Amos 1989; Tumarkin 1983; Kapferer 1988:149–67; Ingersoll and Nickell 1987).

Our sense of death is that it transforms presence into absence. Presence, in its manifold variations, may be understood in social, phenomenological, embodied, and existential terms. But to our knowledge, in all such paradigms of knowing and feeling, the immediacy of death is the absence of presence among the living—something like an implosion into a black hole that sucks in being, nullifying presence in its wake. In these moments (brief or lengthy) following death, individuals have memories of the dead, but the latter rarely are connected and cathected with wider penumbra of meanings that make their death significant to greater numbers. (We are tempted to call the extension of these penumbra of meaning, secondhand death—people who know people who knew the dead; people who know people who know people who knew the dead; knowing the dead through the mass media, and so forth.) Memorialism, regardless of the multitude of cultural practices among a wide variety of peoples, has then a most unusual task—to make this absence present so that it serves the agency of the living, whether through mourning, celebration, consultation, and so forth (Handelman 1985; Huntington and Metcalf 1979; Bloch and Parry 1982). For memorialism to succeed, the absence of presence must be turned into the presence of absence; the nullity of the dead transformed into feelings, topoi, and durations of their absence. We will have more to say on this in the concluding section.

The relationship between place and memory, between the groundedness of being and the motility of its horizons of imagination in space and through time, is intimate. Place and memory apparently seek, select, and shape the perceptions of one another. Thus Casey (1987:189) argues that "a given place will invite certain memories while discouraging others," while "memories are selective for place: they seek out particular places as their natural habitats." Perhaps this torquing of the exteriority of the self (place) and its interiority (memory) are one way in which dreamscapes are turned into landscapes (Ezrahi 1992:482), to the extent that signs of place substitute for the self in remembering:

> Let the memorial hill remember instead of me,
> that's what its here for. Let the park in-memory-of remember,
> let the street that's-named-for remember,
> let the well-known building remember . . .
> Let the flags remember,
> those multicolored shroûds of history: the bodies they wrapped
> have long since turned to dust. Let the dust remember.
>
> (Amichai 1987:13)

In the landscapes contested by Israel and her Palestinian and other Arab neighbors, it is violent death that most frequently is understood as national sacrifice. In its religious senses, sacrifice is by definition violent death, in which the body is rent and life torn from its remnant in order that something of greater worth be received or preserved (Smith and Doniger 1989:224; Herrenschmidt 1978). In nationalist discourse, one that dwells incessantly on the holistic unity of national entities, metaphors of sacrifice often signify the willingness of individual citizens—the parts of such national wholes—to die on behalf of and therefore in place of the whole. The bodies of the sacrificial dead are perceived to embody the national whole. In substituting for the death of the national entity, the sacrificial dead are no longer parts of a national whole, but themselves embody its holism. Through synecdoche—the part-whole relationship—the ontological status of the part is elevated to that of the whole.

In this chapter we address the commemoration of national death in Israel through the construction of memorials. We limit this discussion to memorials whose erection is either done under the auspices of or is recognized by the relevant institutions of the state (see Azaryahu 1992:65–67 for a discussion of private monuments to sacrifice in Israel). Our discussion takes up a statist variant of how, in Durkheimian terms, the dead are used for the needs of the living. Mosse (1990:36), in discussing the formation of the cult of fallen soldiers in post-Revolutionary France, calls this the nationalization of death. Therefore we emphasize that the death we refer to is "public," in that it is expropriated and made the public property of extensive sectors of the population. Indeed, it is death that has many publics. So, too, different publics claim rights to use such death: to explain the intentions of the dead in their dying; to speak in the name of the dead; to give meanings to these deaths; and to make relevant the multiple affiliations of the dead to different places and categories of population.

Following Halbwachs (1992) on collective memory, we argue more generally that such memorials are intended to evoke sentiments of national identity and common goals. Thus national unity is solidified, materialized, and (of the highest value) embodied in the land through the construction of signs of collective commemoration that signify through death the especially intimate link between the individual and the collectivity, between nation and land. This is the national landscape of commemoration. In particular we explore certain conditions that influence the degrees to which memorials are elaborated symbolically on the surface of the land. In this regard, these memorials are principled rather than conditional formations. That is, the symbolic elaboration of these memorials cannot be attributed to contingent calculations of differences in political motives, in fiscal means, in the social networks of the dead nor to personal desires, as is often the case in acts of private commemoration. Instead, such memorials are intended as principled declarations of national topoi, in their representation of the rootedness of ideology in the originary land. Yet this quality of deep embedment in the landscape (that finally becomes the cosmogenic emergence of the people from the land) is processual (at least in the Israeli case) in order to continue to be rooted.

Kuchler (1993) makes the distinction between landscapes of memory and landscapes as memory, attributing the former to modern Western perceptions. The landscape of memory is a picture of landscape, a static, inscribed surface on which memories are fixed and labeled, and from which the social and cultural referents of these memories can be read off. Landscape as memory indexes the practice of landscape (as landscaping, one may say) as memory-work that unceasingly reforms the shaping and shapes of its own significance. The distinction is useful, yet itself overly rigid. Thus in the modern era, memories and landscapes of national death increasingly mutate (and migrate) in order to continue to be perceived at any given moment as eternal. The landscape as memory produces the landscape of memory, and perhaps their relationship is dialectical (and dialogical), as the work of Henri Lefebvre suggests.

To embellish for a moment on the dialectics of space of Lefebvre (Shields 1991:50–56), one may argue that what Lefebvre (1991:41–2) called representational spaces open up spaces of representation that are configured into national landscapes. That is, the cultural encodings of ideology, history, and knowledge, explicit and implicit, enable the imaginings of versions of lived spatializations that both reproduce and critique dominant social orders. This is so even in the enclosed discourses on the commemoration of national death—the configuring of national landscapes of memorialization is processual and changing, and different epistemologies of memorialism compete with and undercut one another through time even as their conflict often is made mute at the holistic, encompassing level of national unity.

In Israel there are three major types of place that articulate the relationship between sacrificial death and the land—the relationship that embodies and empowers the land with the presence of absence. These are the military cemetery, the military memorial, and the Holocaust memorial.[3] Each type visualizes some relationship of the dead to the land, such that their absence on its surface signifies their presence within its earth. That is, each type of place represents death on the surface of the land in ways that constitute claims for national landscapes. Through these representations, these places contribute to the molding of landscapes of collective memory.

In the body of this chapter we discuss relationships between the presence of the body of the dead within the land and the visual representation of death on the surface of the land, relationships that create landscapes of national sacrifice. There are broad but significant contrasts in visual representation among the three kinds of place mentioned in the previous paragraph. These contrasts are related to the degrees to which the dead, the embodiment of sacrifice, are present in the land and thereby embody it with the presence of their absence. The highest degree of presence is in the military cemetery, where the body of the dead is indeed in-place. The lowest degree of presence is in the Holocaust memorial, from which bodies and significant places of death both are absent. In between is the military memorial: this articulates relationships between the sacrificial dead and the living in connection to places that are significant to both. Nonetheless, the bodies of the dead are absent there. Our argument is that the greater the presence of the sacrificial dead, as outlined above, the less problematic is this relationship between living and dead.[4]

THE MILITARY CEMETERY

As a child he would mash his potatoes
to a golden mush.
And then you die.
A living child must be cleaned
when he comes home from playing.
But for a dead man
earth and sand are clear water, in which
his body goes on being bathed and purified
forever.

(Amichai 1986:92–93)

In Israel the military cemetery is the place that contains the body of sacrifice, and that thereby embodies the land. This synthesis of body and land makes the military cemetery the exemplar of the presence of national death. The graves of soldiers are almost always set apart from those of others. These graves are located either in a separate location, the "military section," within a civilian cemetery or in a cemetery given over wholly to military death. As noted above, military death (as in many states of the modern era) is predicated upon notions of sacrifice for the sake of the higher values of the state and its people (Mosse 1990:35–36). The soldier-citizen is thought to offer his life so that the state and its citizens will live. Just as the state exists through the viable constitution of its territory, so military death is intimately related to the land that such death is said to protect and propagate in some way. Therefore, in modern nationalism an intimate relationship is struck between the body of the dead soldier and the substance of the land he battled to defend (see Mosse 1979). As the soldier sacrificed himself for the land in life, so in death the land takes him in, and his presence there empowers the intimacy of their relationship—the holistic integration of culture and nature through self-sacrifice, often to be memorialized precisely in this way. The body, one may say, belongs to the land, while the land is felt to acquire contours that resonate with the bodies buried within it.[5]

Our discussion refers in particular to the military cemetery located in Jerusalem on Mount Herzl, and called by the name of this location. This cemetery has its own particular physical contours that differ in certain respects from most other military cemeteries in Israel. Nonetheless, in the most important details it can be treated as a nearly generic example of these venues in Israel.

Mount Herzl was planned as the central ceremonial and memorial center of the state, following independence in 1948. The remains of Theodor Herzl, the visionary of Zionism and pivotal to its secular pantheon, were brought from Austria and reinterred on the top of this mountain in 1949, and in the following years the space around Herzl's tomb was developed as the burial ground for Zionist and Israeli leaders. In the early years of the state, the annual commemoration of Herzl Day was a central event in the enactment of national cosmology; and a museum dedicated to his life and work was constructed close to his tomb. The state ceremony that opens Israel's annual Independence Day uses his tomb as its axial focus (Handelman 1990: 191–233). The northeastern side of the mountain, sloping toward the dense urban neighborhoods of Jerusalem, was turned into the military cemetery (Benvenisti 1990). On a lower, more distant ridge of Mount Herzl, jutting from its western slope, but turning its face from the city toward the sea in the direction of Europe (Friedlander and Seligman 1994), Yad Vashem—the Holocaust Martyrs' and Heroes' Remembrance Authority—was erected. Further on we discuss Yad Vashem as the exemplar of Holocaust memorialism in Israel. Despite the apparent cosmological and commemorative unity of places in Mount Herzl (Herzl memorialism, the military cemetery, Yad Vashem), there are conflicts among these spaces of representation.

The graves—over four thousand of them—begin within a few dozen meters from the plain arch of the entrance. Unlike the often barren terrain of the Jerusalem hills, the cemetery mountainside is quite heavily forested. The trees, mainly pine and cedar, were planted when the space was developed as a cemetery. This side of the mountain was heavily terraced, to create small islands of level ground at different heights and angles of perspective, embedded in the slope of the mountainside. The graves are placed in the main on these small clearings. Clusters of trees and other vegetation separate the levels of terraced clearings from one another. The terrain created at each level is like that of a series of shaded groves, connected by pathways and steps.

From no vantage point in the entire cemetery is it possible to see its whole landscape of death. One's perspective is continually foreshortened and enclosed by the trees and the rounded slopes of the mountainside, and so one's gaze is drawn into the clusters of graves in their terraced groves. Soldiers who fell in the same war or action often are buried in the same area. Visitors to a particular enclave often know of more than one of the dead buried there. Here the constitution of place can be likened to that of small communities, whose inhabitants are the dead, set intimately within the natural landscape. These communities of the dead, from their different levels on the mountainside, look out and down at the vista of city and more distant hills. In this cemetery the dead in their place are elevated above the living.[6]

In Israel, by law the disposal of the corpse must be in accordance with religious tradition (Jewish, Muslim, Christian). In Judaic traditions the presence of the corpse is of extreme importance, since the body will become the site of resurrection and redemption at the End of Days, the end of time. Ultimately, the body is the site not only of the being that was, but also of the being to be. Following military actions, every effort is made (even many years later) to retrieve the remains of soldiers for proper burial. Thus the gravesite, the surface representation of the presence of the dead body, is of major significance.

The gravesite in the military cemetery is shaped by regulations of the army, the Israel Defense Forces (IDF). All graves conform to army regulations, and are highly similar in composition. Each gravesite contains a holder for a memorial candle. The headstone is of local stone; the body of the grave consists of a rectangle of stone raised above the surface of the ground, and covered by earth planted with the evergreen shrub, rosemarin. The effect is that of the body within rock and earth vital with life. In terms of the surface representation of the military gravesite, the dead not only rest, but nourish the living earth of the national landscape with their last remains. The memories of death evoked here are close to imageries of life. Like the cemetery as a whole, each gravesite literally embodies the intimate spatial and temporal relationship between the dead and the land, while the entire cemetery landscape itself resembles a natural extension of the land that is cared for carefully and especially well. This careful cultivation of the cemetery accords with the Zionist vision of the reclamation of wasteland (but also with changing conceptions of cemetery landscaping, influenced by Romanticism and Enlightenment perceptions in nineteenth-century Europe [see Mosse 1990:40–45]).

There is a strong sense of continuity here, for each self-sacrificed body put into the soil reproduces and authenticates the nationalist vision of the relationship between the nation-state and its territory. First and foremost it is the body, the authentic witness to the conjoining of intent and action in self-sacrifice, which enables gravesite and cemetery to signify the holistic unity of greater national entities. Just as the military cemetery is a version of the entire national territory in the idiom of self-sacrificial death, so too the military cemetery can be broken down into its component gravesites, each of which is the equivalent of all others. Each gravesite, then, is a microcosm of the entire nationalist landscape of self-sacrifice, and therefore through this synecdoche its relationship to the whole territory of the nation-state is easily construed as metonymic. Thus even a single gravesite with the appropriate headstone is sufficient to recall the entirety of a topos of national death. The gravesite, a part, can bring into temporary existence and contextualize an entire landscape of place and narrative. Indeed, the gravesite of self-sacrifice creates a center that is both personal and national. It becomes a center "in the sense of a past against which all future will be made" (Golden 1990:17).

According to the information on the headstone (sometimes referred to by bereaved parents as "the little head pillow"), the sacrificed body has a personal identity (the name of the dead), an age (date of birth, date of death), a genealogy (names of parents), and a place of origin. The date and place of death articulate the deceased with the history of the state (or, in some instances, pre-state history), and the struggles of its peoples for independence and survival.[7] The text also articulates the dead to state institutions through the symbol of the Israeli Defense Forces, and through the military classifications of army number and military rank at death. The only variation in the inscription concerns the context of death, which also relates the degree of sacrifice of the dead. In descending order of prestige, the permitted categories are: "fell in battle" (that tells the reader of the conscious intentionality of self-sacrifice on the part of the dead), "fell while doing his duty" (i.e., while on some kind of active service in uniform), and "fell during military service" (that covers all other instances of death while in uniform, including traffic accidents, and so is the most ambiguous of the three categories).

In terms of all these coordinates, gravesite and body belong fully to the land that encompasses them, but that also is made over—embodied—by the presence of the dead under the ground. And whatever the stories (Berdoulay 1987) generated by the headstone text and the memories the grave evoke, they tend to be more intimate tales that also are articulated easily with greater national landscapes, as is the corpse that gives them birth. The typification of the dead as national sacrifices virtually ensures that these intimate narratives also will be articulated in some way with various national aims (see also Katriel and Shenhar 1990). The centrifugal currents of sentiment generated by each body in the military cemetery conversely pull in the living, in private acts of remembrance, care, and commiseration, or during statist ceremonies of commemoration. These are the living who belong to the dead, since (although often older in age than the dead at the time of their death) they are the continuation of the latter, existing through the sacrifice. Through the symbolism of self-sacrifice, bereaved fathers become the offspring of their dead, heroic sons. Often the living are kin, intimates, and comrades-in-arms of the dead.[8]

> I stood in the cemetery dressed in
> the camouflage clothes of a living man: brown pants
> and a shirt yellow as the sun . . .
> "I shall never forget you," in French
> on a little ceramic plaque.
> I don't know who it is that won't ever forget:
> he's more anonymous than the one who died.
>
> (Amichai 1986:94)

The body of sacrifice is the most powerful presence of national death in Israel. Although its placement requires the consecrated ground of a cemetery, this venue could be located almost anywhere on the land. The body of sacrifice is at home everywhere in the land. The body is the authentic witness to the sacrifice that is thought to shape national contours. In all of these respects, the body makes and authenticates place. However, given the intimate, metonymic affinity of the dead soldier to the land, the military cemetery in Israel is constructed with comparatively little representation (i.e., metaphorization, symbolization, or explanation). The dead are placed within the land and covered with a plain marker and a simple text. The gravesite is a metonym, rather than a metaphor, of sacrifice. It is where the sacrifice is. Here the aesthetic of place nears the self-explanatory.[9]

THE MEMORIAL PLACE

Dicky was hit.
Like the water tower at Yad Mordekhai.
Hit. A hole in the belly. Everything
came flooding out.

But he has remained standing like that
in the landscape of my memory
like the water tower at Yad Mordekhai.

He fell not far from there,
a little to the north, near Houlayqat.

(Amichai 1986:94)

Apart from military cemeteries, hundreds of memorials to self-sacrificial military death mark and shape the landscapes of the country.[10] Some signify where sacrificial death took place, stressing that "it happened here." Others commemorate the dead of military actions, and are placed within the general locale of theaters of operation. Many others emblazon the local provenance of the sacrificial dead, and are located in or near the villages and towns the dead belonged to. Almost every community has a memorial to its fallen soldiers. Still others highlight the membership of the dead in particular military units of various scale and complexity, and are located in military bases or in an area of the country associated especially with a particular unit. Some memorials commemorate hundreds of persons; others, a single individual. The word used generically for these memorials is *gal-ed*, which in biblical terms (Genesis 31:48) signifies a heap of stones as an eternal sign; indeed, as witness to a covenant. In military memorialism, the sign is a witness left on the land, in place of the dead who are there no more.

Despite their numerous differences, these memorials are thought to share a common orientation to the land, one recently enunciated clearly by a former minister of defense and assassinated prime minister (Rabin 1989:7): "We build neither arches of triumph nor palaces of heroism. No one knows as we do that wars . . . are lengthy journeys in pain and bereavement. . . . The little with which we, the living, can reward our dead friends is with the memory that follows them and is with us. . . . The memorials are signposts [*tziyuney derekh*] of the historical and geographical map of the wars, actions, and accidents. . . . The history of this land is carved in the memorials of wood, stone, and iron." Through these memorials, the memory of self-sacrifice is placed on the land, and shapes its contours of national death. The land is sign-posted in space and time, in coordinates of nationalist sacred geography and history.[11] In turn, the signpost 'carves' the landscape with remembrance, for those who are attuned to these aspects of place and history. Interestingly, Mosse (1991) argues that war memorials in Israel "are more peace monuments than those [war] monuments [of Western Europe], which are aggressive to the core."

But these memorials share another attribute: the absence of the most essential witness to self-sacrifice, the dead body that is its highest authentication. This absence is crucial for the extension, substitution, and aesthetics of memorialism. Unlike the military cemetery, the memorial's attempted embodiment of sacrifice is necessarily a number of removes from "the presence of absence," teetering closer to "the absence of presence." In the previous section we argued that the presence of the body within the land is paralleled by the quite minimal representation of its presence on the surface of the land. This aesthetics of place is not given to monumentalism. The body in-place not only makes that place, but its presence is virtually self-explanatory. The presence of self-sacrifice requires no further mediation in constituting and authenticating the relationship between land and people.

In its absence the body cannot be duplicated. This absence can only be represented in various ways, from different angles and perspectives, and in different media. The absence of the body creates or accentuates a dynamic of representation to fill that emptiness with presence, the presence of absence. In the process, it is this absence that can be reproduced endlessly, in ways that the presence of the body cannot. The presence of the body speaks to the uniqueness of authenticity; its absence, to the multiplicities of reproduction.

This helps explain the profusion of memorial places in Israel. The absence of the body of sacrifice allows the memory of the dead to be organized publicly in terms of numerous categories of affiliation with the living. In this way, many publics partake of and use the memory of the dead for their own purposes. So, too, the dead acquire numerous identities that link them to locality, community, social groups, historical period, and military event. Moreover, the absence of the body gives to many others greater freedom to speak in the name of the dead than does the gravesite itself. The presence of absence is more variegated and contradictory within the multiplicity of memories evoked by the memorial, than were the living persons whom the memorial represents. Thus, memorial places parcel out the ownership of the dead as the cemetery cannot.

Every major war has been followed by a spate of private memorials, erected primarily by comrades-in-arms and kin of the dead. Early on, the state decided to organize memorialism from the top (as military funerals are, although the immediate family of the dead soldier has the right to reject burial in a military cemetery, thereby foregoing a military funeral). The desire of parents to memorialize their fallen son or daughter clashed with the capacity of municipalities, army units, and the state itself to honor individually each of the dead. State intervention in memorialism arrogated ultimate authority to the greater collectivity, at whose command voluntary self-sacrifice was enacted in battle. This is the semiotic complement to the singular body of the military dead becoming the synecdochal whole through self-sacrifice, for here the statist whole reabsorbs all of its human parts, dead and living. The aesthetics of statist memorialism here, as in many other nation-states, tends toward giving a common statist identity to the dead by making them equivalents of one another—by standardizing the forms of memorial name-plaques, by grouping the dead on such plaques according to military units, and so forth. The singular uniqueness of the individual dead soldier can then be substituted for the uniqueness of any other, for in statist vision all are ultimately equal citizens of the Jewish state.

The state also worries about overcommemoration, about a profusion of privately erected memorials placed willy-nilly in the national landscape of sacrifice, and thereby perhaps altering its shaping (Azaryahu 1992:69). These more singular and spontaneous expressions of comradeship and family, which may well exclude any explicit recognition of the statist hierarchy, would create a littered landscape of national sacrifice (the detritus of family outings), in place of the ordered landscape envisaged by the state, one that reflexively and continuously indexes statist authority. Through the years of ongoing negotiation over the creation and placement of private memorials, various compromises have emerged. Some memorials were moved, others reshaped, and still others became part of a more collective memorializing. Many others were left as they were. In return, the state (through the IDF) gives its official recognition to such memorials, thereby removing them in part (and at times in full) from the more private sector of memorialism.

The great majority of memorials stand on the land, open to the sky. Many are constructed of stone, either dressed or irregularly shaped. Many are continuous with the natural landscape; others appear to sprout or thrust from this. For example, the memorial to General David 'Mickey' Marcus, killed in the 1948 War of Independence, is an irregular, elongated, pyramidal shape that stands high in the hills in the vicinity of Jerusalem. Erected in 1957, the monument is close to the place where he was killed, and is constructed of stone from the locale. The memorial belongs to the place, in its location and the materials of its construction. One may say that the memorial is native to the place, as the place is to the broader landscape. Simultaneously, the monument takes the form of a common visual analogue for courage and bravery—its tapering height reaches toward the heavens, while its bulk is impressed firmly on the land. The memorial is a metaphor for the absent self-sacrifice. Given this absence, the body is metaphorized and made into a certain shape of memory, its form transmuted to one that is larger and more powerful than human life. Here the constructed presence of place re-presents and compensates for the absence of body.

By contrast, other memorials of natural stone hug the ground, inverting the power of the absent sacrifices and demonstrating above-ground their powerful intimacy with the very substance of the land in-place. Still others seem to confront and dare the elemental in their design. The memorial to those who broke through to Jerusalem, to lift the months-long siege of the Jewish part of the city in the 1948 War of Independence, appears to tear at and pierce the naked sky. Six rugged, irregular lengths of sharp corrugated iron, the longest twelve meters, are extruded by the rocky hillside of their location at a forty-five-degree angle, pointing in the direction of Jerusalem. Here human qualities of desire, focused intensity, and effort are metaphorized through positioning, shape, angle, and texture.

The absence of the body enables the same sacrifice to be memorialized in different places, through different signs, giving each commemoration a different affiliation but more or less the same value. Northwest of Jerusalem, a small plaque screwed into stone commemorates six soldiers who were killed in the conquest of Radar Hill during the 1967 Six-Day War. Following on the names of the six, the brief text reads, "From their friends in the Portzim [i.e., breakthrough] battalion." Battalion members placed the plaque on the hill, close to the location of their friends' death. The names of the six also are included in the lists on the memorial to the dead of the Har-el Brigade, to which the battalion belongs. In this instance the presence of the six is copied from location to location, once signifying the impressed place of sacrificial death and the memories of comrades, and then membership in a more inclusive military unit.

Such substitutions are commonplace, demonstrating over and again the metaphorization of name, place, and memory in the absence of the authentic body of sacrifice. The basic point derives, of course, from Benjamin's (1969:220) comments on art in the modern West. Benjamin argued that the authenticity of a work of art requires its singular presence in time and space, "its unique existence at the place where it happens to be." Its authenticity is its ultimate authority (to appear in its own right; to be seen for itself). In this respect the authentic work of art can only exist at a single set of coordinates of time and space. In other words, it can occupy only a single place. The absence of the body often seems to generate more complex metaphors of substitution in the placing of memory on the surface of the land. And, no matter how elaborate these metaphorical forms of structures become, their presence points over and again to the absence of what they represent. However, these substitutes for the body are not Baudrillard's simulacra that render reality as collages of copies of itself, and therefore inauthentic, in the terms of this chapter. Nor are these substitutes for the body "floating signifiers" (Poster 1990:63), cut loose from their referents to be moored to any number of possible signifiers in order to create imaginary worlds. Always foregrounding the presence of the absent dead in these war memorials is the cultural authenticity of their sacrifice, the powerful existential reality of their being.

Place also may be metaphorized, its significance moved from one locale to another. The metaphorization of presence often builds fragments of authenticity—in effect, "relics"—of the immediate context of death into the construction of memorials (Azaryahu 1993). For example, a memorial in Ophira, in Sinai, commemorated the deaths of five members of a radar unit who were killed by an Egyptian missile in the first hours of the Yom Kippur War of 1973. Erected by comrades from the same unit, the memorial was constructed from pieces of radar equipment damaged in the attack. Following the Israeli withdrawal from Sinai, the memorial was moved to the Judean hills, within Israel. However, there it was placed on a base of stones brought from the area in Sinai where the memorial was first erected. In effect, a bit of the Sinai landscape, of the authentic place of death, was reconstituted within Israel through the metaphorization of space. Memory was, one may say, brought home, the now alienated territory of Sinai embedded in the home landscape.

Such fragments or parts are authentic pointers to the absence that is the heart of the sacrifice. The relics, or other found objects, "were there." Through these parts, the enveloping context of battle, of moments of death, is metaphorized as *lieux de memoire* (Nora 1989). The living can reach out to touch, not the place of the dead, but a substitute that itself was in touch with their presence. The use of relics abounds, and here we give only a few illustrations.

The memorial to a tankist killed on the Golan Heights during the desperate stemming of the Syrian breakthrough at the outset of the 1973 Yom Kippur War includes two sprocketed tank wheels and a short section of tank tread. A lengthy section of tank tread, lying on its side in a three-quarter circle, demarcates a memorial to three tankists killed in Sinai during the same war. The centerpiece of a memorial to fifteen scouts of a paratroop battalion killed in the Yom Kippur War is a halftrack, its tread passing under and caught by the living rock. A plaque on a decapitated jeep is the memorial to a soldier killed in the Six-Day War when the jeep he was riding in went over a mine. A memorial to paratroopers consists of a damaged aircraft of the type they parachuted from. Outside the plane, a plaque asks the visitor to enter the body of the plane in order to concentrate memory on those who fell.

Many of these memorials are highly personalized artifacts, constructed to demonstrate affinities to particular landscapes, their histories, and certain categories of people. Numerous memorials, as we have noted, were designed and built at the behest of people who were kin, members of the same community, or comrades-in-arms. During the War of Independence, Hill 69 (as it was designated) guarded against the route of the Egyptian advance northward. Twenty soldiers were killed trying to defend the position. In the 1950s, at the initiative of the bereaved families, an elaborate memorial was erected there. The text of the memorial plaque reads in part: "Here on Hill 69 . . . in bitter battle with the Egyptian invader, they gave their life defending their motherland. . . . Their name will stay with us forever."

The Pilots' Forest is constituted from small groves containing numerous plaques and some memorials in memory of air force pilots. These memorials often contain pieces of destroyed aircraft. Plaques and memorials were done at the initiative of family and friends of the dead. For example, one memorial was erected by friends and dedicated on the dead pilot's birthdate. One may well say that such memorials belong, first and foremost, to these people.

As we have discussed this so far, the relatively elaborate representation of death in memorials is in part a function of the absence of the authentic body of sacrifice below ground and a corresponding metaphorization of body and place above ground. There are two other aspects that need mention. One concerns the relationship between the scale of memorialism and the totality of its representation. The other relates to the linking of military memorialism in Israel to Jewish armed resistance in Europe during the Holocaust.

Generally, the representation of military death in Israel increases in scale and elaboration when the size of the units concerned and the numbers of dead greatly increase. A prominent example is the memorial in remembrance of the dead of the steel division of the armored corps in the 1967 Six-Day War. It was erected first in the Israeli town of Yamit, in Sinai. Following the Israeli withdrawal from Sinai, the memorial name-plaques were moved to Israel. There, in the desert area of Pitkhat Shalom, close to the border of the Gaza Strip, an identical (although expanded) monument was built. The monument covers some fifteen dunams (almost four acres) of desert flats. In the center of this landscape is a tower, twenty-five meters high, constructed of five half-cylindrical columns that support an observation platform. Radiating from the tower, spread over the landscape, are four hundred concrete pillars of varying heights. At the top of each pillar is a damaged part of an armored corps vehicle or weapon. Each pillar symbolizes the Pillar of Fire (*Amoud Ha'esh*), the heavenly sign of the Exodus that led the Israelites out of bondage from Egypt. In this memorial, the pillars of mechanized fire-power stand guard, defend the land, and are elevated in value. But the pillars also represent the sacrifice, each holding up toward the heavens a relic of battle. So, too, the vehicles and weapons were operated by soldiers, who again (as pillars) are metaphorized as larger-than-life, in height, strength, and vision. There is a memorial room at the base of the observation tower, containing the bronze memorial name-plaques, grouped by unit.

This monument departs from the others we have discussed in certain respects. Although the great bulk of the memorial is open to the elements, it moves toward the creation of a total environment through monumentalism. Its component pillars are not only highly abstract; they also bear a limited relationship to the surrounding desert. Rebuilt once from scratch, the memorial turns in on itself, holding and enclosing the names of the dead. This monumental copy of the Sinai memorial contains its own sacrificial core, the original name-plaques moved from Sinai, themselves of course representations of the presence of the absent dead. The enclosed room containing the names of the dead is itself a smaller-scale total environment, sealed from the surrounding landscape. Clearly impressive in scale, bulk, and conception, the overall effect nonetheless has something of an imposing and imposed alien presence in the land. The pillars stride over the land, transforming and totalizing it into a different landscape. These kinds of representation and elaboration of absence are more distant from the memorialism of the military cemetery, and move closer to the memorialism we discuss the next section—that of the Holocaust.

At Kibbutz Yad Mordekhai, near the Gaza Strip, a ruined water tower stands overgrown by foliage, its concrete walls punctured by shell holes. The tower was left as a memorial to one of the fiercest battles of the War of Independence, the repulsion of an attack on the kibbutz by a large Egyptian force. The water tower is in keeping with the military memorialism discussed in this section: it is native to the place, an integral part of the landscape, and a relic of the battle. In front of the tower is the statue of a heroic figure with grim visage, his shirt torn open to the waist, exposing a powerful chest. One strong hand clutches a grenade at the ready (see also Young 1989b). The statue was put in place in 1951. Its figure is that of Mordekhai Anielewicz, in 1943 the commander of the Warsaw Ghetto uprising. In that year the kibbutz was renamed in his memory.

The statue is intended to represent more than the courage of the uprising. Indeed, it is the juxtaposition of water tower and statue that is significant. Brought into conjunction, the figure was intended to signify the antecedents of the 1948 fighting, and the tower the continuity between heroic Jewish armed resistance in World War II and that of the kibbutz fighters in the War of Independence.

Especially interesting is the figuration of the Ghetto fighter in the person of Anielewicz. Here, representing a far-off location, the presence of the body returns. This figure is neither an abstract metaphorization of the heroic body nor a relic of sacrifice. It is a copy, stereotypic in certain respects, in keeping with the social realist style of the sculptor (Young 1989a), but elaborately faithful in so many flourishes to the authenticity of the human shape and its proportions (Young mentions that the sculptor used kibbutz people as models for many of his realist figures). There are other examples of this kind of sculpture (not all from the same period) in military memorialism; nonetheless the sculpting of the realistic human body, whether freestanding or in relief, is comparatively rare in Israeli memorialism of military sacrifice. In general, the presence of this kind of copy is associated with an even greater degree of absence than that discussed in this section. This is the absence both of the authentic body of sacrifice and of the place of sacrifice, which typifies Holocaust memorialism in Israel. The memorial at Yad Mordekhai demonstrates the difference between the memorialization of the sacrificial body through authentic place or relic, and that which depends wholly on copies. In the latter instance the figuration of the real body returns, but as an elaborate copy, above ground.

In this section we have argued that when the body of sacrifice is absent it is the memory of the body through the memorialization of place, and of belonging to place, which rises in importance. These places of memorialism are continuous in the main with the landscapes of Israel. They are in place in this terrain. However, there is greater elaboration in representation as the absence of the body is filled with metaphoric allusions to its presence. As in cemetery memorialism, here, too, there are kin, intimates, and comrades who constitute a personal public that attends the military memorial. These patterns are altered quite drastically in Holocaust memorialism in Israel.

THE HOLOCAUST MEMORIAL

The slaughtered children are heaped in a big stack, they are added, thrown onto the pairs of adults. Each corpse is laid out on an iron "burial" board; then the door to the inferno is opened and the board shoved in. The hellish fire, extending its tongues like open arms, snatches the body as though it were a prize. The hair is the first to catch fire. The skin, immersed in flames, catches in a few seconds. Now the arms and legs begin to rise—expanding blood vessels cause this movement of the limbs. The entire body is now burning fiercely; the skin has been

consumed and fat drips and hisses in the flames. One can no longer
make out a corpse—only a room filled with hellish fire that holds something in its midst. The belly goes. Bowels and entrails are quickly consumed, and within minutes there is no trace of them. The head takes the
longest to burn; two little blue flames flicker from the eyeholes—these
are the eyes burning with the brain, while from the mouth the tongue
also continues to burn. The entire process lasts twenty minutes—and a
human being, a world, has been turned to ashes. . . .
    The fire burns boldly, calmly. Nothing stands in its way, nothing puts
it out. Sacrifices arrive regularly, without number, as though this ancient, martyred nation was created specifically for this purpose.
        Zalmen Gradowski, "The Czech Transport: a Chronicle of
            the Auschwitz Sonderkommando" (March–April 1944)
                        [in Roskies 1988:563–64]

In the twentieth century, Zionist ideologies constructed ideas of a Jewish
homeland in Palestine as the antithesis of Jewish life in the (European) diaspora. The new Jews in Palestine, and then in Israel, were to be everything
their diasporic counterparts were not. These sentiments were given acute if
ambivalent expression in Israeli Jewish responses to the Holocaust, following the founding of the State of Israel. The Holocaust refers to the killing of
an estimated 6 million Jews by Germans and their collaborators during
World War II. From the various perspectives of Israeli Jews, the meanings attributed to the Holocaust have undergone major changes since World War
II (Segev 1993; Ezrahi 1985–86; Friedlander and Seligman 1994).
    In the pre-state period, and then in the early years of the state, there were
strong proclivities to understand the behavior of European Jewry during the
Nazi period in negative terms, as that of persons who responded passively
to their own destruction. European Jewries were often referred to as "sheep
led to the slaughter," in contrast to the spirited actions of Israeli Jews who
made themselves masters of their own fate (Segev 1993). However, two other
developments of rhetoric and narrative modified this denigration.
    One emphasized the flareups of armed resistance to oppression and ex-
termination, of which the Warsaw Ghetto uprising was made the exemplar.
As in the memorialism at Yad Mordekhai, active resistance was made to
bridge, through time and space, the cognitive and emotional abyss between
European and Israeli Jewries. Just as some Jews in Europe became active heroes, so many, many more were heroic in the homeland. The second com-
plemented the first, and enunciated the theme that a great many of the
European Jews who died during that period did so, wittingly or not, for the
'Sanctification of the Name' (*Kiddush HaShem*), that is, they died for the
sake of their Jewish identities and Judaism. Still later, virtually all Jewish

Holocaust death was referred to in this way. In religious terms, this kind of death refers to "martyrdom," and it joins the "martyrs" to all those other catastrophes through the ages in which Jews were menaced and killed because they were Jews.

The shaping of such narratives is complex, in both religious and secular terms. In religious terms, these narratives raise issues of divine plan or at least, patterning, and so of the motivation of God, the possibility of divine punishment, and of the unwitting role of the Nazis themselves in this.[12] In secular terms, the idea of divine intervention and martyrdom is understood metaphorically, as allegory that expresses the immensity, tragedy, and horror of the life lost. Even if one accepts the idea of sacrifice embedded in martyrdom, it is difficult to find the conscious willingness to self-sacrifice in this (unless it is thought to be in accordance with divine plan), to parallel that applied to heroic military death. So, too, the religious narratives complicate the validity and value of the heroic, secular response to oppression in the diaspora.[13]

There is a strong consensus among Israeli Jews that, regardless of the lack of unequivocal documentary evidence, the Nazis intended the planned, total extermination of the Jewish people (Taylor 1985; Lang 1990). There is no doubt that with all its complications, the Holocaust is understood as national death. The years of settlement and then of statehood in Israel were understood as practices intended to contrast sharply with, to oppose, and to tear apart bridges to diasporic existence. State and diaspora were to go their separate ways, the former victorious, the latter destroyed. However, in recent years the existence of the state increasingly is being interpreted as the answer itself to the Holocaust (Friedlander and Seligman 1994). In these terms, the national death intended by the Nazis helped produce the rejuvenated nation of Israel in its national home. So, too, runs the argument, that had the state existed with the rise to power of the Nazis, European Jewry would have had the refuge denied them everywhere else in the Western world, and the enormity of the Holocaust could have been averted. This is in keeping with the ideological tenets of Zionism that the State of Israel is the homeland of all Jews; that all Jews have the legal right to return to their homeland; that Israel is the legitimate representative of the interests of Jews everywhere in the world; and that the state therefore is the defender of Jewry wherever it is threatened.[14]

It is in these senses that the dead of the Holocaust are of the remarkable kind that belong to the State of Israel. And yet this kind of belonging is more problematic in the case of the Holocaust dead, as they lived and died elsewhere. One difficulty concerns the meanings that are attributed to their death; the other, the relationship between their death and the State of Israel. In the first instance, there are difficulties in arguing that their deaths were those of intentional self-sacrifice. Yet it is existentially devastating to claim that they died for naught. Thus the argument that they died for the Sanctification of the Name gives the meaning of faith to their death. In comparison to the military dead, the Holocaust dead have a more tenuous and uncertain relationship to the Israeli landscape. This is expressed in the construction of their memorialism.

In 1953 parliamentary legislation led to the establishment of Yad Vashem, The Holocaust Martyrs' and Heroes' Remembrance Authority. Yad Vashem is one of a small number of major Holocaust memorials in Israel. Unlike military memorialism, that of the Holocaust is not spread widely and densely over the landscape. Instead it usually is concentrated in centers that specialize in this kind of commemoration. This, too, speaks to the more difficult relationship of Holocaust memorialism to the landscapes of Israel. Yad Vashem is the most prominent of Holocaust memorials in Israel, in part because of its official standing and central location. Moreover, its close proximity to the military cemetery on Mount Herzl is especially evocative.

Yad Vashem means "a place and a name," and is taken from Isaiah (56:5), in which God states: "I will give in my house and within my walls a place and a name better than of sons and of daughters: I will give them an everlasting name, that shall not be cut off." This immediately implicates the problematic relationship alluded to above. On the one hand, the State of Israel is conceived of as the land of the Jews. On the other, in the perceptions of Israeli Jews, the Holocaust forms of mass death could not have happened within the landscapes of present-day Israel. Following (and prior to) the establishment of the State of Israel in 1948, there was little official need to encourage consensus among Israeli Jews with regard to the value of military memorialism. Commemoration of the war dead was virtually taken for granted. But perceptions of Holocaust remembrance were quite different in the earlier years of the state. Thus, the 1953 Knesset Law (Law on Commemoration of the Holocaust and Heroism) that established Yad Vashem defined the mandate of this institution in part as follows: to "gather, study and publish the entire testimony concerning Holocaust and heroism and endow the nation with its lesson; [to] . . . foster an atmosphere of unanimity in memory" (State of Israel Yearbook 1954:250–51). The Knesset understood that in Israel, unlike memorialism for the war dead, knowledge of the Holocaust had to be fostered in order to be turned into memory, and deliberately had to be cathected with a unanimity of feeling, because this consensus was lacking.[15] The presence of the Holocaust dead was absent, despite the large number of survivors who settled in Israel.

Holocaust memorialism does make present the absent dead. It gives identities (names) to, and makes place for these dead within the Israeli landscape. But to do this, highly specialized places must be constructed for Holocaust memorialism; and in their composition these places are made to have a more arbitrary and artificial relationship, indeed a discontinuous relationship, to the surrounding landscapes. Within these modes of commemoration both the bodies and the places of Holocaust death are absent, as they are from the entire landscapes of Israel. Present is their memory, but to fix memory in the presence of such absence is a complicated matter, especially among a people sidling among fragments of a partly postmodern world.

Within the distinctive environments of Holocaust memorialism there is only representation that elaborates representation. Present are the disembodied names of the dead, the signs of distant lands, and the memories and metaphors they evoke in others. Unlike military memorialism, Yad Vashem builds its presence wholly upon absence. Or, one may say that within the Israeli landscape, Yad Vashem transforms the absence of the Holocaust dead and their places of death into presence, but that at the heart of this presence there is the absence of both the authentic bodies and places of sacrifice. The extent of this absence is reflected in the extent of the metaphorization and reproduction of that which is absent.

The entry to Yad Vashem (facing away from Mount Herzl, toward the sea and Europe beyond) is a voyage to otherness—not to another Israel, but elsewhere. The monumental, ornamented gate at the border has qualities of a checkpoint. The parking area follows, and then beyond this another border, although it is not called this. Yad Vashem is built along the top of a ridge. Most of the major edifices front along the southern exposure of the ridge. The outermost path that runs from the parking area along the southern edge of the ridge is called "The Avenue of the Righteous Among the Nations." On either side of the long pathway are carob trees, which were planted by gentiles who saved Jews during the Holocaust at risk to their own lives. This risk taking is a condition of recognition as a righteous gentile. In front of each tree is the name-plaque of the gentile so honored, and the name of that person's country.[16] Within the Israeli landscape the voyage to Yad Vashem is one through discontinuity, to a foreign land whose physical border is marked by gentiles, not Jews. These are the good gentiles; the evil ones are hidden from view, deep within this land.

The major memorial structures of Yad Vashem are of two kinds, closed and open. In the main, the closed structures are buildings that enclose space designated for specialized functions, and that are named and furnished accordingly. Neither the functions nor furnishings of any of these buildings are identifiable from their facades. The exteriors hide their interiors from the external gaze, as the killing grounds of the death camps hid themselves innocuously from outside glances. By contrast, the open structures are freestanding sculptures or monuments that stand under the sky, utterly exposed to the external gaze and to the natural elements of the Israeli landscape. Generally speaking, the functions of the enclosed structures are most embedded in the commemoration of Holocaust genocide, while many of the open ones point more to the heroic, fighting response. The latter are closer to the forms of military memorialism in Israel; the former, more distant.

We commented earlier that Yad Vashem is characterized by the presence of absence. To this we can add that its built environment struggles through numerous media and perspectives to give shape, meaning, and significance to this absence—historically, pictorially, textually, statistically, metaphorically, allegorically. Commemorative ceremonies are held in the Hall of Remembrance (*Ohel Yizkor*), a cavernous structure of boulder-like stone walls, off-center concrete ceiling, and massive iron doors. In the mosaic floor are inscribed, in Hebrew and Latin script, the names of the twenty-two largest Nazi concentration and death camps. In one corner is the Eternal Flame. In front of this is a covered rectangular receptacle, set into the floor, within which are interred the ashes of bodies destroyed in death camp crematoria. The hall was inaugurated in 1961 with the interment of the ashes and the lighting of the Eternal Flame. The area of the receptacle was consecrated as sacred ground (i.e., burial ground) with the participation of a unit from the IDF Rabbinate. In the early years of Yad Vashem this receptacle was sometimes referred to as the Tomb of the Unknown Ashes. The ashes are the only relic of bodily substance in Yad Vashem.[17] The dark hall is perhaps the largest enclosed memorial in the complex. Within the hall the dominant feeling is that of the bursting emptiness of absence, contained by massive walls and ceiling, focused on the single flame and the imagery of ash, ephemeral dust. We emphasize that to create this kind of emotional space of foreign places and the memories and imagination they are enabled to evoke within the Israeli landscape, this local landscape, its sights and sounds, must be kept without. Were this memorial open to the sky and the elements, the wrenching emptiness of its internal space would dissipate, permeated and overwhelmed by the local environment.[18] Enclosed as it is, the hall is metaphorized as sacred space, the ashes as sacred ash; every man entering the enclosure is requested to don a skullcap, as he would in a cemetery. To our knowledge the only official male visitor who refused to do so was Kurt Waldheim, who came when he was secretary-general of the United Nations.

The Children's Memorial (inaugurated in 1987) fills a dark void with a multitude of metaphorical images of light. The cavelike memorial, built into the ground, commemorates the estimated million and a half children who perished in the Holocaust. Inside, the only source of light is that of five memorial candles. Through the use of mirrors, their little flames are multiplied infinitely, over one's head, under one's feet, on all sides. Entering from the brightness of the natural landscape, one is abruptly suspended in a pitch-black void punctuated by thousands of tiny lights receding to infinity, the only sound that of a disembodied voice reciting the names, ages, and countries of the dead children. One gropes blindly for the way through. With time, and the adjustment of retinas to the darkness, the lights become merely reflections, artful representations; and then their presence evokes a terrible anguish of absence. There is indeed nothing—nothingness—behind the artifice except the machinery of artifice, no uplifting revelation, no moralistic liturgy. The sense of loss is overwhelming.

The Children's Memorial is the only one at Yad Vashem that works active, cognitive transformation into its design of experiencing: from representing the presence of absence to realizing that this absence is just that—nullity, the utter absence of substance, not the resistance of stone, the entanglement of text, nor the representational embodiment of photograph. There is no solace here, no narrative that finally raises the spirit. Moreover, this memorial also works directly and immediately on the body of the visitor, effecting transformations in his or her state of being, regardless of whether the person cooperates or comprehends: endocrinal and kinesthesic changes occur in the body's response to darkness and sensory disorientation, just as they continue to occur as the body adapts to the darkness and the person sees more.[19]

In the Hall of Names the dead are represented and memorialized by name. For each, there is an information sheet, a page of testimony, which contains details given by relatives, friends, and others, which register the dead in the name of the Holocaust. Here the dead are individuated, their collective presence evoked by the very density and quantity of these sheets, packed tightly one on the other within file boxes. The collection of names began in 1955, and by now some 3 million names have been recorded and filed alphabetically in the Hall of Names. In 1987, at the opening ceremony of the annual memorial day for the Holocaust, at Yad Vashem, the president of the State of Israel bestowed collective 'remembrance citizenship' on the Holocaust dead. From this perspective their presence was metaphorized by incorporating them within the idea of the state, the sole national refuge for their memory.

The Historical Museum represents the Holocaust and its dead pictorially and textually. To quote from the official guide to Yad Vashem, in the Historical Museum, "the story of the destruction of European Jewry is told through authentic photographs, artifacts, and documents." This museum exhibit was composed by historians as a book of history illustrated by photographic examples. The textual and pictorial narratives—the pages of this book of history—are ordered chronologically; and the visitor leaves the museum through a separate exit, thus preserving the historical coherence of the chronology. The photographs and texts stress the factuality of exact historiographic disclosure, highlighted by the contrast between the near pedantic accuracy of the texts and the pain, terror, and torture of the photographs. The narratives cover the Nazis' rise to power and the persecution of the Jews in the Third Reich; the mass killing of Jews; Jewish armed resistance; the liberation of the camps; and the successful struggle of many of their former inmates to reach the Land of Israel, where the Holocaust finally ends, in this version of the showing and telling of catastrophe.

The section of the museum on armed resistance is entered through a tunnel, slanting upward, which according to the official guide symbolizes "the sewers which served as hiding places and escape routes for Jewish fighters in the Warsaw Ghetto." In this section of the narrative, self-sacrifice through battle comes to the fore, and the visitor ascends from the pit to the surface, to the exterior of the Holocaust, as did the fighters and then the sojourners to Palestine. On departing the museum, the visitor passes the 'symbolic tombstones' on which are inscribed the number of Jews by country killed in the Holocaust.

Through varied media, these major closed sites tell, reflect, and represent the stories of the inexorable destruction of Jewish presence in Europe. However, many of the larger-scale open structures—the monuments and sculptures—provide a contrastive emphasis. The open structures reveal themselves utterly to the external gaze, as proclamations on the land. The smaller of these are tucked into the folds and curves of the cultivated landscape. They are more continuous with the themes of genocide and the destruction of presence. Appositely, the larger ones abruptly thrust up from the land, to hold gaze and dominate perspective. These open structures, geometric and figurative, are dedicated to resistance and heroism by Jewish ghetto fighters, partisans, and soldiers, during World War II (Young 1989a, 1989b).

The three largest form a set of triangular coordinates that corresponds geometrically to the general shape of the ridge. Near the entrance to the Yad Vashem complex, the Pillar of Heroism, simple and severe in design, soars some twenty-one meters straight into the sky from the highest rise in Yad Vashem. Its inscription commemorates all forms of Jewish rebellion and resistance during the Holocaust, including those who died sanctifying the name of God.[20] At the other end of the long ridge the horizon is dominated by the massive monument to all the Jewish soldiers, ghetto fighters, and partisans of World War II. It is composed of six oblong granite blocks, three on each side, which between them form a window-like space in the shape of a Star of David. This space is bisected by a giant needled sword that reaches toward the sky. The blocks represent the 6 million dead, the Star the Jewish people, and the sword the fighting opposition to the Nazis. Almost equidistant between these two memorials, and forming the third angle of the trian-

gle, is the powerful, larger-than-life monument to the Warsaw Ghetto uprising. This sculpture is a copy of that erected on the site of the Ghetto in Warsaw (Young 1989a). Its realist figures, of both sexes and of different ages,
are armed, at the ready, in the midst of battle.

Recollect that the outermost path along the southern edge of the ridge is
a bulwark dedicated to the Righteous Among the Nations. Following on
this, the symmetric triangulation of the three memorials of heroism constitutes a second border or bulwark within the outer one. Then, inside and
within this space of representation, is constituted the absence of place and
of bodily substance of the Holocaust dead—through emptiness, ash, reflection, and photographic mirror-images.

Within the landscape of Israel, Yad Vashem converts the absence of presence of the Holocaust dead into the presence of their absence. But this utter
absence from the land means that its presence can only be alluded to,
metaphorized, and allegorized through various media. So, too, the use of
these media signifies degrees of reproduction, illusion, and distance. The
problem of the utter absence of the Holocaust dead and of their places of
death is insoluble. This is indicated by the kinds of memorialism through
which solutions are sought. First, the presence itself of this absence is constituted through various media. But then the presence of this absence generates attempts to fill the void that has been made present. Yet the very media
used to substantialize and so to excise the void are themselves only copies
that continually reconstitute the presence of absence. Thus the dynamic set
in motion by the absence of body and place generates the ongoing and increasing representation of memorialism.[21]

We stated earlier that the journey to Yad Vashem was a voyage to a foreign land within the Israeli landscape. To this we now add that Yad Vashem
indeed builds Europe within Israel in order to convey the Holocaust. Only
this totalistic and highly specialized simulation, one that is discontinuous
with and alien to the Israeli landscape, can memorialize the utter absence
that is at the heart of the Holocaust. Yet then there are significant consequences for memorialism and the constitution of place. Despite the collection of names and details of the dead, the Holocaust dead are quite
anonymous at Yad Vashem. So, too, their relationship to the living is problematic. Those directly affected, the Holocaust survivors, diminish with
time. Unlike military memorialism, which is revitalized continuously by ongoing warfare, the Holocaust continually recedes from the present.[22]

The memory of the Holocaust must be kindled in the offspring of
survivors, in their children, and in numerous others if Holocaust memorialism is to survive. Where military memorialism is the especial, intimate preserve of kin and comrades, of those who belong to the dead and to their
places of burial and memorialism, Holocaust memorialism is thrown open

to everybody (indeed, the living "every body" that parallels the anonymous "any body" of the incinerated Holocaust victim). The vast majority of visitors are strangers to the dead, and include numerous foreign tourists. So, too, foreign dignitaries visiting Israel are taken routinely to Yad Vashem at the beginning of their itineraries, there to be guided through the Historical Museum and then to place wreaths on the anonymous ashes in the Hall of Remembrance. This sequence is important: these visitors first learn of the Holocaust, studying it, as it were, from an Israeli Jewish perspective. For these visitors this act turns the absence of presence of the Holocaust dead into the presence of their absence; and then this presence of absence is ritualized and memorialized (perhaps one could say, *memorized*). Symbolically, these dignitaries cross the border into Israel through Yad Vashem. Ironically, the totalistic environment of memorialism constituted there from stone, metal, glass, flame, and paper, it is the living trees of the righteous gentiles that take root, live, and grow in the soil of the Land of Israel.

THE PRESENCE OF ABSENCE: TEST CASES OF THE CORRELATION

Spilt blood isn't roots of trees,
But its the closest to them
That man has.

(Amichai 1971:93)

We have suggested that in the modern state a crucial problem of memorialism is how to turn the absence of the sacrificial dead into the presence of their absence. The Israeli materials we discussed suggest an inverse correlation between the presence of the dead within the land and the absence of their symbolic representation on the surface of the land. The less the degree of presence, the more elaborate the representation.[23] This aesthetic of elaboration substitutes for the presence of the dead, visualizing and shaping their absence, thereby turning this into the presence of absence. The presence of absence evokes the consuming sacrifice that is essential in modern, romantic nationalism.

In this section we discuss Israeli instances that seem to contradict the correlation between absence and symbolic elaboration. In the concluding section we argue that the correlation is significant for Israeli Jewish nationalism, because it focuses attention on the importance of part–whole relationships in nationalist ideologies.

A number of monumental structures of representation stand within the military cemetery on Mount Herzl, seemingly in contradiction to the inverse correlation between presence and representation. However, these memorials are constructed in memory of the absent body of sacrifice. One monument commemorates the volunteers from the Jewish community in Palestine who were killed in World War II. Its centerpiece is a large boulder, from the area of Jerusalem, which is set onto the rocks of the mountainside. The boulder is pierced clear through with the sign of the Star of David. The Star is shaped into and through the natural land. One's gaze through this hole in the boulder is molded by the shape of the Star, itself given form by the natural stone that holds it together. The absence implicated by the emptiness within the Star signifies the loss driven into the substance of the strong, firm land (the boulder) by these deaths; the shape of the Star signifies the presence in the land of the national idea, carved out by the sacrificial absence. Indeed, the monument metaphorizes the presence of absence in the shape of nationalism, but an absence that is integral to the forming, to the presence, of the land.

Other monumental structures in the cemetery are given forms that metaphorize the shape of place or location of death. The memorial to 140 seamen lost in the sinking of their vessel by the Germans in World War II is constituted as a reflecting pool, with a structure at one corner that in outline resembles a ship's superstructure. The four sides of the bottom of the pool are lined with name-plaques for each of the dead. This extended visual metaphor constructs sea, ship, and the drowned dead, all within the cemetery. The memorial to the sixty-nine submariners lost in the disappearance of their vessel, the *Dakar*, is constructed as a massive submarine-like shape with a rudimentary conning tower. The memorial is partially sunk within the ground, and encloses an interior memorial chamber lined with name-plaques of the dead.

Within the cemetery, as outside it, where the bodies of the sacrificial dead are absent, their presence is made tangible through more elaborate representation on the surface of the land. Indeed, in some of these monuments this representation approaches the simulation of totalistic environments (i.e., ship, sea, and the bottom of the waters; the interior of a submarine-like structure) within which the distant contexts of death and traces of the dead can be made explicable.

Of particular interest in this regard is the cemetery memorial to those who were killed defending the besieged Jewish Quarter of the Old City of Jerusalem during the War of Independence. During the siege, dead defenders were buried in a common area within the Quarter. After the Quarter fell to the Jordanian forces, it was not possible to retrieve the remains of the dead defenders. In 1957, a memorial structure to these fallen sprouted in the Mount Herzl cemetery. Partially below ground level, the long, covered structure is intended to resemble in outline an alleyway in the Old City. Covering the walls of the low, linear thoroughfare are the name-plaques of the memorialized dead. After the Old City was taken by Israel in the 1967 War, the remains of these soldiers were moved to ordinary graves in the cemetery. On the site that had served as their common grave in the Jewish Quarter, a permanent memorial marker was placed. Here the absence of the sacrificial body within the cemetery produced a representation there of the presence of the place of sacrifice. This creation of context itself contains representations, names, of the dead. However, when the bodies of sacrifice were buried permanently, simple gravesites with minimal representation above ground were sufficient. In all of the above examples, the elaboration of memorial representation in the military cemetery occurs in the absence of the sacrificial dead, and so reproduces the inverse correlation we outlined.

Recently, Yad Vashem completed its largest memorial to destruction in the Holocaust. In contrast to the major closed structures that commemorate genocide at Yad Vashem, the Valley of Destroyed Communities (as it is called) is in the open air, thereby seeming to contradict our analysis. The valley is located on some six acres of flattened rocky hillside immediately below the massive monument in the shape of the Star of David that commemorates all Jewish armed resistance during World War II. This monument immediately becomes the guardian of the valley, as the visual contrast between the heights of heroism (the monument) and the depths of destruction (the valley) marked architectonically. The valley commemorates the five thousand Jewish communities destroyed in Europe. The valley is blasted and carved meters deep into the living rock and earth of the Land of Israel. From the hill above, it is intended to resemble a schematic map of Europe, cut into the landscape. From within it has the vision and feel of a labyrinth; only the sky and the massive, sheer walls are visible, as the valley floor turns this way and that through the schematic contours of the map. Engraved on the rock faces of these cliff walls are the names of the communities, grouped together in locations that correspond to their approximate positioning on the map.

The valley is a place of desolation without redemption, the Holocaust vision of Europe. To know the Holocaust, one journeys to Europe, entering into the entire space of its map. There, within the absence of presence, one learns the stories of the presence of absence. Although the site is outside, under the sky, one must enter it to know it; and from within it is a sealed, totalistic environment, no more open to the Israeli landscape than the other closed memorial structures of Yad Vashem. Although the intention is to make this site an integral part of the broader national landscape, the valley is a brand of elsewhere burned into the flank of the Land of Israel. Once again, this site makes its place within Israel by making a part of Israel into another place; and in so doing, Holocaust memorialism differs radically from that of military death.

MEMORY, METONYMY, AND METAPHOR IN
NATIONAL MEMORIALISM

To know everything it is possible to know,
and that's everything,
because it is impossible to understand.
(Israel Radio advertisement for The Encyclopedia
of the Shoah, whose publication was
cosponsored by Yad Vashem)

The correlation between absence and symbolic elaboration is significant for Israeli Jewish nationalism because it focuses attention on the importance of part–whole relationships in nationalist ideologies (Handelman 1994). In ideal terms, such relationships are intended as metonymic. This is most problematic with regard to Holocaust memorialism, and foregrounds how Israeli nationalism would have to change in order to fully incorporate the Holocaust into its narratives of national identity and solidarity.

Nonetheless, precisely because of its disjunctions with the Israeli landscape, the Holocaust Memorial tells us more than do the others discussed here about the process that informs all memorialism of national death in Israel—how the absence of presence is filled with the presence of absence. Absence, in Jewish national memorialism, is rarely permitted to become a zero signifier, a sign in a symbolic composition (linguistic, architectural, theological, cosmological) that deliberately is left vacant, such that it is empty of specific meaning but full of a virtual infinity of potential meanings with the capacity to reorganize the whole composition (see Ohnuki-Tierney 1994). The indeterminacy that such emptiness can generate is anathema to national symbolism (Handelman and Shamgar-Handelman 1990, 1993; Shamgar-Handelman and Handelman 1986, 1991)—although the Children's Memorial teeters on the edge—and perhaps also to Judaic traditions in which the injunction to remember is central.

How, then, is the absence of presence dealt with? We suggest the following, preliminary formulation. Memorialism of a past that one has not experienced seems to depend on the paradoxical formulation of memory constituted by information that is wholly in and of the present. This is paradoxical because here "memory" and "the present" are simultaneously active while each negates the other (Handelman 1992). Such memory is a relationship to a past that the present can never reach directly. One way of solving this conundrum is to furnish memory in and of the present with images of the past, representations that at times are artifice, and that the person perhaps knows little or nothing about. Through this substitution (via enculturation, education, knowledge, and so forth) these images of the past are implanted and cathected in memory of the present.

As these images or representations of the past are made integral to the present, the memory of these images becomes part of the person's past. Memory and image change places. Images of the past that are shown in the present constitute the absence of presence. Thus there is memory in the present of images of the past. But then these images become memories of the past—the presence of absence. In this way, memory in and of the present—memory of images of the past—is turned into images in the present of memories of the past. The person experiences present as past, and remembers this past in the present. The absence of presence is filled with the presence of absence. This is the process by which "collected memories" (Young 1993) become collective memory. As noted, in terms of the kinds of memorialism we have discussed in this chapter, this process of creating absence and then filling it with the presence of absence is most prominent in Holocaust memorialism, because of its simulation of totalized worlds of experience that are foreign to the Israeli landscape.

We commented earlier that a single, simple military gravesite is sufficient to bring to mind the self-sacrifices that sustain the entire land and people of Israel. In nationalist vision, the place of burial is the synthetic conjunction of space and time. Nationalist dreamscapes pursue the seamless holism of people in place through time. The sacrifice buried in the land is perceived as proof of the identification between people and place, such that there is no gap, no disjunction between them. The gravesite is a part that signifies the entirety of nationalist holism. The gravesite contextualizes, makes meaningful, the holism of this vision. The vision of the synthetic holism of people in place through time is retrievable time and again from a single military gravesite, just as this holism signifies all military gravesites as integral parts of the national entity. The military gravesite is a metonym of the holistic vision of people in place through time.

However, once the body and place are separated, disjunction enters metonymy, and processes of metaphorization set in to reconstitute the loss of synthetic holism. Thus the representation of the military memorial that marks place in the absence of the body becomes more elaborate. Just as metonymy thrives on continuities among the parts of a whole, their absence or disjunction generates metaphor that strives to reunify holism (see Eco 1985). In the memorialization of Holocaust death in Israel, disjunction, the metaphorization of absence, and the need to fill this absence with unconsolable presence reach their apex—and the presence of absence slips and slides over and again into the absence of presence.

Neither the Holocaust dead nor their places of death are native to the Israeli landscape. The dead are neither in place nor in memory. Their time and temporal experience are not those of the Israeli Jewish vision. Belonging elsewhere, elsewhen, the Holocaust dead can be synthesized into the nationalist vision of holism only by making disjunction integral to this holism. Then the powerful metaphors and allegories generated by these contradictions can be used to articulate the Holocaust dead to the Land of Israel. The dimension of time becomes crucial to this endeavor. Linear time depends upon sequencing, on ideas that connect before and after. Time enables narrative, narrative enables lineal history and its telling (Ricoeur 1984). Holocaust memorialism in Israel is first and foremost narrative, often metaphorical and allegorical even as it is historical. These stories strive to create a narrative structure and sequencing that incorporate into a greater synthetic whole the disjunctions between the Holocaust dead—elsewhere, elsewhen—and the Land of Israel. Most showings of the Holocaust in Israel are also organized as tellings—they have strong narrative components. However, because of the disjunctions between the Holocaust and Israel, each telling must be holistic.

Each military gravesite is the coded narrative of the metonymic whole. Each grave condenses the whole national story, over and again, because that metonymic whole is constituted by the landscape of people in place through time. Under ordinary circumstances these stories do not need elaborate representation in order to signify the holism of the national entity. By contrast, each viable Holocaust memorial must once more simulate an entire context constituted of implanted memory, history, and narrative that bridges and articulates the disjunctions. Only within this simulated whole—Europe through time, in Israel through time—do the various parts of the Holocaust acquire their fuller, awful significance. Ironically, these disjunctions are not erasable, for they are essential to the historical narratives that strive to bridge the absence of the diaspora in Israel. And, so long as Israel is not made into the diaspora, these disjunctions will continue to generate sentiments of ambivalence and compassion, alienation and identification. Indeed, it is these sorts of ambiguities that are diagnosed by our surface reading of the absence and presence of representation in memorials of national death.

> Is all this sorrow? I guess so.
> "May ye find consolation in the building
> of the homeland." But how long
> can you go on building the homeland
> and not fall behind in the terrible
> three-sided race
> between consolation and building and death?
> (Amichai 1986:94–95)

ACKNOWLEDGMENTS

Our thanks to Jonathan Boyarin, Sidra Ezrahi, Michael Feige, Thomas Laqueur, and Richard Werbner, for their comments on an earlier version of this chapter. Our work on national memorialism has been supported by the Shaine Foundation of the Hebrew University.

NOTES

1. Baudrillard's (1983:2) postmodern vision of territory in contrast to that of modern states is apposite here: "Simulation is no longer that of a territory, a referential being or a substance. It is the generation by models of a real without origin or reality: a hyperreal. The territory no longer precedes the map, nor survives it. Henceforth, it is the map that precedes the territory. . . . It is the map that engenders the territory." In keeping with this vision, one may argue that in accordance with these postmodern conceptions, once we are aware of their artifice of construction, national memorialism lacks any claim to authenticity, any referent to a reality of sacrifice, as does the state. But see note 19.

2. The suffix "scape" points to a unifying principle that constructs a part of the land as a unit, such that the part is understood to signify the whole of the land, just as the whole signifies its parts. See Cosgrove (1984:13). In this conception, the perceptual relationship between landscape and land is that of synecdoche. Landscape becomes particular ways of seeing and experiencing (Bender 1993:2).

3. Here we address the memorialism of Israeli Jews. Were we to discuss memorial activities of Palestinian citizens of Israel or of the West Bank, especially during the Intifada years, there would be certain contrasts and complementarities. Both Jews and Arabs used and use the memorialization of war dead to authenticate claims to territory, sometimes in direct competition with one another. For example, following the 1967 War and Israel's capture of East Jerusalem, Jews and Arabs erected improvised, private memorials for their respective war dead all over that area of the city. The Israeli authorities replaced the Jewish memorials with uniform marble plaques inscribed with the names of the dead, but at first did not react to Arab memorials. However, on the first anniversary of that war, with Jewish and Arab mourners grouped around their respective memorials, tensions ran high. Eventually only one Arab memorial was permitted, and this in the teeth of strong Jewish opposition. Benvenisti (1983:54) cites a public opinion poll of the time in which 67 percent of Israeli Jews opposed the erection of Arab monuments to their war dead, while 18 percent felt that "losers have no rights," and 28 percent believed that "those who intended to exterminate us should not be commemorated." Even more so than the battles of political economy, those of symbols that authenticate territorial claims are waged without quarter. See also Benvenisti (1990:92).

During the occupation of the West Bank and the Gaza Strip by Israel, but especially during the Intifada years, the Israeli authorities did their utmost to suppress the memorial activities of Palestinians. Both sides have recognized the terrible power of nationalist memorialism to focus political sentiment and to galvanize political action.

In this chapter we do not discuss a fourth kind of memorial, that of ancient graves that are aligned by Israeli Jews as their "ancestors." Sidra Ezrahi refers to such sites as "cemeteries without bones." Examples include the fall of Masada (A.D. 73) (Paine 1994) and the Bar Kokhba revolt (A.D. 132–135) (Zerubavel 1995). In May 1982, shortly before the Lebanon War, the Begin government sought to create such a site by holding an elaborate state funeral in the Judean desert for bones that were attributed (amid considerable controversy and dissent) to persons who fought with Bar Kokhba (Aronoff 1986). Through this symbolic practice, that government tried to mobilize support for its West Bank settlement policies by embodying the immediacy of the ancient in the landscape.

4. In contrast to the sacrificial dead, the presence within Israel of Adolph Eichmann, the Nazi war criminal, was turned into utter absence. He was executed; his body was then destroyed by fire. The border authorities took his ashes out on the Mediterranean, beyond Israeli territorial borders. There, at dawn, the break of a new day, his last traces were expelled, the ashes thrown into the sea to vanish without trace.

5. The voluntarism of sacrifice has deep resonances in Judaic biblical tradition, in the paradigmatic intent to sacrifice of the Aqedah. This refers to the preparedness of Abraham to sacrifice to God his beloved only son, Isaac, and of Isaac's willing acceptance of this (Hayward 1980). The highest form of national death in Israel (and in other modern states) is predicated not only upon sacrifice, but on the more hermetic and totalistic notion of self-sacrifice. Sacrifice of oneself connotes also sacrifice by oneself, as a conscious and utterly voluntaristic act for the sake of higher values. In its political and religious rhetoric and allegory, self-sacrifice is understood as the evolution of being, of its transformation or transportation to a higher plane. Self-sacrifice contrasts with suicide, the devolution of being, killing oneself for wholly egoistical sentiments through which one is trapped completely within one's mirror-image of self. By contrast, self-sacrifice is always orientated to someone or something beyond oneself, to an other, however this is understood. In this regard, it is also selfless sacrifice, the voluntary extinguishing of self for the sake of the other. Complementarily, the other (here the state and its people) are obligated especially to keep the memory of the selfless sacrifice of its members within, as it were, the "body" of the state, its national landscapes. The most prominent place of this kind is the military cemetery.

Three prominent roles commonly are discussed in relation to sacrifice: the sacrificer, the sacrificed, and the "sacrifiant" (Herrenschmidt 1978), the latter referring to the agency or person on whose behalf the sacrifice is offered and made. In these terms, the especially high value attached to self-sacrifice stems from its conjoining of sacrificer and sacrificed, of the praxis of intent and action within the single person. For that matter, given the synecdochal relationship of part and whole between the slain soldier (the part) and the state and people (the whole) that he defended, all three sacrificial roles are conjoined within the single person of the dead soldier.

In Judaic traditions there is a strong connection among earth, creation, and death. In Hebrew, the land of Israel is commonly referred to as "place of birth" (*moledet*). In Zionist usage this has acquired the meaning of 'motherland' (the term is embodied in the feminine form), and it may be contrasted with a place one merely "comes from" (*houledet*).

6. As noted, the terrain of this military cemetery is not typical of others in Israel. It is also a more elitist graveyard, containing not only the military dead of the Jerusalem area, but also famous fighters who were reburied there, and also a variety of monuments that we address further on. Nonetheless, given the symbolic prominence of the cemetery, its simplicity of representation is telling.

7. Over the years the state has shaped an increasingly greater totality of sacrifice and heroism that contributed to its making, by incorporating into its official pantheon figures and groups who were distant in time from that of statehood (e.g., the Nili group who spied for the British against the Ottoman Turks during World War I, and who were executed), marginal underground groups (Etzel and Lechi) whose primary targets often were the British before the 1948 War of Independence, and who at that time clashed repeatedly with the Palmach, the underground army of the dominant socialist-Zionists, and Vladimir Jabotinsky, the founder and guru of Zionist revisionism whose remains were reburied in 1963 on Mount Herzl, not far from Herzl's tomb.

8. In Israel there is no tomb of the unknown soldier (see Mosse 1990:94–98), because Israelis claim that all soldiers are known and that each is known by his name. There are, however, those whose place of burial is unknown. For these soldiers there are name-plaques and other memorials in various locations (Azaryahu 1992:70–71, 74).

9. Burial and belonging are tightly linked, certainly in Jewish tradition. Eisen (1986:10) comments that one may sojourn in the Land of Israel without necessarily possessing it. But to die here, one needs a holding (*achuza*) for a burial plot. Ezrahi (1992:482) notes that "Israel's first real-estate transaction in ancient Canaan was the purchase of the burial cave of the Machpelah [the Tomb of the Patriarchs, in Hebron]."

This linkage of burial and belonging seems to hold true in the present; and the landscape of burial shapes the contours of Israeli nationalism in relation to territory. After the 1967 War, Israel deliberately placed agriculturalists on the desert lowlands along the Jordan River, on territory captured from the Jordanians. The Israeli Labor governments of the time envisaged a future peace agreement with Jordan in which Israel would keep this strip of territory along the Jordan as a security border, but return the heavily populated mountainous bulk of the West Bank (where little Jewish settlement was planned at the time) to Jordanian control. This strategy was called the Allon Plan, after the then foreign minister, Yigal Allon. However, to this day, these agriculturalists bordering the Jordan have rarely if ever buried their dead there. Instead they have used cemeteries across the Green Line in pre-1967 Israel.

10. Shamir (1989, 1991) has compiled descriptions of over nine hundred military memorials, but this listing likely is still incomplete.

11. See Paine (1990) for a discussion of 'place' as the intersection of space and time.

12. The etymology of the English language term "holocaust" connotes religious sacrifice consumed by fire. By contrast, the modern Hebrew term for the Jewish genocide is "Shoah," which has no religious or sacrificial connotations, but means simply, "destruction, ruin." See Garber and Zuckerman (1989:199–200). For a more complex exegesis of "Shoah," see Tal (1979). Garber and Zuckerman state that Elie Wiesel was the first to term the Shoah the Holocaust. Although we gloss over this here, the problem of terminology and the implications of its contradictions are of extreme importance. Thus in Holocaust memorialism in Israel, the term "Shoah" is used routinely together with the insistence that these dead died for *Kiddush HaShem,* the Sanctification of God's Name, which in English language usage is translated as martyrdom. On *Kiddush HaShem,* see Schindler (1977).

13. The rhetoric of martyrology hones the problem of claims to the Holocaust. Does it belong to the Jewish people, so that the outside world should be made conscious continuously of its evil intentions toward Jews? Or is the Holocaust one extreme expression of the universal possibility of evil? Or of certain social conditions that for various reasons have especially made Jews targets and victims (Bauman 1989)?

14. The serious shift in Israeli attitudes towards the Holocaust likely began with the Eichmann trial in 1961, and crystallized further with the 1967 Six-Day War. Friedlander and Seligman (1994:370) suggest that "The perception [by Israeli Jews] of the possible destruction, in the weeks preceding the Six-Day War, reinforced the identification with the fate of European Jewry within wide strata of the [Israeli] population." We question this. The isolation of Israel prior to that war was perceived by Israelis as the problem

of the Israeli state and its people. During that period there were few allusions to or comparisons with the fate of Jews in the Holocaust. But in the immediate aftermath of the war, Israeli Jews learned from American and European Jews, who visited Israel then in great numbers, that Israel had been on the brink of imminent Holocaust. The strength of Israel's self-identity as the post-Holocaust state of the Jewish people coalesced especially in the wake of the 1967 war.

In turn, American Jews learned about the public representation and monumentalism of Holocaust from Israeli centers like Yad Vashem, since at that time Holocaust memorials in the public spaces of Western Europe were either tiny or tucked into corners, and were virtually nonexistent in the United States. During the next two decades, Holocaust memorialism flourished in the United States, culminating in the museum on the Mall in Washington.

In Israel the rise to power in 1977 of Begin's extreme nationalist Likud Party publicly politicized the Holocaust and began to make Israel diasporic as never before. Begin gloried in the authenticity of prewar Jewish *shtetl* tradition in Eastern Europe, in the growth of traditional (religious) ways of life (Yeshivot flourish in Israel today as they almost never had in Central and Eastern Europe); and he and his minions used Holocaust metaphors and allegories at every opportunity to justify government actions in the spirit of narrative of "the few against the many" (Gertz 1986), including the 1982 Lebanon War and the Israeli siege of Beirut. At that time, Begin wrote to Reagan: "May I tell you, dear Mr. President, how I feel these days when I turn to the Creator of my soul in deep gratitude: I feel as a prime minister empowered to instruct a valiant army facing 'Berlin' where amongst innocent civilians Hitler and his henchmen hide in a bunker deep beneath the surface" (cited in Cromer 1987:289). By the 1990s Israeli teenagers by the thousands had gone on eight-day trips to Poland, sponsored by the Ministry of Education, in search of the authentic relics of Polish Jewry and the places of their annihilation by the Germans, an authenticity that is insufficiently present in Israeli Holocaust simulations. One minister of education (Zevulun Hammer, of the extreme nationalist National Religious Party) likened these trips to "traveling to the Shoah" (On the program, "Six After Six," Israel Radio, September 14, 1992).

In the Israeli narrative of statehood, the Holocaust is increasingly understood as the reason and so the foundation for state formation (Segev 1993), supplanting the earlier Zionist belief that statehood was necessary to break utterly with the dead ends (assimilation or destruction) of the diaspora. Meanwhile, the area around Herzl's tomb today is used mainly as a park by families from a nearby ultraorthodox neighborhood; his museum is deserted; and to provide an audience for the ceremony of his annual state day, the government brings in busloads of captive Ethiopian and Russian new immigrants. If these trends develop further, and there are indications of their increasing power on Israeli Jewish dreamscapes, the Holocaust may yet become a radical critique, in Lefebvre's dialectical sense, of the Zionist state.

In present day Israel, military and Holocaust memorialism have quite distinct circulations. Military memorialism is rarely for export beyond the boundaries of the state. This memorialism belongs first and foremost to the state and its people. Its consumption and contestation are local, as are its pilgrims and tourists. By contrast, Holocaust memorialism is exported and circulates transnationally. Its electronic technologies of showing and telling are competitive with one another, as are its master narratives and meanings in different countries (for example, in Israel and in the United States). So, too, publics whose centers of power are outside Israel contest the shaping of Holocaust memorialism within Israel. Thus in 1995, gays held a memorial ceremony in the Hall of Remembrance at Yad Vashem, which was disrupted by orthodox Jews for whom homosexuality is anathema. And ultraorthodox Jews (*haredim*) threatened to boycott Yad Vashem if photographs of Jewish women stripped naked and herded by Nazi guards were not removed, since the immodesty offended ultra-orthodox visitors.

Foreign visitors to Israel, Jews and non-Jews, easily detach Holocaust memorialism from the national contexts of its embedment. Holocaust memorial centers are turned into places of pilgrimage and tourism where pan-Jewish or universal meanings are sited. In this regard, as pilgrims and tourists from many places intermingle, the significances they attribute to Holocaust memorialism may shift towards the hybrid. This is distant indeed from the meanings of Holocaust memorialism for Israeli Jews, yet follows in part from the ongoing recreation of the diaspora in Israel. In the hybridization of statist and foreign perspectives, the former pulls Holocaust memorialism toward its positioning in changing national narratives; while the latter relates to the autonomy of Holocaust memorialism, yet utilizes venues (and times) of commemoration whose shape and momentum are statist.

15. In a similar vein, in April 1957 the Yad Vashem World Council passed a resolution stating that "The Council considers it desirable that Memorial Day [for the Holocaust dead] be observed in a similar manner in all parts of the country [Israel] and that this manner be determined in cooperation with the government" (*Yad Vashem Bulletin,* No. 2, December 1957, 25). So, too, in 1962, the head of the Yad Vashem Executive declared that "We have made a close study of how to make memory of the Catastrophe strike root [in Israel] (*Yad Vashem Bulletin,* No. 11, April–May 1962, 99).

16. The Avenue was inaugurated on Memorial Day, May 1, 1962. Among the first of Righteous to plant a tree was Oskar Schindler (*Yad Vashem Bulletin,* No. 12, December 1962, 99).

17. The ashes are a signal reminder of the significance of embodiment (however ephemeral its remains) and burial in Judaism, and of the implications of these for Israeli nationalism and its relationship to religion. In 1947 a former Polish partisan "illegally" brought into Palestine ashes from the death camp of Treblinka (*Yad Vashem Bulletin*, No. 22, May 1968, 64). Yad Vashem's use of the term "illegal" was intended to evoke the "illegal immigration" (*Aliya Bet*) of Holocaust survivors through the British sea blockade against all such immigration before the founding of the state. Thus ashes of the martyred dead also suffered the depredations that living survivors underwent in order to make their place in the Israeli landscape. Ashes of Holocaust martyrs were first interred at Yad Vashem in 1958 (*Yad Vashem Bulletin*, No. 3, July 1958, 36), prior to the building of the Hall of Remembrance. A burial society consecrated the burial plot as a cemetery. After the completion of the Hall of Remembrance, the ashes were transferred there.

At the initiative of a senior official of the Ministry of Religious Affairs, ashes from the death camp of Flossenburg were buried on Mount Zion, in what became The Cellar of the Holocaust (*Martef HaShoah*). These ashes were the first focus of traditional memorial services for the Holocaust dead in Israel. In religious tradition, Mount Zion is the burial place of King David. So, too, the Messiah will come from the lineage of King David—so the linking of the ashes of the Holocaust dead to Mount Zion invokes the ever-spiraling symbolic linkage in Jewish tradition between destruction and redemption (Friedlander and Seligman 1994; Handelman 1990). The same rhythm (moving from low to high) but phrased primarily in secular terms is embedded in the Mount Herzl complex—Yad Yashem signifies the destruction; the military cemetery, the sacrifice needed for redemption; and Herzl's tomb, the redemption itself through the creation of the state (Handelman 1990).

18. A comment on the Hall of Remembrance (Lishinsky 1983:16–17) states: "My own thought is that on this Jerusalem hillside . . . it marks one absolutely sacred patch of earth. You may retort: and if that is the case, why was it necessary to erect a building, construct walls, a roof, a gate? The patch of earth could just as well have been marked by a simple palisade. The eternal flame would burn under an open sky; ceremonies and prayers would be conducted directly beneath the heavens . . . in fact, that is often what happens." Indeed the 'simple palisade' describes military memorialism. Toponyms as forms of commemoration were extremely popular in the first years of the state, and among these was the planted memorial forest (Azaryahu 1992:63). Such a forest was planted by Yad Vashem, and as it grew it disappeared into other forests planted for other purposes, and quite lost the distinctiveness of its memorialism in the greater Israeli landscape.

Were the Holocaust to be commemorated as Lishinsky suggested, it would dissipate into the Israeli landscape.

19. The Children's Memorial is built as a developmental, architectural sequence that moves from its exterior, figurative layers done in the style of socialist realism, to its interior core, designed in the indeterministic style of a postmodern architectural vision. One enters the memorial from the outside by passing the bas-relief of a young boy's face, the donor's son who perished in the Holocaust. This figurative representation was a condition of the donor's subsidization of the memorial. One then enters a lit ante-chamber, facing a wall covered with black-and-white photographs of children who died in the Holocaust. Only then does one pass into the black landscape of flickering reflections. Here the Children's Memorial comes closest to Baudrillard's postmodern vision of reality as simulation. The sudden loss of direction, the blurring of vertical and horizontal borders, the onset of tiny surges of vertigo, the need to feel rather than see one's way through, all imbalance and fragment the totality of reality that is itself a fragmented totality—the infinity of separate lights that have no connection between them except the nullity of darkness. This memorial is likely the most seductive to the senses (Baudrillard 1990) at Yad Vashem in its mastery of artifice to evoke both the lost innocence of childhood (the infinity of tiny lights) and its loss (the recognition of the artifice behind them). As eyes adjust to blackness, the body once again sees more than feels, and we lose the reality of fragmentation that this memorial conveys. One exits from this cave into near-blinding daylight, high above a vista of valley and mountains, an authentic and integrated vision that once more eye and body must adjust to. The exit from this memorial is no less brilliant than the entry.

20. We take note here of comments by some Israeli Jews that, from a neighboring ridge, people who are familiar with the location of Yad Vashem, but not with its contents, sometimes mistake this memorial to courage for the chimney of a death camp crematorium. In so doing, they inadvertently raise the difficulties of making the Holocaust continuous with the Israeli landscape.

21. During the 1980s there was a significant increase in the 'historical artifacts' given to the Yad Vashem museum and archives by Holocaust survivors, conscious of their age and seeking a 'home' for these authentic, personal mementos (Mais 1988:18). By contrast, the Museum of the Jewish Diaspora deliberately uses only copies of artifacts to describe the history of Jewish life in the diaspora. Golden (1996) argues that this policy says something about "the inauthenticity of the life that is on display."

22. To some degree this is offset by the fact that areas of Yad Vashem are 'living memorials' (Barber 1949:66) that have more immediately instrumental purposes—archives, library, teaching, and so forth. Of course, all the work done there is related intimately to Holocaust memorialism, and therefore to the intensity of national absence of which we write.

23. Thomas Laqueur (personal communication) maintains that this relationship is not shared with the commemoration of military dead in the West (see Laqueur 1991). However, we have not argued for the universality or essentialism of this inverse correlation in logics of the memorialism of national death. The generality of the logic on which the correlation is premised remains to be discovered.

Of greater significance to the human condition (and certainly to that of death, a subtext of this chapter) is the problem of that which we are calling presence and absence, and the creation of the presence of absence. This, by the way, is no less a problem for postmodernist thinking, given its strands that emphasize the loosening of structures, social fragmentation, and social simulation.

REFERENCES

Amichai, Yehuda. 1971. *Selected Poems.* Translated by Assia Gutmann and Harold Schimmel with the collaboration of Ted Hughes. Harmondsworth: Penguin.

———. 1986. *The Selected Poetry of Yehuda Amichai.* Translated by Chana Bloch and Stephen Mitchell. New York: Harper & Row.

———. 1987. *Poems of Jerusalem.* Jerusalem and Tel Aviv: Schocken.

Azaryahu, Maoz. 1992. "War memorials and the commemoration of the Israeli War of Independence, 1948–1956." *Studies in Zionism* 13:57–77.

———. 1993. "From remains to relics: authentic monuments in the Israeli landscape," *History and Memory* 5:82–103.

Aronoff, Myron J. 1986. "Establishing authority: the memorialization of Jabotinsky and the burial of the Bar Kochba bones under the Likud." In *The Frailty of Authority,* M. J. Aronoff, ed., 105–30. New Brunswick, N.J.: Transaction.

Barber, Bernard. 1949. "Place, symbol, and utilitarian function in war memorials." *Social Forces* 28:64–68.

Baudrillard, Jean. 1983. *Simulations.* New York: Semiotext(e).

———. 1990. *Seduction.* New York: St. Martin's.

Bauman, Zygmunt. 1989. *Modernity and the Holocaust.* Ithaca: Cornell University Press.

Ben-Amos, Avner. 1989. "State funerals of the French Third Republic." *History and Memory* 1:85–108.

Bender, Barbara. 1993. "Introduction: landscape—meaning and action." In *Landscape: Politics and Perspectives*, Barbara Bender, ed., 1–17. Oxford: Berg.

Benjamin, Walter. 1969. "The work of art in the age of mechanical reproduction." In *Illuminations*, Hannah Arendt, ed., 217–51. New York: Schocken.

Benvenisti, Meron. 1983. *Jerusalem: Study of a Polarized Community.* Jerusalem: The West Bank Data-Base Project.

———. 1990. *Jerusalem's City of the Dead.* Jerusalem: Keter. (Hebrew)

Berdoulay, Vincent. 1987. "Place, meaning, and discourse in French language geography." In *The Power of Place*, J. A. Agnew and J. S. Duncan, eds., 124–39. Boston: Unwin Hyman.

Bloch, Maurice, and Jonathan Parry (eds.). 1982. *Death and the Regeneration of Life.* New York: Cambridge University Press.

Casey, Edward S. 1987. *Remembering: A Phenomenological Study.* Bloomington: Indiana University Press.

Connerton, Paul. 1989. *How Societies Remember.* Cambridge: Cambridge University Press.

Cosgrove, Denis E. 1984. *Social Formation and Symbolic Landscape.* London: Croom Helm.

Cromer, Gerald. 1987. "Negotiating the meaning of the Holocaust: an observation on the debate about Kahanism in Israeli society." *Holocaust and Genocide Studies* 2:289–97.

Davis, Natalie Zemon, and Randolph Starns. 1989. "Introduction." *Representations* 26:1–6. (Special issue, Memory and Counter-Memory).

Eco, Umberto. 1985. "At the roots of the modern concept of symbol." *Social Research* 52:383–402.

Eisen, Arnold. 1986. *Galut: Modern Jewish Reflections of Homelessness and Homecoming.* Bloomington: Indiana University Press.

Ezrahi, Sidra. 1985–86. "The Holocaust in Hebrew literature." *Salmagundi* 68–69: 245–70.

———. 1992. "Our homeland, the text . . . our text, the homeland: exile and homecoming in the modern Jewish imagination." *Michigan Quarterly Review* 31:463–97.

Friedlander, Saul, and Adam Seligman. 1994. "The Israeli memory of the Shoah: on symbols, rituals and ideological polarisation." In *Now Here: Space, Time and Modernity*, Roger Friedland and Deirdre Boden, eds., Berkeley: University of California Press, 356–71.

Garber, Zev, and Bruce Zuckerman. 1989 "Why do we call the Holocaust 'The Holocaust'? An inquiry into the psychology of labels." *Modern Judaism*, 197–211.

Gertz, Nurith. 1986. "Social myths in literary and political texts." *Poetics Today* 7:621–39.

Golden, Deborah. 1990. "Memory in and out of the body: an enquiry into the links between memory, place and Jewish identity." Ms.

———.1996. "The Museum of the Jewish Diaspora tells a story." In *The Tourist Image: Myths and Myth Making in Tourism.* Tom Selwyn, ed., 223–250. New York: John Wiley & Sons.

Halbwachs, Maurice. 1992. *On Collective Memory.* Edited by Lewis A Coser. Chicago: University of Chicago Press.

Handelman, Don. 1985. "Rites of the living, transformations of the dead." *Reviews in Anthropology* 12:220–31.

———. 1990. *Models and Mirrors: Towards an Anthropology of Public Events.* Cambridge: Cambridge University Press.

———. 1992. "Passages to play: paradox and process." *Play and Culture* 5:1–19.

———. 1993. "The absence of others, the presence of texts." In *Creativity/Anthropology,* Smader Lavie, Kirin Narayan, and Renato Rosaldo, eds., 133–52. Ithaca: Cornell University Press.

———. 1994. "Contradictions between citizenship and nationality: their consequences for ethnicity and inequality in Israel." *International Journal of Politics, Culture and Society* 7:441–59.

Handelman, Don, and Lea Shamgar-Handelman. 1990. "Shaping time: the choice of the national emblem of Israel." In *Culture Through Time: Anthropological Approaches,* 193–226. Stanford: Stanford University Press.

———. 1993. "Aesthetics versus ideology in national symbolism: the creation of the emblem of Israel." *Public Culture* 5:431–49.

Hayward, Robert. 1980. "The Aqedah." In *Sacrifice,* M. F. C. Bourdillon and Meyer Fortes, eds., 84–87. New York: Academic.

Herrenschmidt, O. 1978. "A qui profite le crime? Cherchez le sacrifiant: un desir fatalement meurtrier." *L'Homme* 18:7–18.

Huntington, Richard, and Peter Metcalf. 1979. *Celebrations of Death: The Anthropology of Mortuary Ritual.* New York: Cambridge University Press.

Ingersoll, Daniel W., and James N. Nickell. 1987. "The most important monument: the Tomb of the Unknown Soldier." In *Mirror and Metaphor: Material and Social Constructions of Reality,* Daniel W. Ingersoll and G. Bronitsky, eds. Lanham, Md.: University Press of America.

Kapferer, Bruce. 1988. *Legends of People, Myths of State.* Washington, D.C.: Smithsonian Institution Press.

Katriel, Tamar, and Aliza Shenhar. 1990. "'Tower and Stockade': dialogic narration in Israeli settlement ethos." *Quarterly Journal of Speech* 76:359–80.

Kuchler, Susanne. 1993. "Landscape as memory: the mapping of process and its representation in a Melanesian society." In *Landscape: Politics and Perspectives*, B. Bender, ed., 85–106. Oxford: Berg.

Lang, Berel. 1990. *Act and Idea in the Nazi Genocide*. Chicago: University of Chicago Press.

Laqueur, Thomas W. 1991. "Memory and naming in the Great War." Ms.

Lefebvre, Henri. 1991. *The Production of Space*. Translated by Donald Nicholson-Smith. Oxford: Blackwell.

Lishinsky, Yosef. 1983. "Yad Vashem as art." *Ariel* 55:14–25.

Mais, Yitzchak. 1988. "Institutionalizing the Holocaust." *Midstream*, December, 16–20.

Mosse, George L. 1979. "National cemeteries and national revival: the cult of the fallen soldiers in Germany." *Journal of Contemporary History* 14:1–20.

———. 1990. *Fallen Soldiers: Reshaping the Memory of the World Wars*. New York: Oxford University Press.

———. 1991. "The Holocaust, death, and scenes of war." Lecture at Confederation House, June 6, Jerusalem.

Nora, Pierre. 1989. "Between memory and history: les Lieux de Memoire." *Representations* 26:7–25.

Ohnuki-Tierney, Emiko. 1994. "The power of absence: zero signifiers and their transgressions." *L'Homme* 130:59–76.

Paine, Robert. 1990. "The Law and the land: tensions of time in Israel." In *The Politics of Time*, Henry Rutz, ed. Washington, D.C.: American Ethnological Society.

———. 1994. "Masada: a history of a memory." *History and Anthropology* 6:371–409.

Poster, Mark. 1990. *The Mode of Information: Poststructuralism and Social Context*. Chicago: University of Chicago Press.

Rabin, Yitzhak. 1989. "Introduction." In *Gal-ed: Memorials for the Fallen in the Wars of Israel*, Ilana Shamir, ed., 6–7. State of Israel, Ministry of Defense. (Hebrew).

Ricoeur, Paul. 1984. *Time and Narrative*. Vol. 1. Chicago: University of Chicago Press.

Roskies, David G. 1988. *The Literature of Destruction: Jewish Responses to Catastrophe*. Philadelphia: Jewish Publication Society.

Segev, Tom. 1993. *The Seventh Million: The Israelis and the Holocaust*. New York: Hill and Wang.

Shamgar-Handelman, Lea. 1986. *Israeli War Widows : Beyond the Glory of Heroism*. South Hadley, Mass.: Bergin and Garvey.

Shamgar-Handelman, Lea, and Don Handelman. 1986. "Holiday celebrations in Israeli kindergartens: relationships between representations of collectivity and family in the nation-state." In *The Frailty of Authority*, M. J. Aronoff, ed., 71–103. New Brunswick, N.J.: Transaction.

———.1991. "Celebrations of bureaucracy: birthday parties in Israeli kindergartens." *Ethnology* 30: 293–312.

Shamir, Ilana 1989 (ed.). *Gal-ed: Memorials for the Fallen in the Wars of Israel*. State of Israel, Ministry of Defence. (Hebrew)

———. 1991. Gal-ed: Memorials for the Fallen in the Wars of Israel—Additions and Corrections. State of Israel, Ministry of Defence. (Hebrew)

Schindler, Pesach. 1977. "The Holocaust and the Kiddush Hashem in Hassidic thought." In *Religious Encounters with Death*, F. E. Reynolds and E. H. Waugh, eds., 170–80. University Park: Pennsylvania State University Press.

Shields, Rob. 1991. *Places on the Margin: Alternative Geographies of Modernity*. London: Routledge.

Smith, Brian K., and Wendy Doniger. 1989. "Sacrifice and substitution." *Numen* 36:189–224.

State of Israel Yearbook. 1954. Jerusalem: Government Printing Press.

Tal, Uriel. 1979. "Excursus on the term: shoah." *Shoah* 1, no. 4:10–11.

Taylor, Simon. 1985. *Prelude to Genocide*. London: Duckworth.

Tumarkin, Nina. 1983. *Lenin Lives! The Lenin Cult in Soviet Russia*. Cambridge, Mass.: Harvard University Press.

Williams, Colin, and Anthony D. Smith. 1983. "The national construction of social space." *Progress in Human Geography* 7:503–18.

Young, James E. 1989a. "The biography of a memorial icon: Nathan Rapoport's Warsaw Ghetto Monument." *Representations* 26:91–121.

———. 1989b. "The texture of memory: Holocaust memorials and meaning." *Holocaust and Genocide Studies* 4:63–76.

———. 1993. *The Texture of Memory: Holocaust Memorials and Meaning*. New Haven: Yale University Press.

Zerubavel, Yael. 1995. *Recovered Roots: Collective Memory and the Making of Israeli National Tradition*. Chicago: University of Chicago Press.

5

Tiyul (Hike) as an Act of Consecration of Space

ORIT BEN-DAVID

EDITOR'S COMMENTS

Orit Ben-David's "Tiyul (Hike) as an Act of Consecration of Space" discusses hikes organized by the Society for the Protection of Nature in Israel. Ben-David shows that these hikes can be understood as combining two aspects: the ritualistic and the taxonomic. The ritualistic aspect of the hikes is evident in their contemporary expression of valued actions found in earlier versions of Zionism: on actualization (hagshama) of a link to the land. Thus she suggests that for many Israelis hikes are a means for 'marking' territory and for declaring ownership of the land. In other words, hikes, like similar rituals found the world over, are means for effecting a legitimate connection between people and land. The symbolic aspect of the hikes lies in their designating a distinction between culture and nature, between civilized areas and 'untouched' spaces.

On Saturday, November 4, 1989, about four thousand members of the Society for the Protection of Nature in Israel as well as members of various youth movements, set out to protest against the intention of the air force to expropriate an area in the Arava (a valley that is part of the great Rift Valley between the Dead Sea and the Gulf of Aqaba) in order to turn it into a site for military exercises. This particular site was selected because a broadcasting station for the Voice of America was to be erected in the area that serves at present as an exercise area for the air force. Erection of the broad-casting station would necessitate extension of the training zone, which would in turn prevent many nature lovers from hiking in the region, because entering training areas is forbidden except on certain public holidays. In or-der to demonstrate their commitment to prevent this move, which they viewed as extending civilization, thousands of hikers from all over the coun-try converged on the Arava.

In the framework of the demonstration, the participants hiked in the area for five hours in desert landscape void of any point of scenic interest or his-torical significance. It was a tiring walk in the hot sun, and an effort had to be made to complete the course. The hikers perspired, looked at the scenery, listened to the sounds, and smelled the plants. For a short period they were "part of nature."

In an explanatory leaflet that was handed out to the participants by the organizers, it was stated: "This is an area of unique natural resources and primeval scenery as yet untouched by man. . . . It is completely unacceptable that due to outside interests and alien considerations the citizens of Israel should be forced to give up this priceless scenic heritage. . . . We [Society for the Protection of Nature] call on you to come and join us and help remove the threat."

I suggest that the hike cum demonstration in the Arava is a declaration of territorial claim, and a consecration of the space in the sense of expropriat-ing space from a social group (the air force in this case) and keeping it as a nature reserve, where people can always indulge in the social activity known as *tiyul* (a hike).

The demonstration previously described affords just one example of the consecration of space by means of a hike, but this is a recurrent feature in the walks of the Society for the Protection of Nature in Israel (SPNI). In or-der to demonstrate the above idea this chapter will only refer to hikes in na-ture sites since it deals with the special function that the natural environment has for individuals.

Hikes have usually been examined by sociologists and anthropologists as a form of tourism (Dvir 1972; Cohen, Ben Yehuda, and Aviad 1987; Graburn 1983). Researchers deal with the roles of the tourists or their hosts, and focus on individuals who have left their own society to visit a new soci-ety usually far from home.

I wish to illuminate another aspect of this subject since the hikes organized by the Society for the Protection of Nature are aimed at individuals who are tourists in their own society, and therefore these hikes cannot be examined by the same theoretical concepts. Instead this chapter examines these hikes as a symbolic social activity that distinguishes between two categories—"na-ture" and "society"—and restates the social and national definitions of these categories. This symbolic act enables members of the SPNI to consecrate space, to distinguish it from society and what it represents (daily life), and thus to come back again and again using nature every time to restate their definitions. I also propose that the *tiyul* functions in Israeli society as a means for the legitimation of personal and national identity.

THE SOCIETY FOR THE PROTECTION OF NATURE IN ISRAEL

The Society for the Protection of Nature in Israel was founded in the early 1950s as a nonprofit organization with open membership in order to protect the state's natural assets. Unlike the Green Movements in Western countries the SPNI is not a political movement; it serves as a focal point for all Israelis (no matter what their political conceptions) concerned about the quality of life and the preservation of the country's natural and historical heritage. The SPNI is a unique movement in the sense of its activity. It offers a combination of teaching geography and nature studies, tourism, research, and actual nature protection.

The main aims of the SPNI as registered in its articles of association are to conserve landscapes and relics of the past, to protect plant and animal life, and to develop research and educational material in order to achieve these aims. The SPNI directed its main effort toward educating Israel's population to respect, understand, and love nature and to encourage the assumption of personal responsibility for the country's appearance.

Historically this body emerged as a continuation of the European boy scouts and German *Wandervogel,* the Jewish youth movement, and later the Palmach (the strike force of the "Hagana," a voluntary Jewish self-defense organization active in the years 1941–48). Today the SPNI numbers about 45,000 full-time members; approximately 400,000 persons (youth and adults) participate annually in its activities.

Members of SPNI take part in lectures, hikes, and outings organized by nineteen local branches situated throughout Israel. Many of these trips are short walking tours, free of charge and open to anyone who shows up at the appointed time and place. The SPNI Touring Department also offers special "off the beaten track" tours and outings suited to those of all ages and physical capabilities. These range from trips for the experienced hiker, which entail traversing long distances over rough terrain, to outings suitable for the entire family. The wide range of tours offered includes trips for hikers and nature lovers as well as trips to archeological sites. The tours themselves are handled by a network of twenty-five field study centers located in various geographical areas throughout Israel.

Each field school has a hostel providing all necessary services, classes for nature study, and accommodation for the staff. The SPNI employs a staff of about four hundred people, including a number of women who act as guides on SPNI tours during the course of their army service. The more senior guides are usually males, aged twenty-two to twenty-five, who have completed army service and, on occasion, even university training, mainly in the scientific disciplines such as biology, geology, and geography. SPNI guides pass a strict selection process, and then undergo a three-month training period in which they study the geology, geography, biology, and, to some extent, archeology of the area in which they will guide tours in the future.

Israeli guides are easily identified because of their typical style of dress. They wear wide trousers, faded (sometimes even torn) t-shirts, walking boots, and wide-brimmed hats or *kaffiyes* (Arab head dress). Each guide carries a big rucksack containing, among other necessities, plastic water bottles and didactic aids like maps. This "uniform" was originally the typical clothing of Israelis in the Palmach and later in the youth movements. It enables the guides to feel that they are rooted in the environment and are truly part of it, or at least lead others to feel like that.

Another way to feel part of the area, part of nature, is to speak the "native" language—Arabic. Thus guides often interpolate Arabic words in their speech. They practice Bedouin rituals like baking pitah (a kind of Bedouin bread) over an open fire in the field, or preparing tea from herbs. They also tell their audience short stories taken from bedouin folklore. The bedouin are people of the desert and, by imitating their way of life, the Israeli guides are managing the impression of a greater sense of belonging.

Fieldwork was carried out in the years 1984–86 in one of the southern field schools of SPNI in the Negev. The site of this field school was located some distance from the nearest settlement in order "to let visitors feel the separation from civilization and become part of nature," as the manager of the field school defined it. The field school includes a hostel of 25 rooms with 130 beds, classrooms, an office, a dining room, and accommodation for the staff. All buildings are single-storied. The field school manager made it his business to ensure that all electricity and telephone wires were installed underground, so as not to mar the scenery, and further endeavored to preserve the desert character by planting indigenous flora. The staff numbered five women guides, working in the framework of their army service, two senior guides, four maintenance people, a secretary, and a manager who had himself once been a guide.

THE HIKE—SOME SCIENTIFIC APPROACHES

The topic of the hike has been used as a focal point for research in various studies. Educationalists (Vilnay 1953; Yonay 1955) see the hike as a frame-

work within which important social and cultural values are implicitly in-
stilled in hikers. Examples of such values are physical training, a wide knowledge of the geography and history of an area, and love of the homeland.

Another type of literature deals with the hike from the aspect of tourism,
recommending paths to explore and incorporating advice and suggestions
for the hiker (Ilan 1967; Vilnay 1935; Itzhaki 1978; Dvir 1972, etc.). Thus
some sociological studies have examined the hike within the framework of
a study of tourism. The common factor is the concept that tourists leave
their familiar social milieu and daily routine for a limited period and enter
different surroundings. Some researchers claim that this kind of activity
causes tourists to leave their own society and its social center to search for
another and different social order in the society that they are visiting. This
is the approach taken by Cohen et al. (1987). According to them, tourism
is an act of looking for centrality, or as they call it, an "elective center"
located outside society and its culture. A specific kind of tourism, mainly
that of young people, is essentially a search for a new meaning to life. This
type of approach, which draws a parallel between the phenomena of
tourism and of pilgrimage, is derived from the same worldview that inter-
prets the act of tourism as a form of departure from existing society. This
approach is based on the ideas suggested by Turner (1974:197–207) about
pilgrimage. He maintains that the group that embarks on a pilgrimage distances itself hundreds of kilometers from the geographical area from which
it sets out. Pilgrimage moves individuals from the familiar and habitual to
a far place and liberates them from the obligatory everyday constraints
of status and role. It also removes them from one type of time to another.
In the pilgrimage situation individuals are no longer involved in the combination of historical and socially structured time that constitutes the social process in their home community, but kinetically reenact the temporal
sequences. Graburn (1983:11) finds a common factor between touring and
setting out on a pilgrimage. According to him touring is a structured departure from daily life.

Indeed, some sociological approaches regard the tour as a kind of modern
ritual, such as MacCannell (1976). He sees tourism as a "modern ritual" in
which the populace "gets away from it all." Tourism thus is a period of separation characterized by "travel away from home." Katz (1985) regards the
tour in Israel as an activity belonging to a kind of civil religion, thereby combining both ideas, that of the tour as a pilgrimage and that of the tour as a
lay ritual. He explains that the hike, which constitutes one of the various
components of Israeli civil religion, is connected to the belief in the inseparable relationship between the people of Israel and its territories. The *tiyul*
as a secular ritual is carried out by secular practices (walking).

Other researchers treat the act of touring as a rite of passage. Graburn (1983) claims that touring, like the process of adolescence, army service, and marriage, signifies the transition of the individual from one social status to another. Many of the papers mentioned above deal with a special type of tourist activity, in which individuals are transferred physically from their own social milieu to another.

The hiking tours of the SPNI cannot be regarded as pilgrimages as defined by Turner, for in these excursions the participants are not distanced to any great extent from their place of residence. Although removed from the daily grind, they neither leave their social milieu nor depart from their obligations or status. On the contrary, it is actually their close connection to the society from which they stem that encourages this specific activity. In other words, people who join an excursion of the SPNI wish to define their social status (as will be shown more fully below). The act of social definition evolves from the social environment and is thrust back on it. In these excursions a real separation from society does not take place. Moreover, although there are certain elements (a different set of customs, and a different pattern of behavior) that distance the symbolic act of the hike from daily life, the physical or mental withdrawal defined by the other researchers does not exist. The participants in the SPNI's tours continue to speak the same language and are in the company of people from the same social environment. Moreover, the hike is not a kind of rite of passage for either the guides or the participants. There is no indication here of passing from one stage to another. The young female guides perform their duties in the framework of their army service while the more senior male guides take up their duties after they have completed army service or university studies. The participants, regardless of age, come from every stage and walk of life.

The fact that neither guides nor participants change their social status when setting out on an excursion indicates that the hike has no attributes of a rite of passage. Indeed, being a member of the SPNI and participating in its walks affords a special social status (in Israeli society, members of the SPNI are perceived as belonging to the upper middle class), a fact that is not denied by the members even when they are not on a hike.

Oren (1985) suggests that the hike is a symbolic act involving its own characteristic rituals. I accept the idea that the hike is a symbolic act in which individuals fashion their own social world. I propose to view the hike as an act in which the individual simultaneously consolidates both social and national identities.

Turner (1974:197) describes the actor-pilgrims as participants in symbolic activities that they believe are efficacious in changing one's inner being. The hikers of the SPNI do not believe in changing their inner lives, but being and wandering in nature help them determine that very same inner meaning of their social and national identities.

SOCIETY AND NATURE IN THE
SOCIETY FOR THE PROTECTION OF NATURE

One of the most striking features of the hike was the way both guides and hikers would constantly engage in the exercise of classifying the objects and features of their surroundings into two categories: "society" and "nature." To each category they would assign features derived from and contrasting with the other.

The act of classifying things and features into categories was previously described by Levi-Strauss (1966:10), who conceived this action as a striving of the savage mind for order. This perception is also offered in reference to members of SPNI. For those members the category known as nature (as it is conceived by those who define it) is made up of every aspect or form of behavior connected directly or indirectly to its natural environment, an environment perceived as unchanged by man and his technology. This category, then, is made up of flora, fauna, and scenery. It includes a flexible approach to time; food that is uncooked and untreated; cleanliness, silence, and isolation from all mass media; fresh air; and the guides of the SPNI. The category known as society, on the other hand (again as conceived by those who define it), is made up of those phenomena and systems of behavior that are man-made and constitute the culmination of human development. This category includes buildings, roads, factories, electricity, pylons, the Voice of America station, a more rigid time structure, cooked and processed food, dirt, noise, air pollution, mass communication media, and the hikers.

The separation into categories is understood as an antithesis—society as opposed to nature. Each category is mutually exclusive. This is illustrated by the following axis:

Society ←——————————→	Nature
Man	Flora and fauna
Hikers	Guides
Buildings, roads, factories	Scenery
Processed and preserved food	Uncooked natural food
Dirt	Cleanliness
Noise	Silence
Air pollution	Clean, fresh air
Communication media	No communication media

Between society and nature there is an ongoing dialectic. Society goes out to nature; society needs nature, but also destroys it.

This outlook is expressed directly and linguistically in the rhetoric of the hikers. On one hike a hiker called to a friend who was about to take a photograph: "Wait till the people have moved away. People spoil the scenery." On another hike one of the guides said, "People deface the scenery. This site was spoiled because it was near the road and people came along and ruined it."

The guides incorporate all other hikers, including members of the SPNI, in the category of society, considering them as destroyers of nature while regarding themselves as part and parcel of nature. As explained above, the guides express this point of view not only verbally but also by the way they are dressed and by the kinds of ritual activities they practice. The guides' sense of being part of nature derives from the feeling that the locality in which they work belongs to them. In fact, the "real owners" are the Bedouin living in the area, which leads the guides to try to become as much like them as possible.

The guides also offer proof of their closeness to nature by displaying knowledge and command of technical terms. When a guide asks on a hike, "What is the difference between a locust and a grasshopper?" or explains in detail how a certain plant preserves its seeds, she is announcing to the hikers that she is close to nature and well versed in its hidden mysteries. The small difference between a locust and grasshopper is almost unnoticeable to the lay person, and only a professional would be able to answer such a question. While asking such questions the guide displays knowledge. Being well versed means being close to nature.

The very name of the organization, the Society for the Protection of Nature, provides, in itself, evidence of this outlook. The society that protects nature. From whom? From society. The category called "society" is, as already stated, made up of everything that is a product of civilization. On one of the hikes organized for youth a guide spelled out her credo to the hikers in the following way: "This place has been preserved. There are no roads, no electricity poles, no smoke or factory waste and for this reason it is different. You may not enjoy it, but there are people who go out of their way to look for it. This place refreshes them and so they come out here and breath pure air and escape all the turmoil of the city." Factories and electricity poles are contrasted with pure air and scenery.

While out in the field the participants share the view that food eaten on the hike should be "natural," that is, not cooked, preserved, or grilled. On such excursions participants eat only sandwiches and fruits while on the hike. It is not fitting to eat hot food or to separate the meal into courses. Levi-Strauss (1986:142–43) suggests that people cook their food because they wish to bring about a cultural transformation of the raw. Thus it can be said that fresh, uncooked food is wilder, more "natural," and therefore more suitable to be eaten on those hikes.

Nature is perceived as clean. People will regard sand in their food at home as something quite unacceptable whereas sand in the food on a hike is an integral part of the general atmosphere. Douglas (1966:2) maintains that dirt is essentially disorder, and it exists in the eye of the beholder who makes an effort to reorganize the surrounding environment. Sand, dust, and animal dung are part of nature, and as such are not considered dirt; conversely, human litter is not part of nature and therefore creates disorder and is considered dirt.

Because nature is conceived of as clean, people do not wash their hands with soap and water before eating. Instead, they clean them with sand. One woman commented thus: "After washing your hands and soaping them with glasswort (a type of plant) you may eat your fruit." As the custom of washing hands before meals had not been carried out, she was suggesting an alternative. The sand replaces soap and so is looked upon as a cleansing agent on the hike, although in daily life it is regarded as dirt.

The maintenance of silence is also included in the category of "nature." On one hike a sobbing child was hushed by her mother with the words, "You're disturbing the silence." Drawing on Leach's (1976:63) suggestion that people create noise in order to mark the boundary between the self and the world outside, the necessity to remain silent can be explained as the wish to erase any boundary between the self and the environment. Thus the silence of hikers and guides, in their view, constitutes merging into the scenery and becoming one with nature.

On the various hikes in which I took part there was complete isolation from all forms of mass communication. The participants showed no desire to listen to the news, read the paper, or discuss topical matters during the walk. (Israelis are usually high consumers of mass communication media). This temporary escape from society and its problems intensified the experience of the *tiyul.*

So far I have illustrated how both guides and participants in the hikes organized by the SPNI engage in classifying phenomena by dividing them into two categories, nature and society. The conception that such a separation indeed exists enables them to compare society and nature, using nature as a mirror to reflect and understand their social structure. Levi-Strauss (1966:222) points out that the reciprocity of perspectives, in which man and the world mirror each other, can seem repetitive. The dialectic between nature and society, in which the natural order encroaches upon the social by means of a system of classification of effects and objects, turning the natural into an inseparable part of the social, is a universal phenomenon. Furthermore, in the

opinion of Radcliffe-Brown (1965:131) the phenomenon of people using nature as a mirror to their society can be found in both primitive and modern
societies alike and is expressed by religion.

How do the acts of separation and parallelism occur?

A process of separation and association of the two categories is realized
in the course of the walk by means of a rhetoric of nature preservation put
forward by both hikers and guides. The rhetoric used by the participants is
an implied message that goes beyond the sense of the words. In every walk
in which I participated people would draw parallels all the time. The guides
gave various explanations about the flora and fauna, and people would
come up with analogies from daily life.

On one family excursion one of the guides found a beetle. She picked it up
and began talking about its life cycle, explaining how it could store heat by
day because of its black color, in order to protect itself from the cold of the
desert night. One hiker commented on this: "The beetle has its own solar
system. It doesn't need batteries." The hiker used social expressions, like batteries, to describe the natural world and in fact his message was that there is
similarity between the two categories. On another hike, while walking in a
wadi a guide noticed a nest of wasps between the crevices of the rock. She
began to talk about wasps and the way they worked to build their nest and
feed their offspring. A hiker interjected: "The wasp is a really good worker;
it doesn't need unemployment benefits." Even in the demonstration described at the outset of this chapter the nature lovers drew parallels. At one
specific stage of walking along a particularly wide path, one of the hikers
turned around and called out in loud voice to those behind him, "This is the
superhighway of the desert."

Terms like "solar," "superhighway," and "unemployment benefits" are all
social expressions belonging entirely to the worldview of the hikers. By ap-
plying these terms to objects that belong in nature they are indicating that in
their view an analogy exists between nature and society. The creation of
these analogies reflects the possibility that in the minds of the speakers a realization of this parallel between the two symbolic systems exists. This is not
just a metaphoric way of speaking, but a state of mind.

Not only the hikers but also the guides indulge in the practice of drawing
comparisons and parallels between nature and society. On a youth excursion
a guide told her charges: "There are creatures living under every kind of
stone. If anyone picks up a stone, be sure to put it back, for it is like lifting
the roof off your home." On another occasion a guide described a feeding
location that many desert animals frequented as the Dizengoff Center (a
shopping center in the heart of Tel-Aviv) of the desert.

Another way to draw parallels is by personifying nature, an act in which
guides constantly indulge. On one walk through a wadi when a hiker asked

if the walls of the wadi had been quarried by men, she received the answer: "No, everything is made by nature." Nature is an entity capable of doing things. Guides frequently use expressions like "The hikers have defaced the scenery." This is another example of humanizing nature, and a way of emphasizing its comparability to society—although, paradoxically, society is conceived of as harmful to nature.

Why is the act of classification and the drawing of analogies carried out? If we can accept the supposition that people usually act according to their own worldview, the parallel between nature and day-to-day reality is inherent in the worldview of guides and hikers alike. The separation into categories is absolutely basic to an understanding of their social world.

I would like to propose that in the framework of the hikes of the SPNI both guides and hikers use nature for the same purpose: it serves as a basis for the construction of their social world. Nature is a mirror in which society is reflected not only as it really is, but as it "should be." I maintain that people who protect nature are those who wish to preserve their own status. In this sense, the hike seems to be an activity for defining not only categories of civilization and nature, but also the very categories of the social order.

How is this so?

As already described above, participants in a family excursion drew analogies between day-to-day reality and nature, implying that according to their perception such a parallel exists. One can claim that the ideology central to the SPNI is the preservation of nature (as mentioned above) and it may therefore be deduced that members of SPNI wish to preserve nature. I suggest that people who accept the SPNI's ideology perceive the existence of an analogy between their own reality, their personal status. In addition to the hikers' desire to preserve their personal status, they also want to preserve their national status.

TIYUL AS A MECHANISM OF LEGITIMATION

Like any other symbolic action (see Moore and Myerhoff 1977:7), the hike is characterized by the active involvement of its participants. The hike is a unique experience. For example, hikers go by foot, exert themselves climbing mountains, sweat, and become fatigued. This physical exertion is accompanied by a sensual experience that further enables them to feel that they have become a part of nature. People taste rocks (in order to identify their geological classification), smell flowers, and finger stones and plants. Their sense of hearing comes into play as they listen to the bird's song, the snake's whisper, the wind's roar and the water's rumbling. With their eyes they absorb the panoramic views presented by the scenery.

On one of the hikes the guide took all the participants to see a cave. One of the hikers had decided not to go along with the group and waited for them by the side of the road. Later, another member of the same group said to him, "You have missed the real experience"—thereby implying that in his point of view when on a hike one should take an active part. When the first hiker did not join the group to see the cave, he broke the understanding that everybody should take part in every act of this symbolic frame. Although the director of the field school offered participants on a family vacation the opportunity to stay behind (at the field school) if they got tired, no one accepted this invitation, because active participation is the most important part of the *tiyul.*

Most sociologists and anthropologists agree that territory is man-made and therefore a cultural phenomenon. By claiming for territory individuals declare their ownership (Lowenthal 1961:253) and mark boundaries between themselves and others (see Altman 1975:107). The body constitutes a central marker of various space preserves (Goffman 1972:41–42). In the act of hiking both the individual and the group mark out territory, claiming possession by use of the body—that is, by the act of walking.

There is much evidence in various ethnographies of walking as an act of marking territory. The Norwegian colonization used this mechanism in Iceland (Maurer 1852), the aborigines in Australia (Rapoport 1977), and King Hassan in Morocco (Geertz 1983:134–46). In Israel walking in the frame of *tiyul* has always been one of the most important educational activities and was meant to strengthen the ties between the youth and their homeland.

The Society for the Protection of Nature and its field schools emerged from the historical and social background of the traditional excursions initiated by the youth movement, from excursions of the Palmach, and from groups formed to study the homeland in all its aspects. These studies, called *yediat ha'aretz* (knowledge of one's native country), include study of the Bible, geology, geography, biology, history and archeology all of the land of Israel. It is interesting to notice that the meaning of the word "yediah" in Hebrew is twofold: knowing, but also having sexual intercourse. By use of this term a person may express his wish to get to know the country (*ha'aretz*) which is of course Israel, intimately.

One of the first active participants of the SPNI described the principles on which its Ideology is based, emphasizing the importance of the hike as a means of sinking roots and developing a sense of belonging to Israel which is part of the Zionist ideology (Feldman 1984:20). The concept of the hike as a tool of bonding between youngsters and their land still exists in the present. In Israeli high schools there is an educational program called Shelah (The name "Shelah" in Hebrew is the abbreviation of Field, Nationality, and Society. It is a compulsory course in the Israeli high school) in which the youngsters take part in trips organized by SPNI. Every year the guides of SPNI take about 300,000 youngsters on trips which last 3-4 days. The youths walk in the midst of nature and study the environment for at least 8 hours daily.

As the young so their elders. They walk about on the SPNI *tiyul* for hours, and feel that they are thus strengthening their bond with the country. On some of the hikes in which I participated, people climbed up one hill in order to see the view from the top and right afterwards climbed another hill to see the very same view. Climbing was an end in itself. On one occasion a man in his sixties climbed a mountain. When he got to the top he declared: "We have conquered the hill." In fact it was not only the hill that he had conquered but his body as well. The demonstration described at the outset of this chapter, is another example of the fact that by walking people are making a declaration of ownership. The fact that the hike serves as a mechanism to strengthen the link of the Jewish people to their land was explicitly stated by one of the SPNI founders: "Our link to the land is less than that of other nations, and there is no better way than hiking, especially when there is tension, to strengthen this link. . . . There are important parts of the country which are not inhabited by Jews and they are in danger. Hiking is thus a tool for displaying a Jewish presence in those areas" (Azaria Alon, Israeli Broadcasting Service, 1.9.74). Parts of the country are threatened not only by the Arabs (the fear is of Arabs living in surrounding countries as well as those resident in Israel), but by other members of society. Since the country is in danger it should be protected. Indeed, while walking serves as one way to strengthen the link to the country, preservation of the land constitutes yet another way, and the SPNI fulfills both missions. An interesting symbolic shift has taken place in the course of Israeli history, from a struggle against nature to a struggle for protecting nature. At the beginning of the century, while the Israeli pioneers sought to attain recognition for the Zionist enterprise, they waged a struggle against nature. The Israeli pioneers changed the landscape by building houses and roads, draining swamps, and cultivating the soil. They believed that in this manner they would reinforce their right to settle the land (Kimmerling 1983). Planting trees in the framework of the *Keren Kayemet le Israel* (The Jewish National Fund) was an additional way in which the pioneers could both struggle against nature and create legitimation (Dolev-Gandelman 1987). Paradoxically, their fight against nature strengthened their right to ownership, because they expropriated the land from nature and brought it into the "social" realm. The Israeli pioneers imposed features of culture such as roads and buildings on nature and thereby marked out their possession.

After the creation of the State of Israel, and thus the attainment of "external" recognition of the Zionist enterprise, it seemed that the need to

struggle against nature no longer existed. It was then that the idea of protecting nature emerged. This idea is actually the same thing in a new form.
The first conquest was to change nature, the second to preserve it. In 1954,
when the Society for the Protection of Nature was established, its main goal
was to protect nature from the inroads of physical development that were
"threatening" the natural environment with partial destruction. Yet side by
side with these keepers of the natural environment there are parts of the population who continue to redeem the land in the "old way" (namely, those
who build houses and pave roads in some parts of Israel in order to prove
ownership).

TIYUL AS CONSECRATION OF SPACE

By the act of hiking people strengthen their feeling of the legitimacy of their
claim to the land and also establish the basis for national identity. One may
therefore claim that territory is identity.

In the frame of the *tiyul* people draw a parallel between elements they see
around them in nature and social phenomena. In order to be able to do so
they must first make a distinction between the two. Indeed, the participants
in hikes organized by SPNI make a clear distinction between things that they
conceive as belonging to nature and those belonging to society. This distinction enables them to isolate nature and its components, to protect it, and in
fact to sanctify nature in the sense of distancing it from society.

In all the excursions in which I participated there was a clear boundary
between society and culture ("the profane") and nature ("the sacred"). Douglas (1966:8) says that in modern societies sacred things and places are to be
protected. In fact, the root of the Hebrew word *kadosh* (*k-d-sh*), which is
usually translated as holy, is based on the idea of separation.

People generally arrive for an excursion by bus or in private cars, which
are left at the entrance of the site. Form that point they continue on foot. The
parking place constitutes the border between society and what it represents,
and the world of nature. Although the act of consecration does not convert
the natural sites into holy places, the nature lovers have an almost fanatical
wish to preserve sites in the framework of nature, and not let society control
them, keeping those sites as "no man's land" (Rapoport 1982:169).

The demonstration against the decision to build a broadcasting station for
the Voice of America in the Arava exemplifies this phenomenon. On that Saturday people came from all over the country to protest against the intention
to deprive nature lovers of a piece of land they believed belonged to nature
(and, therefore, to them). The guide who conducted my group said: "It is a
region with unique natural features and an unspoiled primeval landscape."
By so saying he wished to explain that the area was wild and therefore not

available to society, while at the same time investing it with a mythical connotation. Thornton (1980:17) argues that the Iraqwe people take natural features out of the wild and bring them into the familiar. In another sense, natural features are given values and meaning that relate these features to their cultural system. As I have already described, the Israeli hikers do very much the same as the Iraqwe. While hiking, they classify universal components, and arrange elements and events of nature to conform with their own sense of order. But after they do what Thornton calls "appropriating," the hikers of the SPNI prefer the territories to remain "wild" so that they can return again and again to repeat the process of "appropriation," which is their mechanism for self-determination.

Talking of man and nature separately is not only a convenient rhetorical device but a defensible way to view reality (see Tuan 1971:3). In sum the act of separating nature form society enables the hikers to consecrate nature sites in order that they remain places to which they can return in order to use them as a mirror of their society.

CONCLUSIONS

The central feature of the arguments presented in this chapter is that the hikes organized by the SPNI are used as a mechanism for creating a basis for legitimacy. Territory is a man-made entity, and the way individuals or specific groups define and organize space and territory reflect their activities, values, and purposes. In the act of hiking people emphasize their possession of the land both physically and by consecration. These hikes are very popular in Israel; they are rooted in Israeli culture and began long before the creation of the state. Every year many youngsters and families join in this activity throughout the country. Hikes help the Israelis stress their bond with the country and their link to their land. Understanding this phenomenon helps explain the way in which concepts of territoriality and space are used in political terms. The Israelis' claim as their own territory, which is now Israel, and their wish to gain world recognition have not been fully realized. It is therefore not surprising that they feel threatened, and need to reassure themselves of their right to the land. Hikes are the kind of activity that enable individuals to emphasize both personal and national identity.

ACKNOWLEDGMENTS

This chapter was originally presented as an M.A. thesis at the Department of Sociology and Anthropology, Tel-Aviv University, 1989. I wish to thank Professor Emanuel Marx for his generosity of mind and spirit, which accompanied me throughout my research. He was kind enough to comment on this chapter. I am also most grateful to Dr. Eyal Ben-Ari for his input at all stages. Last but not least, I warmly thank Mrs. Judith Fadlon for her fruitful comments and her passion to reread many drafts.

REFERENCES

Altman, I. 1975. *The Environment and Social Behavior.* Monterey, Calif.: Brooks/Cole.
Cohen, E., N. Ben Yehuda, and J. Aviad. 1987. Recentering the World: The Search for Elective Centers in a Secularized Universe. *The Sociological Review* 35(2), 320–46.
Dolev-Gandelman, T. 1987. The Symbolic Inscription of Zionist Ideology in the Space of Eretz Yisrael: Why the Native Israeli Is Called Tsabar. In *Judaism Viewed from Within and from Without,* H. E. Goldberg, ed. Albany: State University of New York Press.
Douglas, M. 1966. *Purity and Danger: An Analysis of the Concepts of Pollution and Taboo.* London: Ark.
Dvir, O. 1972. *Where Shall We Hike This Weekend?* Tel-Aviv: Levin Epstein. (Hebrew)
Feldman, Y. 1984. Out of the South a Blessing Shall Break Forth. *Teva Va'Aretz* 23(3):4–6. (Hebrew)
Geertz, C. 1983. *Local Knowledge: Further Essays in Interpretive Anthropology.* New York: Basic.
Goffman, E. 1972. *Relations in Public: Microstudies of the Public Order.* Harmondsworth: Penguin.
Graburn, N. H. H. 1983. The Anthropology of Tourism. *Annals of Tourism Research* 10:9–33.
Ilan, Z. 1967. *From Going To and Fro in the Earth: Rambling Guide in Liberated Areas.* Tel-Aviv: Culture and Education. (Hebrew)
Itzhaki, A. (ed.). 1978. *Israel Guide.* Jerusalem: Keter.
Katz, S. 1985. The Israeli Teacher-Guide, the Emergence and the Perpetuation of Role. *Annals of Tourism Research* 12:49–72.
Kimmerling, B. 1983. *Zionism and Territory: The Socio-Territorial Dimension of Zionist Politics.* Berkeley: University of California, Institute of International Relations.
Leach, E. 1976. *Culture and Communication: The Logic by Which Symbols Are Connected.* Cambridge: Cambridge University Press.
Levi-Strauss, C. 1966. *The Savage Mind.* London: Weidenfeld and Nicolson.
———. 1986. *The Raw and the Cooked.* Harmondsworth: Penguin.
Lowenthal, D. 1961. Geography, Experience, and Imagination: Towards a Geographical Epistemology. *Annals of the Association of American Geographers* 51:241–60.

MacCannell, D. 1976. *The Tourist: A New Theory of the Leisure Class.* New York: Schocken.

Maurer, K. 1852. Beitrage zur Rechtsgeschichte des Germanischen Nordens. *Die Ensttehung des Islandischen Staats und seiner Verfassung.* Munchen: Christian Kaiser.

Moore, S. F., and B. Myerhoff. 1977. *Secular Ritual.* Assen: Van Gorcum.

Oren, A. 1985. The Social Construction of the *Tiyul.* M.A. thesis, Jerusalem, Hebrew University. (Hebrew)

Radcliffe-Brown, A. R. 1965. *Structure and Function in Primitive Society.* London: Cohen and West.

Rapoport, A. 1977. Australian Aborigines and the Definition of Place. In *Shelter, Sign and Symbol,* P. Oliver, ed. New York: Overlook.

———. 1982. *The Meaning of the Built Environment.* Newbury Park, Calif. Sage.

Thornton, R. J. 1980. *Space, Time, and Culture among the Iraqw of Tanzania.* New York: Academic.

Tuan, Y. F. 1971. *Man and Nature.* Washington, D.C.: Association of American Geographers.

Turner, V. 1974. Pilgrimage as Social Process. In *Dramas, Fields, and Metaphors.* Ithaca: Cornell University Press.

Vilnay, Z. 1935. *The Eretz Israel Guide.* Jerusalem: Stimatsky. (Hebrew)

———. 1953. *The Hike and Its Educational Value.* Jerusalem: Sheaalim. (Hebrew)

Yonay, Y. 1955. School Excursions. *Hed Ha'Chinuch* 29:26–27. (Hebrew)

6

Remaking Place

Cultural Production in Israeli Pioneer Settlement Museums

TAMAR KATRIEL

EDITORS' COMMENTS

"Remaking Place: Cultural Production in Israeli Pioneer Settlement Museums" is the title of Tamar Katriel's chapter. Her focus is on current attempts in Israel to promote certain versions of history by creating anew, by reconstructing 'old' places. The case she discusses involves the plethora of museums now being built to commemorate and celebrate the country's socialist-Zionist past and the values associated with this past. As she shows, the construction of such places should be seen in the context of history-making practices that inevitably construct selective interpretations of the past. She especially underscores how, within these practices, a certain selective image of Arabs is created to fit the aims of the museums.

Recent work in the area of cultural studies has highlighted the nature of culture as an essentially constructed, potentially contested process involving a range of public communication forms and contexts (e.g., Appadurai 1981; Johnson et al. 1982; Hobsbawm and Ranger 1984; Dominguez 1986, 1989; Borofsky 1987; Handler 1988; Leong 1989; Brow 1990; Gothercole and Lowenthal 1990). Tradition, in this view, "is a conscious model of past lifeways that people use in the construction of their identities" (Linnekin 1983:241). As studies in various parts of the world have demonstrated, historical museums are major participants in this ongoing cultural production

147

of a shared past and sense of place (Horne 1984; Lumley 1988; Clifford 1988). As such, they serve as major vehicles in the creation of contemporary "imagined communities" (Anderson 1983).

Not surprisingly, many of these museums and historical sites are permeated with a spirit of nostalgia. A nostalgic interest in the past is a well recognized feature of fast-changing, postindustrial societies (Davis 1979). It finds its expression in a variety of history-making practices, of which the establishment of local heritage museums is a major one. Many of the aforementioned interpretive studies of museums and sites, which combine visual displays and verbal interpretation in telling a localized historical tale, have been highly rewarding both as contributions to the general study of cultural production and as a source of insight into the processes of social legitimation and identity formation of particular groups as they are reflected in the preservation and re-creation of their heritage.

Writing about history museums in the United States, Wallace says that "on any given summer afternoon, a considerable number of Americans go to visit the past" (1981:63). In Britain, according to Lumley (1988:1), "new museums are being set up at the rate of one a fortnight." Documenting the recent museum boom in Israel, one recently published museum guidebook states that "there is a passion for museums in Israel, a passion for preserving and interpreting the past" (Rosovsky and Ungerleider-Mayerson 1989:6), while another guidebook states that these "museums have become a central cultural factor in Israeli society, so much that one can speak of a revolution, which finds its expression not only in the number of museums but also in the range of their activities" (Shalev 1990:13). The flourishing during the 1980s of local-historical museums and sites devoted to the presentation of the country's pioneering history is then part of a worldwide nostalgia wave, but it also gives expression to a distinctively Israeli version and politics of nostalgia.[1]

Indeed, more than 2 million people are said to visit the pre-state pioneering past annually in some sixty local-historical museums and sites now in operation, and projections for the future speak of doubling that number within a couple of years. The planning and construction of some fifty more museums and sites are under way, an effort that combines a grassroots preservationist movement and various institutional endorsements.[2] The general feeling among professionals is that there will be a considerable increase in historical museum patronage in the next couple of years, and concerted efforts are made toward this end, including the organization of a national scale Historical Sites week (May 1992), the institutionalization of links with the educational system, and the opening of a special, yearlong in-service training program for museum education in the fall of 1992 under the sponsorship of the Council for the Preservation of Buildings and Historic Sites.

Although these heritage sites have become increasingly and self-consciously differentiated with regards to the geographical area or historical period they cover, they seem to have also developed a largely shared representational idiom, embodying essentially similar "master narratives," which in various ways articulate the central story of Zionist fulfillment. The growing sense of competition between local museums over their slice of the "visitors' market," as this is often expressed, attests to an awareness of this situation. The following account, therefore, while anchored in two particular sites, in fact sketches the contours of a much broader history-making scene.

Many of these small museums are located in agricultural settlements (a good number of them in kibbutzim), and they have become widely accepted institutional contexts for the display, narration, and celebration of the country's socialist-Zionist past and the pioneering values associated with it. Some very active settlement museums are located in what were originally the earliest (late nineteenth century) noncollective settlements (*moshavot*), which have now become urban areas (e.g., Hadera, Rishon-Lezion). Their discourse extends the notion of pioneering (*haluziut*) beyond the agriculturalist-socialist-collectivist definitions found in kibbutz-based museums. The term sometimes used in exchange for *haluzim* (pioneers) is *rishonim* (the first ones to arrive), which is broader in scope given that many of the newcomers to the land actually became city-dwellers.[3]

Even though the massive establishment of local museums is clearly linked to the increasing centrality of the tourism industry in the country's economy, it is notable that these museums cater mainly to a domestic audience. They may occasionally respond to the demands of international tourists, and can usually call on the services of English-speaking guides when this is required, yet most of the museums I have visited have not yet developed an aspiration to become a regular part of the international tourism scene in Israel. The one exception is "The Old Courtyard" in kibbutz Ein Shemer, which aspires and works to become the touristic site where the "kibbutz experience" (past and present) can be marketed to international tourists as part of a larger tour package.

Most visitors to these museums arrive in organized groups, the vast majority of them being schoolchildren of all ages (West 1988). Other groups are various citizens' groups, pensioners' clubs, groups organized in the workplace, soldiers, and so on. Jewish youngsters from abroad make up a large proportion of international visitors as part of their ideological induction. In the past couple of years, these museums have also begun to draw groups of newcomers to the land, mainly from the former Soviet Union and Ethiopia, as part of the cultural initiation ("Israelization") programs organized by *Ulpanim* (Hebrew language learning centers). There has also been a steady increase in the number of visits by individual family groups on weekends and holidays, which has encouraged the development of better labeling for self-guided tours and greater flexibility in the kind and length of tours offered by the guides in attendance.

The analysis offered here is based on three years of ethnographic field-work in pioneer settlement museums in Israel, which consisted of in situ ob-servations of routine activities in a number of such local-historical museums in agricultural settlements, including audio and video recordings of guided tours, interviews, and many informal conversations with museum personnel, as well as the study of visual and written documentation (the display and its labelings, promotional materials, didactic worksheets, visitor books).[4] I have also participated in a couple of miniconferences devoted to museum-related issues over this time, the most relevant of which was the aforementioned conference run under the auspices of ICOM, in which the establishment of a separate section for pioneer settlement museums in this professional orga-nization marked another step in the institutionalization of these museums as nationally recognized cultural resources. Finally, the videotaped material formed the basis of the production of a three-part film documenting various styles and aspects of museum guide performances.[5] The video was then viewed with various groups of museum professionals and the "focus group" discussions thus triggered were taped and became a valuable additional source of data. These various contexts of observation and participation have provided me with rich opportunities to contemplate the significance of these museums as sociohistorically situated "cultural productions" (MacCannell 1976:24), as complexes of ritualized, largely self-addressed messages in and through which collective images are constructed and reaffirmed in contem-porary Israel.

Given their increasing prominence on the cultural and educational scene, and the growing institutional interest and support they command, critical at-tention to the rhetorics they employ as vehicles for the remaking of both Is-raeli time and place seems called for. Such exploration, as we shall see, provides a fruitful point of entry into the intricacies of the broader cultural debate concerning collective identities, group boundaries, and social legiti-mation in which Israeli society is currently embroiled, and which informs much of its contested political and cultural life.

Acknowledging a well-established historiographical tradition that recog-nizes the intrinsically rhetorical nature of historical representation, which concedes that "all history is a production—a deliberate selection, ordering and evaluation, of past events, experiences and processes" (Wallace 1981:88), students of the museum scene recognize that museums, like other history-making practices, inevitably construct selective interpretations of the past. Therefore, as the map of Israel becomes more and more densely dotted with local-historical museums, which sacralize localized versions of home-spun foundation mythologies, it is incumbent upon us to interrogate the popular readings and appropriations of the past established in and through them, adding an analytical voice to the larger, multivocal cultural conversation in which both museums and their observers participate.

In this chapter I offer an interpretive reading of the oldest pioneer settlement museum, which was established in kibbutz Yif'at in 1972, focusing on some of the display and narration practices that highlight the museum's role as a site for ideological statement and as a performative arena. Where relevant, I will make some comparative remarks based on similar fieldwork I have carried out in "The Old Courtyard" of kibbutz Ein Shemer, which since its opening in 1987 has developed into a major touristic site and as a "window to the kibbutz experience."

PIONEER SETTLEMENT MUSEUMS AS CULTURAL EXPERIENCES

"I once thought the museum had a message to convey," a guide at Ein Shemer told me, "but now I realize that what it should do is provide an experience." Even those guides who spoke of "the message of the museum" often formulated their task in rhetorical terms, that is, in terms of the effects they desired the museum visit to have: deepening visitors' rootedness in the land; increasing their appreciation for an agricultural, socialist, and communal way of life; gaining adherence to claims concerning the role of settlement in the country's pre-state history. Throughout my fieldwork, however, the notion of "an experience" (*havaja*) stood out in the discourse of museum personnel and patrons alike as they formulated their expectations of the public museum encounter. It became clear that even though a great deal of information was imparted in the context of any given tour—information painstakingly and systematically gathered as part of the museum construction and maintenance enterprise—visits often tended to be evaluated in terms of the quality of the "experience" they generated rather than in terms of the factual learning they provided. One museum guide stated explicitly: "We are not here to teach history, to do the teachers' work. Let them learn history at school. We are here for the experience." Thus, the tension between what Carey (1988:15) calls "a transmission view of communication" and "a ritual view of communication" is concretely experienced within the museum context. Israeli heritage museums definitely tend toward a ritual view of communication, which "is directed not toward the extension of messages in space but toward the maintenance of society in time; not the act of imparting information but the representation of shared belief" (ibid.:18).

The ritual view of communication is very much in line with MacCannell's discussion of tourist attractions. I therefore propose to consider pioneer

settlement museums as artfully designed sites for the ritualized production
of cultural experiences. MacCannell's perspective and analytic vocabulary
can help shed light on the order of experience generated in these museums.
He says:

> The data of cultural experiences are somewhat fictionalized, idealized
> or exaggerated models of social life that are in the public domain. A cul-
> tural experience has two basic parts which must be combined in order
> for the experience to occur. The first part is the representation of life on
> stage, film, etc. I call this part a *model,* using the term to mean an em-
> bodied ideal. The second part of the experience is the changed, created,
> intensified belief or feeling that is based on the model. This second part
> of the term I call the *influence.* A *medium* is an agency that connects a
> model and its influence. A social situation of face-to-face interaction, a
> gathering, is a medium, and so are radio, television, film and tape"
> (MacCannell 1976:24).

A cultural production, accordingly, involves "a cultural model, its influ-
ence(s), the medium that links them, the audiences that form around them,
and the producers, directors, actors, agents, technicians, and distributors
that stand behind them" (ibid.:24). Clearly, the visual display and verbal narration constitute media of encounter in and through which the museum's idealized model of pioneer life finds vivid articulation, and when they are
rhetorically effective, a cultural experience is generated. Furthermore, the
highly participatory nature of the museum visit lends it a ritual flavor that is
shared by other cultural productions, which "are rituals in the sense that
they carry individuals beyond themselves and the restrictions of everyday experience" (ibid.:26).

Thus, to understand the significance of pioneer settlement museums as
cultural experiences anchored in rhetorically potent ideological statements,
I will explore some of the representational and performative idioms employed in these museums, considering them as media that relate particular
cultural models and their desired influence. A frequently heard, semi-
metaphorically intended statement in those museums is that "we let the tools
tell the story." The tools' testimonial presence and aura of authenticity
notwithstanding, the museum's story and "message" are in fact conveyed
through verbal interpretations of the objects on display. As one open museum director put it: "What are these cabins in themselves? Nothing. It's all
in the stories they enable me to tell." These may be minimal and given in
written form, but usually they are relayed in part or in full in the context of
the guided tour itself. As museum guides repeatedly testify, perceived degree
of attentiveness, interest displays in the form of questions, and explicit signals of appreciation on the part of the audience largely determine the extent

of narrative elaboration found in a particular tour as well as its experiential quality (cf. Fine and Speer 1985).

Thus, while any given museum tour involves descriptive attention to a considerable number of objects along the tour route, some objects routinely trigger particularly elaborate or evocative acts of narration. These "narrated objects" (Stewart 1984) function as synecdoche; they are parts that stand for a whole, traces that epitomize a narratively captured vanished world. The museum thus becomes a concrete "house of memories" (Yates 1966) in which "authentic" objects give testimony to a cherished past via the verbal mediation of the guides. Every museum houses a particular range of objects that tend to become narratively elaborated by all guides, and these will be the focus of the present analysis. Each guide, however, has an individualized fund of self-selected and self-invested stories as well, and these contribute to the formation of individual styles within the museum's wider instructional repertoire, the contours of which must be left for another study.

The narrative junctures I focus on have recurred in one way or another in many of the museum tours in which I have participated in Yif'at. Taken together, they anchor a cultural experience in and through which there emerges a localized sense of the Israeli pioneering past, which, like the "bygone days" of the New Mexican village Briggs has studied, functions "as a communicative resource, providing a setting and an expressive pattern for discussions that transform both past and present" (Briggs 1988:99). Some of the ways in which the displayed objects and verbal interpretations intertwine to create the "museum experience" are described and analyzed in the next section.

NARRATING OBJECTS IN A PIONEER SETTLEMENT MUSEUM

The discourse of pioneer settlement museums is dominated by a rhetoric of place and origins. The establishment of the museums is a celebration and, in a sense, an imaginative reenactment of the pioneering spirit, a remaking of place. Both the ideologically minded groups of pioneers who arrived from Eastern Europe to "build and be rebuilt" in the Land of Israel and the single-minded individuals who worked toward the establishment of the museums commemorating the pioneering enterprise some fifty years later are spoken of affectionately as incorrigible enthusiasts, as "nuts over the cause" (*meshuga'im ladavar*). Throughout the museum tour, stories concerned with the exploits of the original founding fathers are interspersed and echoed by stories related to the laborious establishment of the museum by their offspring. Particular emphasis is placed on the drama contained in the purposeful hunting for relevant, authentic objects, which are often rescued from demise.[6] What we get, then, is a composite tale of a double-layered act of "making place," the original myth of foundation nested within a secondary

heroics of historical conservation. The museum's specific location is therefore highly significant, and, whenever possible, museums are established
around some restored original building or ruin, which serves to authenticate
and thus 'sacralize' it. The question then becomes, in the self-ironical,
metaphorical formulation of a second-generation museum guide from kibbutz Ein Shemer, "how one turns an ankle-high site into towers floating in
the air" (*eih hofhim atar begova karsol lemigdalim porhim ba'avir*). This
statement indicates an awareness of the inventional and dramatic aspects of
the museum enterprise, a self-consciousness I have never detected among the
first-generation guides.

The process through which a sight becomes "sacralized" is a complex one,
as discussed by MacCannell (1976:43–48). He speaks of the necessary step
of *naming* the sight, which in the case of museums determines the nature and
the range of relevant objects encompassed by it; the steps of *framing and elevating*, which involve placing an official boundary around an object (or
site) and putting it on display; the step of *enshrinement* which involves the
sacralization of the framing material (e,g,. container, building, museum) in
which the display is housed; the step of *mechanical reproduction*, which involves material reduplications in the form of souvenirs (miniatures, posters,
postcards, and so on); and, finally, the step of *social reproduction*—a situation in which host communities name themselves after the sight, sharing in
its aura.

The museum of pioneer settlement in Yif'at grew out of a commemorative
local exhibition, which was further expanded and enhanced so as to become
a permanent exhibit and was opened to the wider public in 1974. It was the
first pioneer settlement museum of its kind. It is now named after its late
founder, Oded Arzi, a second-generation kibbutz member who is said to
have brought back the idea of the museum from encounters with heritage
museums in the United States. Through his enthusiastic leadership he managed to get the kibbutz support for the idea and turn the museum into a communal venture. All the tour guides are kibbutz members, as is the museum
director. Three of the regular guides, two women (S. and J.) and one man
(B.), are old-timers (in their seventies). As members of the founding generation, they serve to authenticate the museum story through their very presence as well as through the autobiographical allusions they intersperse in
their narratives. They provide the core guidance but are increasingly aided
by other community members, including youngsters who belong to the third
generation of the kibbutz. The old-timers' stories and storytelling styles have
created available performative models that serve as suggestive examples that
younger guides simultaneously draw upon and distance themselves from in
fashioning their own distinctive styles.

The establishment of this pioneer settlement museum (and the ones that followed) reflects a more encompassing symbolic shift in temporal orientation. It involves the naming of settlement history as a culturally focal past in addition to—or even in competition with—the ancient, biblical past focused on in earlier years in the context of archeological excavations and displays. This renaming and revaluing process involved turning discarded, useless objects into valued "collectibles" as well as refashioning and recycling tales and anecdotes in which these objects and their original users have figured.

The site chosen for the Yif'at museum is a hill overlooking the kibbutz, allowing a breathtaking view of the Jezreel Valley. The climb up the hill and the wall enclosing the museum along which much of the display is organized provide the necessary framing and elevating. The scope of the museum has changed over the years. Its founders originally thought of it as commemorating the history of pioneer settlement generically and have collected specimens from all over the country for the agricultural display. The settlement in the valley dates back mainly to the early 1920s, but the emblem they originally chose—the Tower and Stockade icon (Katriel and Shenhar 1990)—names the heroic settlement period of 1936–39, which is not specifically connected to the distinctive settlement history of the Jezreel Valley. It seems to have been chosen because it has come to symbolize the saga of heroic settlement more generally. One of the moves taken by the museum's new director upon assuming his position was to delimit the museum's scope to pioneer settlement in the Jezreel Valley itself, diffusing the Tower and Stockade emblem. "We have to know what we are about and what we are not," he said to me in explaining this move. While the museum has been undergoing considerable expansion, exhibits have not been removed, so some of the ambiguity remains, as reflected in a guide's comment. "This is a museum for pioneer settlement in the valley but tools were brought here from all over, actually." Interestingly, a similar ambiguity appears in Ein Shemer, whose display, which is much more directly anchored in the particular history of that kibbutz, is nevertheless storified into a generic "kibbutz tale" that becomes larger than its geographical roots. The guides frequently attest to this narrative license in such side-comments as: "Well, it may not have happened in Ein Shemer, perhaps it was in Ein Harod, but it did happen some place. What difference does it make?"

Enshrinement is verbally accomplished at various junctures: tours generally commence at an observation post in front of the museum, at the edge of the hill overlooking the valley, and the guide both visually and narratively locates the museum in its past and present landscapes. The past is sketched in terms of some of the valley's former Arab (Bedouin) inhabitants, the swamps that the pioneers found as they arrived in the valley in the early

1920s, and in terms of the chronology of settlement that has marked foundational points that are historically related to the contemporary landscape. The present is spoken of proudly as an accomplishment of the heroic pioneering era. This expansive bird's-eye view of the valley, with its meticulously cultivated orchards and green fields, serves as a celebratory preface to the tour as a whole, contributing to the enshrinement of the museum—a process that is sustained throughout the tour.

In recent years, the process of site sacralization has reached the stage of mechanical reproduction: a colorful brochure has been produced and beautiful postcards, as well as t-shirts inscribed with the museum emblem or its slogan, "The Valley Is a Dream," both of which appear on the brochure as well. In the case of this museum, there is no indication of social reproduction in the sense that the community names itself after the site, but there is a concerted attempt to construct the museum "experience" in such a way as to allow visitors to inscribe themselves into the museum text. This is particularly the case with schoolchildren, for whom the overall rhetoric of identification generally employed in the museum context is both concretized and intensified through the wearing of "pioneering clothes" and the dramatic reenactments of pioneering life.

In kibbutz Ein Shemer, a full-scale touring package (the kibbutz past and present) includes a guided tour of the kibbutz itself so that contemporary members actually become part of the display, acting out their daily lives in a way that socially reproduces them as part of the museum tale—the "now" counterpart of the museumified "then."

Indeed, while much talking time during the museum tour is spent over informative details, the presentation is essentially dominated by an epideictic discourse, a discourse of celebration and legitimation, whose main significance lies in its capacity to invoke feeling and shape attitudes. It is with reference to the museum's epideictic role that the ideologically saturated "master-narrative," which organizes both the verbal interpretation and the visual display in the museum, takes form. It is the "master-narrative" that all the guides more or less adhere to even though each gives it his or her own personal inflection—the story of the early Zionist pioneers who, in revolt against their diaspora origins, left their homes in Eastern Europe and came to the Land of Israel to find redemption through the production of a new Jewish farmer, attachment to the land, and the creation of new communal ways of life. The guides usually have favorite exhibits in front of which they can tell favorite stories as well as favorite audiences whom they prefer to address. Of the two guides, some of whose stories are cited in this chapter, B. is at his best narrating agricultural stories, and seems to become most animated in the "herdsman corner," where he combines autobiographical anecdotes of his life as a herdsman with Bedouin tales. He says he prefers to guide

children, especially Arab village children for whom traditional farming ways
are not as remote as they are for many of the Jewish children who visit the
museum. S.'s stories become particularly animated as she tells of the pioneers' communal life in the dining-hall, and her preferred audience are old-
timers for whom the tour guide performance becomes an occasion for shared
reminiscing.

The stance toward the ideological statement made by the settlement museum is both reverent and nostalgic. Here and there, however, a retrospective, self-critical, even ironic streak is added to the generally celebratory
tone—for example, in passing, affectionate references to the pioneers as being "nuts," or "naive," for their selfless, enthusiastic participation in extraordinary communal efforts; in open reassessments of central values and
practices of the past; or in "dilemmas" designed as part of the active learning experience of students, which provide a context for debating some of the
pioneering values. The slide show in the Ein Shemer museum is particularly
striking (and somewhat controversial) in that it incorporates a very incisive
and critical look at the kibbutz saga. It admits problems in communal child-
raising practices, the financial debts the kibbutz has accumulated, the fact
that some kibbutz-children have not only chosen to leave the kibbutz but
even to make a life in New York. I believe, however, that these retrospective
critical assessments are largely diffused in the museum context, given its
overall celebratory tone. When the critical voices become foregrounded, as
is the case with the slide show in Ein Shemer, audience response seems to be
mixed: while some people praise the candid critique of past practices and
present difficulties, others resent the fact that "the kibbutz laundry is washed
outside."

As is often the case in historical museums, entering the Yif'at museum visitors are directed along a spatialized temporal line, beginning with an outer,
roof-covered path along the museum walls, which is devoted to the world of
work, followed by a tour of the internal, open-air yard concerned with what
the guides call "way of life," that is, the domestic and social life of the community, which houses sample living quarters—a tent, a communal babies'
cabin, a communal lavatory and shower, and a communal dining-hall considered the social heart of the place.[7] I will follow the typical tour structure
(cf. also Fine and Speer 1985), taking the reader first through part of the
outer circle of work and then move into the inner yard to contemplate some
of the structures of signification that can be gleaned in it.

The "corner" labeled "Traditional Agriculture," which is said to represent
the pioneers' starting point, offers the visitors a glimpse of the technologically
primitive Arab agriculture the pioneers found when they came to the Land of
Israel.[8] The agricultural tales become a way of speaking about the new meeting of Arabs and Jews on this stretch of land, and the new dialectic of cultural

identity thus engendered. Through the narratives woven around them, however, the manual agricultural tools displayed in that corner are associated not
only with the traditionality of the Arab villages in which they were actually
found but also with the antiquity of Jewish agricultural life. The latter link is
accomplished through repeated allusions to the biblical names of the tools
and implements on display and the biblical stories in which they are repeatedly embedded. Take, for example, the following story told by B. to a group
of eight-to ten-year-old summer-camp children (1.8.89) as they all stood facing the implement used as a measure for dry substances until some time ago
in traditional Arab households, and which is known in biblical Hebrew
as *seah*:

> I'll tell you a story, do you remember the story about the Patriarch Abra-
> ham? Oh, he was quite a man! Phee, he had lots of cows and sheep and
> lots of people working for him, and he used to wander from place to
> place, and he lived in the desert. He was the first Bedouin. The Bedouins
> weren't there yet, but he was there already. He was sitting in a tent, what
> was his wife's name? Sara, Sara sat with him in the tent, and three an-
> gels are coming,[9] they are going around in the desert, and they see some
> old man sitting with a young and beautiful woman, so they say, "Let's
> go visit them," so they come, so Abraham says to them, "Tefadalu,"[10]
> please, come in and be our guests," so he says, what does he say to Sara?
> He whispers a loud whisper in her ear: "Go get three measures of flour
> [*seot kemah*]." Here are the measures [pointing to the wall], *from the
> Bible straight here on this wall* (my emphasis). You see, this is what they
> used to measure in, imagine, the Patriarch Abraham in his time. How
> many years already? Oh, it's impossible, I wasn't there, you weren't,
> your parents weren't, and he was already using this to measure.

The tools and implements are therefore attended to and valued not only
for the aura of authenticity they carry as testimonials to a recent past when
"real" work was performed by human hands in a way that promotes attachment to soil and place. They are also textually sacralized through biblical allusions that reconfirm contemporary visitors' link to the ancient Israeli
past, in the meanwhile appropriating the sense of rootedness projected on
them by their actual Arab provenance.

The appropriation of the Arab past, actual and symbolic, is a rarely spoken potential source of tension. It was only in an interview I conducted with
him well into the research (August 23, 1991) that B. elaborated on this tension in recounting an exchange he had had with a group of Arab teachers
who had recently visited the museum, and who had openly raised the issue
of the pre-state history of the place, which was roughly the location of the
now destroyed Arab village of *mdjedel* whose inhabitants fled at the out-

break of the 1948 War. B. said he had had many friendly contacts with the Arabs of *mdjedel* and the nearby village of *ma'alul* during the British mandate since before the establishment of Yif'at in 1952 he had also been an inhabitant of the area, living in a nearby kibbutz. Although quite firm in his belief in the rightfulness of the Zionist enterprise of creating a homeland in Israel for Jewish refugees from Europe and the Middle East, B. strongly empathized with the plight of the Arab refugees as well, presenting them as victims of the war. In line with the ideological position that equates the cultivation of the land with a sentimental attachment to it, and a moral if not a legal right to it, he even refused to let their flight be interpreted as lack of attachment to the land and place and insisted that they were pushed to leave against their will by the Iraqi soldiers who were stationed in the area. By the time the war confusion was over and they may have been ready to return, B. said, the place was already occupied by Jewish refugees from Germany, Iraq, and other locations, who had no other place to go.

B.'s place narrative is clearly shaped by an ongoing internal dialogue of a moral-political nature grounded in a life history that combines warm memories of a childhood spent in a mixed Arab-Jewish neighborhood in Jaffa with a lifetime of service in security matters. His ambivalent attitude toward the Arabs—as much appreciated "children of the land" on the one hand and as treacherous enemies on the other—informs the overall tenor of his performances but becomes especially problematic in encounters with Arab visitors. Since these encounters are his specialized domain and favorite task within the museum's division of labor, these tours become for him a contested arena where his inner conflict comes through, and his version of reality is both reiterated and also put to the test with potentially unsympathetic audiences.

Thus, while S. thrives particularly on the magic attending the conjuring of a shared, cherished past with an audience of like-minded old-timers, for B. the most meaningful tour-guide experience involves the symbolic bridging of gaps with Arabs as his intimately known "cultural others." Unwilling to excise the Arabs from his tale, B.'s personal version of the narrative of Jewish settlement is an essentially troubled tale, its story line charting his own personal vocabulary of motives vis-à-vis the Arabs' displacement whose consequences he deplores even while considering himself as one of many victims of Arab hostilities, recounting painful memories of his own childhood trauma of displacement when his home in Jaffa was destroyed by an Arab mob. Pointing to the beautiful olive grove shimmering in the sun along the slope of the museum hill, he once said to me with obvious feeling: "I never eat those olives. For me they are taboo. They're olives that they planted. How can I eat them?"

This candid and highly troubled version of the local history, however, hardly ever finds its way into the museum's public statements. The largely celebratory story of personal struggle and communal devotion, hardship and creative accomplishment told to Jewish audiences is never questioned in this way. The silences relating to the details of past Arab life in the area, which linger at the edges of the museum's standard story line vis-à-vis its Jewish audiences, go largely unnoticed.[11] Arab audiences, actual and potential, thus pose a problem of narration in the museum context as currently constituted, even while their agricultural ways and social customs are routinely interwoven within the museum tale. As several thoughtful guides said, both in Yif'at and in Ein Shemer, "This is simply not their story." The common strategy of dealing with the problem is to focus on agricultural tools, which is the common technological denominator for both audience populations. But this only works half-way. As B.'s aforementioned story indicates, the museum encounter with Arab visitors harbors an ever-present potential for a radical interrogation of the museum's master-narrative. It may grow into a full-fledged debate as in the above case, or it may be aborted as it was one time in my presence, when B. was guiding a tour of Arab schoolchildren from a nearby village, and a child interrupted his tale with the provocative question. "What was here before the pioneers arrived?" He looked quite skeptical when B. launched into the story of the swamps. His teacher, sensing trouble, told him to keep quiet, saying: "Leave it alone now. The Palestine of the Jews is not the Palestine that we know." The exchange was held in Arabic and later translated to me by B. himself.

The problematics involved in telling the Jewish settlement story to a growing number of Arab groups was attested to by an entry in the visitors' book made by one of the Arab teachers who participated in the tour B. told me about, which followed a highly appreciative comment on the museum visit with the observation: "It's a pity that the Arab contribution to the land has not been stressed enough." A., the museum's new director, is quite aware of this problematic and told me Arab visitors even questioned the name of the museum, the "museum for the beginning of settlement," claiming that this ignores the prior history of Arab settlement and presence in the area. It is precisely these and other voices of potential contention that make the mythologization of Jewish settlement as a foundational act so poignant in the museum itself and in contemporary Israel more generally. So far, Ein Shemer, despite its left-wing political leanings, has received very few Arab visitors. The guides I spoke to about this all said they were interested in correcting the situation but were aware of the problematics involved and would have to give a lot of thought about how to present the museum to Arab audiences.

The museum's core section, entitled "Traditional Agriculture," thus becomes an umbrella term that collapses the pre-Zionist past, alternatively inhabited by timeless Arabs and textualized Jews, into a moment of stasis filled with "authentic," picturesque, and now obsolete tools and implements indexing a time-before-time.[12] Time and chronology, indeed, insert themselves into the story only with the advent of modern Zionism toward the close of the nineteenth century, which brought with it the Western-based celebration of technological progress now recaptured in the linearity of the display, which moves us along from traditional to technologically more and more sophisticated methods of land cultivation. These new methods are in line with central values of a modernized world, such as efficiency, technological control, and material comfort in everyday life, and are not extended to the Arabs who, frozen in time, find it difficult to adapt themselves even to the earliest of agricultural advancements: "The Arabs reaped with a sickle and the Jewish pioneers brought with them scythes so as to make the work easier. The Arabs didn't really grasp the use of the scythe" (ibid.). Another point at which the Arabs' traditionalism in ways of farming bespeaks a more radical "backwardness" relates to their treatment of women, especially the use they made of women instead of mules to draw their wooden plows. One of B.'s stories tells how the Jewish women incited their Arab sisters against this practice, triggering the wrath of the Arab men. At least on one occasion B. speculated that this may have been the reason for the Arab hostilities against the Jews with whom they had been living in peaceful coexistence.

Whereas the linear "grammar" of the display—from the more primitive to the more modern tool in any given category—suggests a wholehearted embracement of technological progress, the verbal interpretation accompanying it is not univocal in this respect. The narrative voice celebrating "progress" is repeatedly interrupted by a nostalgic undervoice filled with longing for a past shaped by heroic values and deeds, an ethos of production glorifying manual labor and a close contact with the land as spiritual fulfillment, not mere necessity. This undervoice breaks through in particular narrative junctures. Consider the story about the pioneer who refused to go along with "progress" and use a newly invented plow endowed with a seat, preferring to walk behind a simple plow, his feet touching the ground. It was told by B. to a group of university students who were visiting the museum as part of my ethnography class.

"Now among the farmers there was one farmer who was very typical. He wasn't religious but he knew the whole Bible by heart, he knew the history of Israel and he knew the history of the valley. And he came to the land [of Israel], and when he was abroad he had one single dream. I tell the kids that he didn't dream to buy a television set or a car or anything, he simply dreamed he would be able to come to the land of Israel and plow the earth here, sow it and plant it. That's what he wanted. And he arrived and he fulfills his dream and he is the happiest person on earth. And then what happens? As long as he works with the simple tools everything is all right. Suddenly some instructor comes and tells him: "You are tying the horses? get onto the chair." So he tells him: "Why should I get on the chair? What am I, a banker or a clerk?" And he refused to accept this. So he tied the horses to the machine and walked beside the chair. The Arabs, they consider the Jews to be clever, so he [the Arab] says: "What is this crazy Jew doing walking beside the chair?" And he says: "Walla [Wow], the Jews are nuts. The Jews have gone completely nuts, why does he have a chair and yet he walks on foot?" Now that Jew , that Yankelevich,[13] he didn't want to waste even one bit of earth, he wanted to feel the earth with his feet because in this earth there passed the prophet Elijah, and King Solomon and King David and the whole history, and all the prophets passed here, so *he* will sit on a chair? He wants to feel that earth, tread on it, and therefore he didn't want it, he didn't walk on the chair. But the Arab he didn't understand that experience. He is already plowing for ages and that one is only beginning to plow and he is only fulfilling his dream, so how can he get on a chair? No. But later he got some plow for which he was forced to get on the chair, and he liked it. They told him: "Yankelevich, get down," but he didn't get down anymore. To get him on the chair was difficult but to get him off it was more difficult. So that was the story with him, and it was a story that really was.

This narrative gives voice to the problematics that surrounded technological "progress" in the ideological climate shaped by "the return to the land" ethos interpreted both as a "return to the Land of Israel" and as "a return to working the land," an "organic" way of life that was antithetical to that of diaspora Jews. Technological efficiency is cast against a world of meaning and value, a world where work to be done as of necessity is cast against a world where work is to be ecstatically experienced as a source of personal redemption.[14] The final twist given to the tale, Yankelevich's final "surrender" and his newly acquired taste for the comforts of modernity, exemplify the self-directed irony that is sometimes added to these stories by way of both denigrating the present and casting a shadow of self-questioning on the highly resounding ideological certainties of the past. The ironical edge is increased by the wordplay associated with the phrase "holding on to your chair," which is used in contemporary parlance to refer to people who self-righteously overextend their claim to public office with undue fervor, an allegation often made against founders-turned-politicians.

Notably, the Arabs emerge from these agricultural tales doubly short-shrifted: they are as mystified by the ideological commitment of the Jewish pioneers as they are baffled by the technological wonders the latter have introduced. The clash between a romantic attachment to the land and a technologically driven, exploitative attitude toward it is obviously foreign to the Arabs' cultural experience. It is the predicament of those Jewish idealists for whom cultivation of the land is not part of a naturalized way of life but of a newly embraced personal and collective ideological identification.

Another narrative context in which the problematics of the agricultural encounter between East and West is articulated involves the following story, which I refer to as "the story of the hybrid plow."[15] The plows used by biblical Jews and traditional Arabs were made of wood and were locally adaptable to fit the condition of the soil in different places and seasons of the year. Initially, the pioneers were incompetent farmers; unaccustomed to local conditions, they were taught how to work by the Arabs (a contribution sometimes referred to, half-jokingly, as "Arab Zionism"). The wooden plows they first adopted from the Arabs kept breaking down in their unaccustomed hands whereas the iron-made, so-called charity plows that were sent to them by Baron Rothschild were unsuitable for work in the hard and dry Israeli soil. The solution combined the best of the two worlds. In B.'s words:

That man Lev Topolsky from Rishon, when he saw the troubles the farmers were having each time the plow broke down, and until you find the right wood from which to make the plow it takes a long time. And then that man who was a blacksmith he turned the wooden plow into an iron plow. It is similar but it is all made of iron, it doesn't break, it is all stable, and its capacity is much greater and therefore it is superior to the wooden plow. Now the Arabs called it a Jewish plow, and the Jews called it an Arab plow. Why? The Arabs know that it was produced by the Jews but the Jews know it is an Arab product.

This hybrid plow, with its Middle Eastern shape and European substance, responded both to the demands of an efficiency-driven agriculture and to the particularity of local soil conditions. The repeated stories of its making encode the vision of the possibility of fruitful, creative developments out of the comingling of Arabs and (European) Jews in the Land of Israel. Nostalgically set in the distant past, and in what appears to be the politically neutral domain of agricultural method, the possibility of mutual enrichment can be fantasized upon even at a time when Arab and Jewish relations reach peaks of hostility (third year of the Intifada). Indeed, hostile acts and conflicts between Arabs and Jews are barely mentioned in the museum tour. The picture of past harmony in Arab-Jewish relations is not even disturbed in discussing the display of guns mounted in the communal dining-room in Yif'at and in a special elaborate display in "The Old Courtyard" in kibbutz Ein Shemer. References to "the enemy" tend to remain so generalized and diffuse that visitors can simply fail to incorporate them into the overall exoticized image of the Arab.

Indeed, the presentation of the past as nonconflictual and harmonious relates not only to the thorny issue of Arab-Jewish relations. Antagonisms within the Jewish population are editorialized out of the picture as well. At one time B. told me as we were having a chat after he completed a tour with schoolchildren: "You know, actually, the people in the *moshavot* [noncollective agricultural settlements first established before the kibbutzim] did not treat the pioneers very well. They did not want to employ them because the pioneers were not religious. They preferred to hire Arab laborers. Of course, this is something I don't mention to the kids." B., like the other tour guides, considered himself not only as a transmitter of heritage but also as its guardian.

As the tour proceeds, the ambivalent attitudes toward modernization is reiterated. Technological progress is celebrated as B. describes the pioneers' delight in a more "advanced" plow. "They played with it. They said, it's very interesting; when you want to you pull it [the handle] up, and when you want to it goes down. It was a plow that fascinated them." A few minutes later, however, the figure of Yankelevich is invoked by B. once again in a nostalgic depiction of agricultural work as a spiritual enterprise rather than as a mechanical one. Yankelevich, overwhelmed by the "historical moment," prays as he walks along the field, sowing the seeds by hand because he "knows that here, in this valley, who worked in this valley? The prophet Elijah, in Megido there were King David and King Solomon. He knows that this is a truly sacred place." And when the green sprouts came out, he "ran out into the field, shouting 'New life! New life!' and he began to caress the sprouts, to kiss them, that's how much he loved agriculture, such a special man, we don't meet them anymore. Today they sow with huge machines, with a radio and a television inside, and everyone has a clock and they work by the clock. Then, there was no such thing. Then, everything had value, with a great love for the land, for sowing it, and for the wheat."

A similarly complex attitude toward the "then" and "now" emerges from the guides' interpretations in the inner yard, which commemorates and celebrates the pioneers' communal domestic life. Just as the agricultural implements anchor narratives that invoke the larger sense of cultural revolution associated with the Jews' return to the land, so the objects assembled in the various corners of the inner yard invoke the social dimensions of the cultural revolution of Zionism. The focus here shifts from the values of work and land to the values of communal feeling and simplicity in ways of life. The pioneer is now presented as the antibourgeois, who has willingly exchanged the genteel porcelain dishware and fine food of his or her parental home for the badly cooked, minimal staple of the communal pioneers' dining-hall. The

77 stop.

coarse, tin dishware displayed on the dining-hall table provide topoi for narrating that aspect of the pioneering experience. For S., whose first steps in cooking were taken in the kitchen of a pioneering group, the story of the pioneers' nutritional efforts is a personal testimony, a tale of woe retrospectively sprinkled with humor:

> The kitchen, you see, the dishware. Look at these dishware, do you see such dishes today? Anyone ever ate from such a dish? Why do you think they ate in such dishes?
>
> Because there was no porcelain then.
>
> There was, there was, but it was simply expensive. This one is simply not breakable, so they used these dishes. Note the cups, there weren't enough of them, there were never enough cups so they would take turns. Now suppose we want to cook a meal. I asked the *econom,* you know what an *econom* is? The one who is responsible for the food supplies. I asked, "Srulik, what's there to cook?" And he would say to me, "You've got a sack of lentils and a sack of beans, perhaps there's some rice here in some tin box; you've got to manage with this." I said, "That's okay for today, but I've got to prepare something to eat tomorrow as well," So he said, "Today make soup out of the beans and porridge out of the lentils, and tomorrow the other way round." And that's what happened, and I began to cook the food, and I know nothing about cooking. Nothing at all. And I knew that the guys are coming, they're starved, so I rang the bell and called them to eat, but what shall I give them? I knew the food I cooked was quite tasteless, I knew it was tasteless because I couldn't cook. They said, "Never mind, in a week or two it'll be over, you'll learn how to cook, you'll handle this later on." And so it was. But at first it was really not very good. So then they simply arranged a train on the table, one plate behind the other, and at the head of the train they put the kettle and they are going "too, too, too," like a train that's about to depart, and the train is beginning to come back to the kitchen with all the dishes and all the food. Of course, imagine my situation. What do you think, was it pleasant? What do you think? It was very hard on me, right? I would go and cry and friends would come and comfort me, but that was the situation. I was supposed to take it as some kind of a joke, but actually they had to finish their meal with only a cup of tea and some bread.

The dining-hall was not only, or primarily, the place for physical nourishment, however. It was the social heart of the community, where group solidarity, which was to become natively known as *gibush* (Katriel 1991), was most fully experienced and cultivated. Thus, the first black-and-white brochure of the museum (now replaced by a less wordy and more colorful

one with some writing in English) vividly describes the central role the dining-hall played in the life of the pioneering group. A similar account appeared orally in most of the tours I witnessed: "The dining-hall itself was the
heart of togetherness (*hajahad*). Here in the dining-hall discussions were
conducted, at times even very arduous soul talks.[16] Here they arranged the
work schedule for the next day. In the dining-hall they danced almost every
night. Dancing gave the strength to start all over again tomorrow." The
place's communal orientation was expressed not only in communal activities such as dancing and singing, but also in the fact that it housed the library
and the musical instruments originally brought in by individuals, as well as
the one radio the group possessed. It also found expression in the pictures of
prominent Zionist leaders that hung on the walls.

The intensity of communal experience sought by the young pioneers is
foregrounded in the story about the debate as to whether seating in the dining-hall should be on chairs or on benches. The decision to use benches was
not a technical matter, but a gesture of invitation as well as a rejection of individually oriented bourgeois values. As B. says (ibid.): "Seating was on
benches. Why benches? Because on a bench you can always move and add
another person. On a chair you can't absorb, that's why it was important to
sit on benches." While the dining-hall benches serve to symbolize the essential openness of the group to new members, the bell placed outside its door
symbolizes the community's responsiveness to the needs of individuals. This
comes through in oft-repeated stories about individuals who would wake up
in the middle of the night, agonizing over some personal problem such as
homesickness for their families, and would summon their bleary-eyed
friends by ringing the bell so that they could share their agony with them.

The ideological embracing of a communal, self-effacing way of life has
not, however, obliterated the personal costs involved in this decision. The dialectical tension between the individual and the community, the private and
the public, is indeed narratively dramatized in the vignettes told at each and
every juncture along the tour route. The dining-hall, the public heart and
symbol of community, and the tent, the private seat of romantic and marital
life, flank the internal yard on opposite sides of it and visually encapsulate
the polarity between the pioneers' private worlds and their communal participation. Thus, while the dining-hall is narrated as an all-inclusive communal hub, the tent stands for the romantic striving for exclusive intimate
relationships that pose a threat to the solidarity of the community at large.

Just as the building of community as narrated in the dining-hall was enhanced by the pioneers' poverty, so the greater material comfort that was
gradually achieved through technological progress is held partly responsible
for triggering the process of communal fragmentation. In B.'s words: "when
electricity arrived and they turned on the first light, then the change began.

Because there was light in the tents too whoever wanted to come to the dining-hall came to the dining-hall, but people preferred to stay in the tents and
began to withdraw more."

However, this shift in attitudes symbolized by the increasing social importance of the tent also involves a profounder reassessment of the individ-
ual/community dialectic. The old-timers say little about the kibbutz
problematics surrounding community pressures and the curtailment of individual autonomy and self-expression (a point I have heard openly raised by
second-generation guides), but some of their stories imply an acute awareness of this central predicament. Stories abound about the problematic living arrangement whereby a third person (nicknamed "primus" after a
popular three-legged oil stove) was assigned as a sleeping partner to a conjugal couple. The stories of the negotiations, spoken and unspoken, which
were needed to ensure a measure of conjugal privacy, while generally recounted with a smile, are sometimes also accompanied by a retrospective assessment of these past practices. B. openly said to a group of school-age
children: "We asked the oldest among the old-timers: 'How could you do
such a thing, inserting a third person into the intimate life?' And one of them
said: 'We needed to break up the family cell, that Yankelevich and his
Zledka, they were always together, they stopped coming to the dining-hall,
stopped attending the parties, and all that.' But some of the others were not
quite comfortable with this, and said there was shortage of living spaces, and
perhaps that's what caused this." Another kibbutz member, a man in his sixties who serves as an occasional guide, told me that the one display in the
museum he finds difficult to interpret is the tent and the "primus" stories associated with it. There was much feeling in his voice when he said: "I don't
understand how they could have done it."

One way such reassessments become incorporated into the museum story
is through the aforementioned "dilemmas" presented to schoolchildren as
part of activity-oriented engagements with the museum displays. Thus, children are invited to enter the pioneers' shoes and debate the legitimacy of the
"primus" arrangement after discussing the tent display, or, after glimpsing
the babies' cabin, they debate whether the newborns' names should be decided by their parents or by the community at large. These "dilemmas," even
while inviting children to identify with the pioneers' world, at the same time
cultivate a sense of distance from the past by highlighting the "exotic" dimensions of the pioneers' quaint way of life. What are presented as "dilemmas" to children were unquestioned practices to the pioneers, and the
solutions children usually arrive at are not in line with those the pioneers
practiced, reinforcing the sense that "things were different those days."

The guides' occasional critical comments about past practices and beliefs
(e.g., "Once they used to begin toilet training when they couldn't even sit

well, today they don't do this anymore") similarly serve as distancing moves within a larger identificatory idiom. Indeed, throughout the tour, oftentimes dressed in pioneers' clothes, children are invited to visualize and identify with the first settlers. The aforementioned distancing moves, though much diffused, nevertheless serve to counterbalance the rather intensive rhetoric of identification that permeates the museum's discourse, keeping visitors mindful of the gap between the past and the present, between the pioneers' world and the contemporary scene. It is this multivocality of the museum conversation that makes it such an interesting cultural arena of ideological articulation.

Thus, by providing an arena for an imaginative, dialectical engagement with significant cultural others—the diaspora Jew, the pioneer, the Arab—these settlement museums invite contemporary Israeli visitors to participate in the construction of a culturally constituted self. Whether they wear "pioneers' clothing" before entering the "time tunnel," a posturing included in some of the activities, or whether they are walking in their own shoes, the inducement to participate in the museum's re-presentation of the past actually invites visitors to "reinvent themselves" in the process. I believe that it is the particular form of this semiludic process of self-invention that gives the "museum experience" its distinctive flavor. To understand the broader significance of this process of self-production in settlement museums, however, we must try and locate it within the larger cultural scene in contemporary Israel.

PIONEER SETTLEMENT MUSEUMS AND ISRAELI CULTURAL POLITICS

In the foregoing analysis I have tried to argue that the recounting of origin tales in the context of pioneer settlement museums marks a performative arena in which a particular version of Israeli cultural identity finds articulation. In a sense, visitors are invited into a "hall of mirrors" in which contemporary Israeli identity is variously refracted against a complex set of partially defining images—the diaspora Jew, the native Arab, biblical ancestors, and heroic Zionist pioneers. At times, visitors' identification with the pioneers is cultivated dialectically through a distancing from the diaspora Jew and the Arab as cultural others. At times, the pioneer image itself becomes the nostalgia-filled cultural other, the embodied ideal with whose heritage contemporary Israelis need to contend. To the extent that its presentational strategies are persuasive, the museum fulfills its cultural mission of creating an "imagined community" (Anderson 1983) of persons bound together through shared participation in evocative storytelling events that generate a sense of communal affiliation by recounting "formative moments from the past" (Lincoln 1989:22).

Thus, the museums's "narrated objects" constitute anchors for the exploration of various dimensions of Israeli cultural identity. Visually and narratively strung together, they provide an idealized tale of "Israeli-ness" as envisaged within the Labor Zionist ethos, with its focus on the New Jew as a dreamer and doer for whom the Land of Israel is a socialist utopian site rather than, for example, a haven for persecuted Jews, as it is depicted in the context of museums for clandestine immigration (*ha'apala*), which tell the story of the arrival of Holocaust survivors during the British mandate.

Notably, as Firer (1985) points out in her detailed study of textbooks dealing with Israel's pre-state history, the emphasis on productive agricultural work and the values of communalism, which is associated with a negative portrayal of diaspora life and values, has been removed from the textbooks published after 1967. As she rightly points out, this textbook revision has responded to broader changes in cultural attitudes, such as greater acceptance of the diaspora world (both past and present), a considerable revival of religious sentiments, changed attitudes toward the Holocaust, and a marked erosion in Israel's socialist heritage. The settlement museum discourse, as presented earlier, has not been modified in response to these changes. In fact, these newly established museums seem to have provided an alternative institutional context in which the traditional, once hegemonic, socialist-zionist discourse can be carried on undisturbed offering a utopian counterstatement to a changing and challenging cultural milieu rather than accommodating its messages to it. A comment I once overheard an old-timer make in the settlement museum of Kfar Tavor to a schoolteacher, who had come to examine the museum's pedagogical potential, brought home to me the self-consciously nostalgic role these museums are designed to play: "Yes, bring the kids here. Let them have some comfort (*nahat*). With all that's happening to this country, the corruption and everything, let them have some comfort." In his voice and manner one could sense the comforting spell these museums hold in promise, a magical feeling that has colored my own "museum experience" throughout much of this research.

What, then, can we make of the recent emergence and institutionalization of these arenas for the production of nostalgic and ideological discourse on the Israeli public scene? The attempt to respond to this question takes us back to the earlier discussion of museum visits as part of a touristic enterprise that takes the form of "secular pilgrimages," which for some citizens of modernity replace the various pilgrimages of the established religions. At the same time that pioneer settlement museums became "secular pilgrimage" centers sacralizing a foundation mythology anchored in the European-based settlement effort of pre-state years, thereby excluding the massive post-Independence settlement of North African Jews from Israeli pioneering mythology, saints' tombs [*kivrei tsadikim*] became centers of folk-religious pilgrimage for Middle Eastern and North African Jews in development towns as part of their ethnic revival movement (cf. Ben-Ari and Bilu 1987; Weingrod 1990).[17]

In other words, just as saints' tombs have been erected to serve as pilgrimage centers within the folk-religious revival of Sephardic Jews in the peripheral urban zones of development towns, so settlement museums have been established as secular pilgrimage centers, mainly in the rural periphery of the country. In each case, a particular segment of the Israeli populace has created new places and occasions for the performance and celebration of competing versions of Israeli identity and cultural experience. Both these versions are partly defined as counterassertions to the identity claims made by the country's official cultural centers—Jerusalem with its aura of orthodoxy, and Tel-Aviv as the heart of profane, cosmopolitan culture. The similarity, however, ends there. While they share the functions of sacralizing the periphery and searching for particularized roots, these two types of modern Israeli pilgrimages chart quite disparate, ethnically anchored "geographies of meaning" within the context of contemporary Israeli culture.

Notably, within the Ashkenazi cultural experience the enshrinement of a native Israeli foundation mythology is not only an act of site sacralization but also a grand gesture of erasure. The expansive proclamation repeatedly made by one of the old-timers and echoed in various ways by all the others—"You see? Here it all began!"—captures the museum's role in elevating and enshrining a particular version of the story of pioneering settlement. The museum's way of accentuating the world-producing import of the pioneering era serves to mystify the place's recent Arab history and its present consequences, to overwhelmingly privilege the story of a particular segment of the (largely Ashkenazi) Jewish population, as well as to construct an Israeli history that is essentially discontinuous with the diaspora Jewish past.

The pioneer settlements are thus inscribed as symbolically potent signs in a culturally compelling imaginative re-creation of "roots." They are fictionalized as places we have all come from (or might have, or, indeed, should have). Truly houses of memory, they are inevitably also houses of forgetting. As no memory is complete, however, no forgetfulness is. Indeed, the concomitant emergence of secular pilgrimages of another kind, which are now routinely undertaken by Ashkenazi Jews and their offspring, and which similarly involve the search for concrete traces of a dispossessed family past in the towns and villages of Europe, notably Poland, suggests that this erasure has not been complete, that there are other tales of origin, competing versions of Israeli nostalgia. The growing awareness among at least some of the museum personnel of the narrative and ideological problematics attending the museum story vis-à-vis Arab audiences suggests the potential opening up of new dialogic possibilities within the very heart of a revitalized Zionist ideological discourse.

Given the present context of ideological erosion and increasing cultural and political marginalization of the socialist-Zionist enterprise and its upholders (the Israeli Labor movement) following their loss of political hegemony in the 1977 national elections (natively known as *mahapah*, reversal), the establishment of museums designed to celebrate this very heritage is clearly a gesture of relegitimation, a move in the cultural politics of contemporary Israel.

The presentation of the past in pioneer settlement museums gives voice to ideals and values that have very little to do with the social, political, and cultural realities of contemporary Israeli life. None of the "key symbols" that populate its discourse are tenable outside the museum walls: the apolitical references to the land as soil, as a cultivation site where Arabs and Jews meet as farmers is a far cry from the contemporary settlement idiom in which the land is territory and agriculture is politicized action. The celebration of the ethos of production and manual labor sounds almost paradoxical in a museum that defines itself as part of a service industry, a touristic enterprise in which the fashionable language of marketing predominates. The rejection of religion-based diaspora life becomes questionable in the contemporary sociocultural situation, which is marked by a growing impact of Orthodox Judaism on the political establishment and public life. Finally, the accented collectivist ideology is utterly out of tune with the individualistic orientation of contemporary Israeli society.

The apparent irrelevance of the "museum message" vis-à-vis contemporary concerns and sensibilities notwithstanding, settlement museums still play an important long-term legitimating role in contemporary Israeli cultural conversation. The official signature given to them through the museums' collaboration with the various branches of the educational establishment reinforces the symbolic potency and cultural authority of the socialist-Zionist tales of origin they weave. At the same time, these repeated visits to the past underscore a sense of distance between what is, what was, and what could have been—a distance both accentuated and bridged by this version of Israeli nostalgia.

ACKNOWLEDGMENT

This research was supported by the Basic Research Foundation administered by the Israel Academy of Sciences and Humanities.

NOTES

1. Cf. Ben-Ari (1991), who studies an example of Japanese nostalgia, arguing for the need to develop localized analyses of the phenomenon of 'nostalgia.'

2. These figures were cited by Y. Feldman, chair of the Council for the Preservation of Buildings and Historic Sites, in a talk given at a conference designed to establish a section for settlement museums as part of the National Museum Association (ICOM), Natanya, May 7, 1991. In personal conversation (January 28, 1992) he said the same number of visitors frequented heritage museums and sites in 1991, "despite the Gulf War."

3. It is interesting to note in this connection that Firer (1985) has found a parallel semantic extension of the notion of pioneering in textbooks that were put into use in Israeli grade schools in the late 1960s, whose effect was to broaden the scope of the notion of "pioneering" beyond the paradigmatic, heroic master-image of the pioneer who "conquers" the land through agricultural labor.

4. The material selected for more detailed presentation in this chapter is based on over thirty hours of recorded tour guides and interviews with museum personnel in the Museum for Pioneer Settlement in Yif'at. These were supplemented by fieldnotes taken in weekly or biweekly day-long visits to Yif'at and other local museums between 1989 and 1991. An average tour lasts about an hour and a half; when visitors are in a hurry, it is shortened (usually with some regret on the part of the guides). Longer tours combine all kinds of activities, including party games, singing, the drinking of herbal tea prepared on an old-time stove (*primus*), reproducing old methods of bread-making, and so on. These can run a whole school day.

5. The fifty-four-minute video was coproduced with Shimon Zafrir, M.A. student and filmmaker.

6. The process whereby discarded objects that have lost their use-value are salvaged from the state of "rubbish" to become culturally valued "durables" is well known in the world of collecting. Cf. Thompson 1979; Danet and Katriel 1989.

7. Expansions made in the museum include the addition of a clinic, a model of a *moshav* (noncollective agricultural settlement) dwelling, and a communal clothes storage room.

8. Cf. Swedenburg (1990) for a discussion of the image of the Arab peasant as a national signifier in Palestinian expressive culture and historiography. The role of the Arab peasant in the discourse of pioneer settlement museums calls to mind Rosaldo's (1989) discussion of "imperialist nostalgia." It deserves more detailed attention.

9. Note the switch to the use of the historical present, which is a very typical feature of storytelling in these museums.

10. B. sprinkles his talk with Arabic words, both when he impersonates an Arab speaker and in referring to Arabic objects, customs, and so on. Having grown up in a mixed Jewish-Arabic neighborhood in Jaffa, and having lived among Arabs for many years before joining the kibbutz, he is the one

entrusted to guide the few Arab groups that visit the museum. He has developed a split language allegiance, and feels that the museum stories "can't be told in one language," as I have heard him say, pointing beyond the language used. In his case, the tour performance also linguistically reenacts the theme of "hybridization" that is so central to the museum's ideological message.

11. Silences of this kind are common in the discourse of museums and historical sites. Wallace (1981) discusses the erasure of black experience from Williamsburg when the site was established; West (1988) points out the silence surrounding class conflict in a museum devoted to the history of the Industrial Revolution. I anticipate that as the incorporation of Arab audiences becomes more standardized, more complex and more highly differentiated versions of the museum story will emerge.

12. In this respect, the "museum experience" seems to replicate the denial of coevalness that Fabian (1983) discusses in relation to the question of how anthropology "makes its object."

13. Yankelevich is a character invoked by B. as a narrative thread along the tour. Yankelevich represents both a typical pioneer and an extraordinary person. In an interview (23.8.91), B. admitted that he strongly identified with this character who, he claimed, has actually lived in another kibbutz.

13. The use of religious parlance to describe the foundational Zionist act of "making place" has also been noted in Katriel and Shenhar 1990.

15. Cf. Katz 1982 for an illuminating discussion of other forms of "hybridization" related to agricultural practices in the pioneering era. Katz (personal communication) claims that the story of the "hybrid plow" is factually incorrect.

16. "Soul talks" were major occasions for self-disclosure and communal bonding in pioneering groups. See Katriel 1986:23.

17. Cf. Katriel and Shenhar 1990.

REFERENCES

Anderson, B. 1983. *Imagined communities: reflections on the origin and spread of nationalism*. London: Verso.
Appadurai, A. 1981. The past as a scarce resource. *Man* 16:201–19.
Ben-Ari, E. 1991. Posing, posturing and photographic presences: a rite of passage in a Japanese commuter village. *Man* 26:87–104.
Ben-Ari, E. and Y. Bilu. 1987. Saints' sanctuaries in Israeli development towns: on a mechanism of urban transformation. *Urban Anthropology* 16(2):243–72.
Borofsky, R. 1987. *Making history: Pukapukan and anthropological construction of knowledge*. Cambridge: Cambridge University Press.

Briggs, C. 1988. *Competence in performance.* Philadelphia: University of Pennsylvania Press.

Brow, J. 1990. *Notes on community, hegemony, and the uses of the past.* *Anthropological Quarterly* 63(1):1–6.

Carey, J. W. 1988.*Communication as culture: essays on media and society.* Boston: Unwin Hyman.

Clifford, J. 1988. *The predicament of culture: twentieth century ethnography, literature and art.* Cambridge, Mass.: Harvard University Press.

Danet, B. and T. Katriel. 1989. No two alike: play and aesthetics in collecting. *Play and Culture* 2(3):253–77.

Davis, F. 1979. *Yearning for yesterday: a sociology of nostalgia.* New York: Free Press.

Dominguez, V. 1986. The marketing of heritage. *American Ethnologist* 13(3):546–55.

—————.1989. *People as subject, people as object: selfhood and peoplehood in contemporary Israel.* Madison: University of Wisconsin Press.

Fabian, J. 1983. *Time and the other: how anthropology makes its object.* New York: Columbia University Press.

Fine, E. and J. Speer. 1985. Tour guide performances as sight sacralization. *Annals of Tourism Research* 12:73–95.

Fine, K. 1988. The politics of "interpretation" at Mesa Verde national park. *Anthropological Quarterly* 61(4):177–86.

Firer, R. 1985. *The agents of Zionist education.* Tel-Aviv: Hakibbutz Hameuhad/Sifrijat Hapoalim. (Hebrew)

Gothercole, P. and D. Lowenthal (eds.). 1990. *The politics of the past.* London: Unwin Hyman.

Handler, R. 1988. *Nationalism and the politics of culture in Quebec.* Madison: University of Wisconsin Press.

Hobsbawm, E. and T. Ranger (eds.). 1984. *The invention of tradition.* Cambridge: Cambridge University Press.

Horne, D. 1984. *The great museum: the re-presentation of history.* London: Pluto.

Inbar, Y. and E. Schiller (eds.). 1990. *Museums in Israel.* Jerusalem: Ministry of Education and Culture, Ariel Publishing House. (Hebrew)

Johnson, R., G. McLennan, B. Schwarz, and D. Sutton (eds.). 1982. *Making histories: studies in history-writing and politics.* London: Hutchinson.

Katriel, T. 1986. *Talking straight:'dugri'speech in Israeli Sabra culture.* Cambridge: Cambridge University Press.

—————.1991. *Communal webs: communication and culture in contemporary Israel.* Albany: State University of New York Press.

Katriel, T. and A. Shenhar. 1990. Tower and stockade: dialogic narration in Israeli settlement ethos. *The Quarterly Journal of Speech* 76(4):359–80.

Katz, S. 1982. The first furrow—ideology, settlement and agriculture in Petah Tikva during its first ten years. *Katedra* 23;57–124. (Hebrew)

Leong, Wai-Teng. 1989. Culture and the state: manufacturing traditions for tourism. *Critical Studies in Mass Communication* 6(4):355–75.

Lincoln, B. 1989. *Discourse and the construction of society: comparative studies in myth, ritual, and classification.* New York: Oxford University Press.

Linnekin, J. 1983. Defining tradition: variations on the Hawaiian identity. *American Ethnologist* 10:241–52.

Lumley, R. (ed.). 1988. *The museum time machine: putting cultures on display.* London: Routledge.

MacCannell, D. 1976. *The tourist: a new theory of the leisure class.* London: Macmillan.

Rosaldo, R. 1989. Imperialist nostalgia. *Representations* 26:107–22.

Rosovsky, N., and J. Ungerleider-Mayerson. 1989. *The museums of Israel.* Tel-Aviv: Steimatzky.

Shalev, A. 1990. Introduction to Y. Inbar and E. Schiller (eds.) *Museums in Israel.* Jerusalem: Ariel Publishing House. (Hebrew).

Stewart, S. 1984. *On longing: narratives of the miniature, the gigantic, the souvenir, the collection.* Baltimore: John Hopkins University Press.

Swedenburg. T. 1990. The palestinian peasant as national signifier. *Anthropological Quarterly* 61(3):18–30.

Thompson, M. 1979. *Rubbish theory.* Oxford: Oxford University Press.

Wallace, M. 1981. Visiting the past: history museums in the United States. *Radical History Review* 25:63–96.

Weingrod, A. 1990. *The saint of Beersheba.* Albany: State University of New York Press.

West, B. 1988. The making of the English working past: a critical view of the Ironbridge Gorge Museum. *The museum time machine*, R. Lumley (ed.), London: Routledge, 36–62.

Yates, F. 1966. *The art of memory.* Chicago: University of Chicago Press.

7

In and Out of Territory

DAN RABINOWITZ

EDITORS' COMMENTS

Dan Rabinowitz has entitled his contribution "In and Out of Territory." While the empirical instance he has chosen to study is of a mixed (i.e., Jewish-Arab) town that lies next to a larger Palestinian Arab city (Nazareth), his analytical focus is on the images and constructs that Palestinian Arabs use in conceptualizing the territory of these settlements. Rabinowitz's interest lies in examining the socially constructed means individuals employ to conceptualize the space associated with their identity as members of a certain nation. Here the picture is far from unitary. Rooted in a profound ambivalence to the state, Arabs living in Natzeret Illit are at once participants in and outsiders to Israel. They wait for things to work out, and seek uneasy alliances with their present situation in the hope for some change in the future in which they will somehow belong more to their place of residence.

A specific terrestrial base either at hand or as part of a chimerical future, is an obligatory component of every effort of what Anderson (1983) has labeled "imagining the nation." It is essential for the suggestion of a physical substrate—the 'homeland' in the literal sense—without which the nationalist idea will remain apriori a groundless blueprint; its promise of natural resources is essential for the concept of the welfare of 'the people.'

But there is more to promised lands than these material aspects. Sanctified as part and parcel of 'the people's heritage,' land becomes a means to translate utopian values into a grid of visible and vital entities (Williams and

Smith 1983:510). The renewal, regeneration, and rebuilding of the nation's terrestrial space are frequently linked to the fundamental, often revolutionary changes that people expect to undergo as part of nation building (Smith 1981). Gupta and Ferguson (1992:7–8) critique the universal tendency to perceive 'National Culture' as inextricable from the primordial homeland and as unproblematically related to well-bounded 'peoples' and 'societies.' Emerging 'national cultures' can thus be argued to consist primarily of bundles of idealistic snapshots representing (1) projective change and (2) the process of regeneration this change is supposed to trigger for the 'people' in its unifying 'land.' Not surprisingly, the newly rediscovered, romanticized, and idealized rural agricultural community features centrally in these imaginations, often as cultural markers that signify historical depth and 'rootedness' (see Malkki 1992).[1]

Studies by geographers and sociologists into cultural constructs of space in urban communities (Suttles 1972, 1984; Jackson 1984) have offered valuable insight into concepts and images that shape the multiethnic, economically varied community in North American and other Western industrialized metropoli. As Gupta and Ferguson observe (1992:6), anthropologists are only now beginning to look at the theoretical aspects of space. My contribution here will be to introduce some key metaphors and concepts used by the Palestinian citizens of Israel (often referred to as 'Israeli Arabs,'[2]) in their attempt to establish spatial meanings.

Kimmerling (1977, 1983) and Shafir (1989) offer insight into the role of territory within Zionism, although the cultural meaning of space is not particularly central to their respective works. Similarly, the cultural constructs of space within Palestinism[3] have not had sufficiently sophisticated treatment, Bisharat (1992) being a possible exception. Land and territory, however, is and has long been a raw nerve in Palestinian political and social domains, an issue as lively debated among the Palestinian citizens of Israel as it is in the occupied territories or with Palestinians abroad. *Yawm el-Ard* ('Land day'), diluted and ceremonial as it has become in recent years, is still the main unifying event on the calendar of the Palestinian citizens of Israel; the Committee for the Monitoring of Arab Land remains a respected institution; the Palestinian ideal of *Sumud* ('clinging'), denoting the indivisibility of people from their ancestral land and their determination to cling to it regardless of indignity and suffering (see Shehada 1982), remains a key idiom within contemporary Palestinian ideology under the Israeli occupation of the West Bank and Gaza.

Though some studies have been conducted recently into metaphors and cultural constructs of territory in frontier situations and in border areas (Anzaldua 1987; Rosaldo 1987, 1988, 1989; Ghosh 1989; Malkki 1992), little has been done from this perspective on the Israeli-Palestinian divide. Elsewhere (Rabinowitz 1992a) I discuss some aspects of frontier territoriality and spatial meanings from the Israeli perspective. This chapter concentrates on the Palestinian angle.

This inquiry is based on material gathered in 1988–89 through residential fieldwork in the new town of Natzerat Illit[4] in northern Israel. At the time Natzerat Illit had approximately 25,000 Israeli residents and 3,500 Palestinians. The Israeli residents tend to perceive the local situation in terms of Israeli turf unfortunately invaded by Palestinians (Shipler 1987:284–87; Rabinowitz 1996). Their ideal vision, to use Suttles' term (1972:21), is an Israeli-defended neighborhood. Inevitably influenced by the wider aspects of the Israeli-Palestinian conflict, they tend to distinguish between the presence of individual Palestinians, which they hold as undesirable but tolerable, and collective assertions of Palestinian presence, which they view as coordinated and intensely dangerous.

The Palestinian residents seem to have a different approach to the issue. For them the town as a place has but a limited representational meaning, to use another of Suttles' terms (1972:170). Rather, they see it as a segment of the metropolitan area of adjacent Nazareth—the older, better-established, and relatively prosperous Palestinian town that serves as regional center for the predominantly Palestinian hinterland, and to which their self-image as individuals is closely linked.

This chapter divides the space of Natzerat Illit into five subcategories, ranging from the exclusively Israeli to the overwhelmingly Palestinian. Observations of the behavioral traits, metaphors, and idioms that establish these different subcategories are analyzed. The Palestinians' discourse of and behavior toward space, I shall argue, reveals the ambiguities of being simultaneously outsiders and participants, rightful and disenfranchised, refugees and hosts in their own homeland.

POPULATION HISTORY OF NATZERAT ILLIT

Natzerat Illit was established by the Israeli government in the late 1950s to assert a Jewish presence in an area which, (see map 1), unlike most parts of the newly formed state, remained predominantly Palestinian even after the 1948 hostilities and mass exodus of Palestinians (for details and analysis of why Nazarenes stayed put in 1948, see Yitzhaki 1982:43–45; Morris 1987:201–2).

Natzerat Illit borders on the old Palestinian town of Nazareth (approximately 50,000 inhabitants in 1989). While almost fused geographically (see Doron 1987), the two towns are politically and institutionally polarized. Nazareth is a stronghold of the Communist Party;[5] Natzerat Illit is a robust bastion of the Israeli moderate Right.[6] Mutual suspicion and dislike between

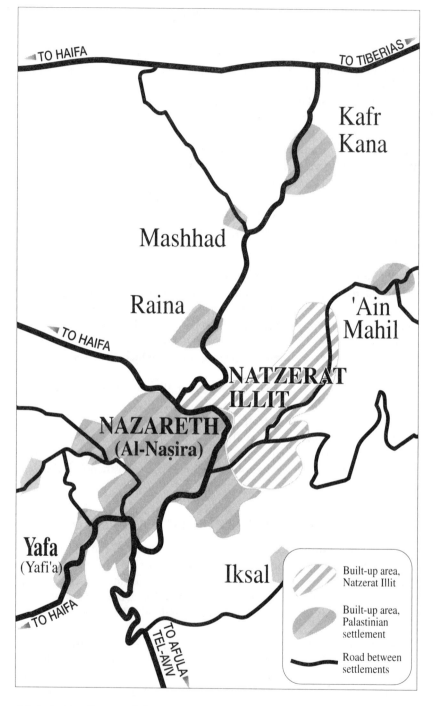

Map 1. Road map of the Nazareth area.

In and Out of Territory

Table 1
Israeli Residents in Natzerat Illit, 1961–89

Year	Population	Basis
1961	4,291	Census
1972	14,400	Census
1983	21,248	Census
1985	22,600	Extrapolated
1986	22,300	Extrapolated
1987	21,900	Extrapolated
1988	21,600	Extrapolated
1989	21,800	Extrapolated

Sources: State of Israel 1988a, 1990:69.

the two towns at grassroots level is reflected in minimal institutional cooperation at the municipal level. The Jewish mayor of Natzerat Illit and the former Palestinian mayor of Nazareth, whose terms in office have overlapped for over fourteen years, at the time of the latter's accidental death in 1994 are believed to have met only three times during the entire period.

The development of Natzerat Illit has been inextricably linked to major waves of Jewish immigration into Israel. Like other development towns, it quickly became a target for newcomers (see Garbuz 1973 for an account of the early period in Natzerat Illit; for a more general analysis of development towns, see Weintraub and Kraus 1982; Spilerman and Habib 1976:803–7). The stream of immigrants directed by central government to the town over the years was backed with substantial investment in infrastructure, housing, and industry.[7]

Central as Nazareth may be to its region and to the Palestinian community in Israel at large, it suffers from a chronic shortage of available land. This reality, partly accounted for by the town's awkward topography, was exacerbated in the 1950s when a proportion of its municipal territory was annexed to the newly formed Natzerat Illit. The shortage of land, coupled with the reluctance of the central government to initiate or encourage development in Palestinian communities in Israel generally and in Nazareth in particular (see Rosenfeld 1988), created an acute housing problem with real estate becoming disproportionately expensive compared to that of Israeli towns of similar size and geographical location.

The process was reversed in Natzerat Illit, where the decline in immigration during the 1980s (see table 1) created a surplus in housing, thus pushing prices down. Inexpensive apartments were increasingly taken up by Palestinian families, mostly Christians from adjacent Nazareth.[8] (This dynamic

Table 2
Palestinian Residents in Natzerat Illit, 1963–87

Year	Population	As Percentage of Total Population	Basis
1963	0	0.0	Census
1972	600	4.0	Census
1980	1,600	9.0	Extrapolated
1983	2,366	10.0	Census
1985	3,000	11.7	Extrapolated
1987	3,200	12.7	Extrapolated
1988	3,300	13.2	Extrapolated
1989	3,400	13.5	Extrapolated

Sources: State of Israel 1988a, 1990:69

Note: The 1972 figure refers to 'Non-Jews.' This category probably includes a number of Christian spouses of Jewish immigrants from Central Europe. The actual number of Arabs was smaller.

process is demonstrated in table 2, as well as in Bar-Gal 1986.) The 1988 Knesset elections voters' roll (State of Israel 1988b) and my own survey of early 1989 indicate that by early 1989 the Palestinian community in the town numbered some 800 households, nearly 76 percent of them owner-occupiers.[9]

THE NOTION OF TENTATIVE PRESENCE

The Arabic name of the ridge where Natzerat Illit is situated is Jebel Sikh (the skewer mountain,) probably in reference to the barren and prickly nature of the terrain. Prior to the transfer of jurisdiction over it from Nazareth to Natzerat Illit in the 1950s, the southern and lower western slopes had been cultivated by small holders and sharecroppers for Nazarene landowners. Other parts had been untended or only seasonally used for pasture by shepherds from Nazareth, the neighboring village of Ain-Mahil to the east, and Ixal to the south.

Palestinian residents of Natzerat Illit are generally aware of the discontinuous nature of past Palestinian ownership of land on Jebel Sikh. They also seem to have a realistic idea of the less than central place the area had within the rural hinterland of Nazareth. Only a few have firsthand knowledge regarding previous owners or cultivators on Jebel Sikh, and even fewer belong to families who used to have land or farming interests there. This partly explains why the Palestinian residents of Natzerat Illit are not particularly preoccupied with the notion of residence in the town as a return to ancestral land. During my fieldwork in 1988–89 this concept was mentioned only in passing, mainly by Palestinian residents who were involved in party politics as part of the communist-led Democratic Front for Equality and Peace (DFP). The notion in fact surfaced more readily from Palestinian residents of Nazareth than it did from those residing in Natzerat Illit itself. The majority of Natzerat Illit Palestinians with whom the issue was raised discarded it off hand. The concept has not turned up as a political issue they tend to rally around.[10]

The Palestinian residents of Natzerat Illit are keenly aware of the geopolitical local context by which they, as newcomers to the town, are the outsiders. While relations and individual acquaintances with Israelis are cordial and open, they are almost universally restricted to next door neighbors. When it comes to local Israelis as a group, Palestinians tend to view the situation with caution, as guests who happen to find themselves in the company of unenthusiastic hosts. Most Palestinian residents of Natzerat Illit have Israeli friends who live elsewhere; only a handful are genuinely friendly with Natzerat Illit Israelis other than their immediate neighbors. And Israeli residents of Natzerat Illit who have Palestinian friends tend to have them in other towns and villages.

This trend is further demonstrated in the reluctance of Natzerat Illit Palestinians to gain representation in local institutions. The first attempt at such representation came in the mid-1980s, more than fifteen years into the presence of Palestinians in the town. It took the rather timid form of a residents' committee representing the all-Palestinian neighborhood of Kūrūm Raina. The committee's objectives were initially limited to the improvement of services rendered by the exclusively Jewish municipality and to the enhancement of environmental conditions in the neighborhood. It was only by 1989 that this effort in local politics matured into a full-fledged political organ— an independent, all-Palestinian list of candidates (herewith the Independent List),[11] which contested a seat on the local council. Even then, much energy was spent on presenting the effort to Israeli eyes as a 'nonpolitical' initiative—a term that in Israeli public life implies preoccupation with utilitarian issues of an essentially technical nature. The more expressive features of the Independent List, such as catering to Palestinians' wishes for more suitable representation of their political and national identity, were systematically concealed from Israeli eyes.

The Independent List began preparing its campaign in late 1988. Significantly, the first public meeting of the campaign took place outside Natzerat Illit, at the YMCA in adjacent Nazareth—an important Nazareth institute and venue familiar to most participants since childhood. In the course of the meeting (which, like all gatherings of the Independent List, had an all-Palestinian audience, not counting the anthropologist, the issue of a venue for future events came up. Someone said it would be appropriate for as many rallies as possible to take place in Natzerat Illit itself. The idea was received with little spontaneous support. Being of sound logic, however, it could not be discarded altogether. A junior member of the organizing committee was asked to look into the possibility of holding meetings in Natzerat Illit's community center (*matnas*) or in alternative venues in the town. As it happened, the inquiry never materialized. The notion of a public venue within Natzerat Illit was not discussed again. All subsequent public meetings and rallies took place in the safety of the YMCA in Nazareth.

Palestinian residents generally perceive Natzerat Illit as a relatively safe place for Palestinian individuals and families. Admittedly, there were occasions on which Israeli vigilantes have attempted to stop Palestinians who purchased or rented apartments from taking possession (see Shipler 1987:283–88). These attempts, which received wide exposure in the local and national media, nevertheless remained marginal, clearly failing to create a popular grassroots movement. The great majority of the 3,500 or so Palestinians who lived in Natzerat Illit in the late 1980s have never been challenged as individuals.

When it comes to visible assertions of the Palestinian collective, however, Israeli residents are genuinely alarmed. A vivid example can be found in the words of a local Israeli real estate agent whose business relied largely on deals between Israeli vendors and Palestinian buyers and who has a number of personal friends and business associates among Palestinians in Nazareth. Faced with the challenge of what is routinely referred to in Natzerat Illit as 'the Arab advent,' he had this to say:

> You have to understand how they [the Palestinians] operate. It is not random. They begin in a given neighborhood, and suddenly all of them go there. Slowly they annex (*mesapkhim*) the whole area. For instance, lower Yizrael street is now 'hot,' So they all go there to settle (*leakhless*). It is really a settlement operation (*mivtsa ikhluss*), with a steering hand (*yad mekhavenet*). [. . .] They clutch (*mishtaltim al*) the town's main arteries. They slowly encircle it (*makifim*). They come from all directions.

Natzerat Illit can thus be characterized as relatively relaxed with the presence of Palestinian individuals, but decidedly apprehensive, even hostile, toward Palestinians as a collective. The analytical significance of this is obvious. The line that separates Israeli tolerance toward individual Palestinian settlers from hostility toward the Palestinian presence as a 'phenomenon' is the same line that separates individual economic considerations (i.e., the sale of property to Palestinians) from the more turbulent public domain, where 'they' (Palestinians) to things to 'us' (Israelis) through the medium of land. The tension this duality creates within the local Israeli community is beyond the scope of this chapter.

The Palestinian citizens of Israel, those of Natzerat Illit included, are not as trained as their Israeli fellow citizens in interpreting trickles of individual families in terms of movements with dynamic intensity and collective intent. Their tendency to see their presence in Natzerat Illit primarily in individual terms is strengthened by their conviction that taking residence in the town is well within their franchise as Israeli citizens and as the genuine natives of the region.

FIVE SUBZONES

The space of Natzerat Illit can be divided into five subzones, from places conceived as impenetrable for Palestinians, through intermediary mixed zones, to spaces both sides perceive as Palestinian. This section reviews these spaces and the idioms that engender them.

The first subzone is space that Palestinians and Israelis view as impenetrable for Palestinians. One case in point is a Ministry of Defense industrial plant east of the town, where, it is widely believed, Palestinians can neither be employed nor visit. Every person entering is subjected to a thorough advance security check, so the chances that a Palestinian will be admitted are poor. There are exceptions, such as the case of specialized maintenance personnel who happened to be Palestinian citizens of Israel, and who were admitted at least on one occasion. Few people, however, are aware of this occurrence. Virtually every Israeli resident of Natzerat Illit I have discussed the matter with genuinely believed the plant to be sealed off to Palestinians. The medium ensuring the establishment of this particular space as a no-go area for Palestinians is clearly state security and military secrecy—domains that Palestinians and Israelis alike see as exclusively Israeli (Rabinowitz 1992b:9).

Another illustration of exclusively Israeli space—albeit in a far less formal fashion—is the local community center (*matnas*). Ostensibly open to all to attend shows and classes, the *matnas* employs no active gate-keeping beyond the security check of bags and cases, which has become routine in public places in Israel since the 1970s. Individual Palestinians have attended films, theater shows, and other events, but tend to be reluctant to make a habit of it. "It was all right, in the sense that no one bothered us," a Palestinian resident once told me of a theater show he and his wife attended, "but we still felt that it was not our place. We were outsiders, and felt uncomfortable." Similarly, while a Palestinian child may occasionally enroll for piano or ballet classes, the overwhelming majority of the Palestinian residents of Natzerat Illit have never set foot in the place. Many of them seem to perceive the *matnas* as a bastion of Israeli Ashkenazi high culture.[12]

This scant use of the *matnas* by individual Palestinian patrons is matched by failure of more organized attempts by Palestinians to use the venue for their own affairs. All bids by Palestinian entrepreneurs to hire the place for cultural events designed for Palestinian audiences were turned down by the center's all-Israeli board of trustees in its capacity as a supervisory program committee. Initiatives I am aware of included a beauty queen contest for Palestinian women that had no other options for a venue in the Nazareth area and was eventually staged in Haifa, and a theater production in Arabic. In this case, it is the idiom of a Western, Ashkenazi high culture—as remote and irrelevant for most Palestinian citizens of Israel as it is for Israeli Jews of Arab or Central Asian origins—which renders this particular space out of bounds for Palestinians.

Three neighborhoods where local Israeli residents succeeded—or are believed to have succeeded—in keeping all potential Palestinian residents away present a third illustration of space established as exclusively Israeli. Two of the three are desirable suburban residential areas in the southern part of town. Having become target neighborhoods for veteran residents of Natzerat Illit who wish to upgrade their living standards, the two neighborhoods enjoyed sustained demand for real estate by Israelis, thus keeping most Palestinian potential buyers at arm's length.[13] A third exclusively Israeli residential area is a humbler housing estate where Soviet Georgian Jews are an overwhelming majority. The idiom engendering this space as Israeli is thus exclusivity in settlement, in keeping with Natzerat Illit's mission as defined in the 1950s—to assert a 'Jewish' presence in an 'Arab' heartland.

Significantly, all three idioms that establish space as a no-go place for Palestinians are anchored in values and ideals perceived by actors as external to Natzerat Illit and its particular predicament. Defense of the realm, the mission of creating and sustaining a new 'Israeli culture' (Dominguez 1989), and the need to have at least parts of the new town in keeping with the mission delegated to Natzerat Illit by the state and the Jewish people are treated as decreed from yonder.

Approximately two-thirds of Natzerat Illit's Palestinian residents (some 500 households) lived at the time of my fieldwork in apartment blocks scattered throughout various parts of town; 57.8 percent of them (96 out of 166 valid cases in my 1989 survey,) occupy buildings where Israeli households are in majority or where the number of Palestinian households is more or less equal to that of Israeli ones. These buildings comprise Natzerat Illit's second spatial subzone.

With the balance of presence clearly in favor of Israelis, it is not surprising that Palestinians tend to maintain a low collective profile, trying to assert themselves primarily as good, friendly, and timid neighbors. Many of them take part in informal gatherings on benches or fences in front of the houses or in semipublic spaces such as patios and miniplazas in and around the block. Palestinian women who live in mixed blocks often become close to older Israeli women, usually of North African origin. Women tend to spend time together in their respective apartments, in staircases, and on lawns, drinking coffee, doing household chores, talking. Babies and toddlers often become a focus of attention and mutual support, with elderly Israeli women helping younger Palestinian mothers with child minding. One case I became aware of had a Palestinian man, a carpenter by trade, building the tabernacle's *sukah* in the communally owned yard of the block where he and his wife lived with seven Israeli families. I later learned that this was no exception. The couple, both in their forties and with no children of their own, take an active part in the block's neighborly routines.

Palestinian residents of blocks comprised primarily of Israelis make a point of keeping away from political controversy. They tend to refrain from taking active part in debates of current affairs, which often end up in heated arguments on aspects of Israeli-Palestinian relations. When they do comment on the subject, they tend to attenuate their stances and utterances to avoid unnecessary tension.

Palestinians occupying apartment blocks in Natzerat Illit tend to see themselves as temporary residents of the town even when they are owner-occupiers. My survey of 1989 indicates that 47.4 percent of them (79 out of 168 valid cases) planned to stay in Natzerat Illit only until they are able to buy or build their own house elsewhere, preferably in their native village or in Nazareth. This partly explains their reluctance to become involved with more formal neighborhood institutions such as the resident's committee (*va'ad bayit*).[14]

The idiom through which this particular type of space is established as 'Israeli' is that of Palestinian self-effacement: the assertion of self as the prototypical good neighbors, coupled with the submissive role of those avoiding all manifestations of their collective, politicized identity as Palestinians.

42.2 percent of Palestinians occupying flats in Natzerat Illit (70 out of 166 valid cases in my 1989 survey) lived in blocks where the majority of units (sometimes all of them) had Palestinian occupants. These blocks comprise the third spatial subzone. Predictably, residents of such Palestinian 'islands' within the predominantly Israeli town tend to be less inhibited in asserting their ideas and identity. They use Arabic freely in semipublic places such as staircases and parking lots. Parents tend to leave windows open and communicate in Arabic with children playing outdoors. Front doors are often kept ajar so women can wander freely into each other's flats. People do not hesitate to open doors or windows for brief surveillance of staircases or

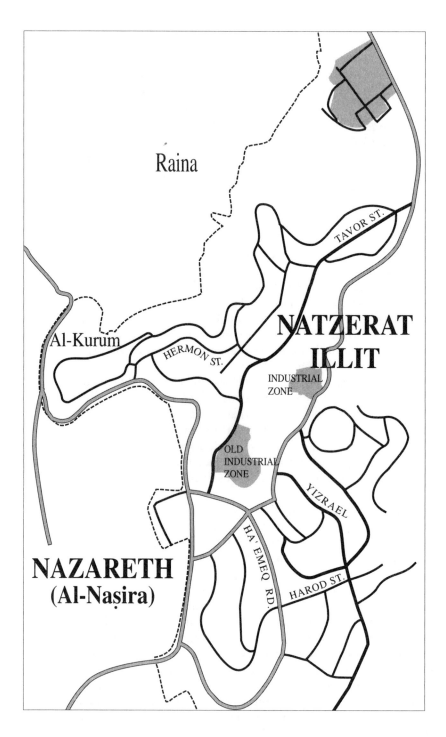

Raina

Al-Kurum

HERMON ST.

TAVOR ST.

NATZERAT ILLIT

INDUSTRIAL ZONE

OLD INDUSTRIAL ZONE

YIZRAEL

HA'EMEQ RD.

HAROD ST.

NAZARETH
(Al-Naṣira)

Map 2. The western section of the municipal boundaries of Natzerat Illit.

entrance halls if a stranger enters the building. A number of these blocks house small clusters of kin, often two or three siblings and their families. Residents' committees tend to be especially active and dynamic. One result is that all-Palestinian buildings sometimes enjoy better maintenance and care than other blocks of similar design.

These elements, while clearly influencing people's sense of space, do not however, redefine these blocks as Palestinian turf. One important factor is size. Unlike residential clusters in Palestinian communities elsewhere, these Palestinian islands are limited in the capacity to handle the full range of social activities. All Palestinian families in Natzerat Illit can in fact be described as displaced components of larger kinship units.[15] Households lean on Nazareth-based kin as foci of familial gravity. Level of activity and visibility of residential units in the mixed neighborhoods of Natzerat Illit are thus inherently constrained, not least because such Palestinian clusters prefer not to stand out as distinctly separate (and obviously 'Arab') in a predominantly Israeli neighborhood.

The medium that establishes the spatial meaning of these blocks as Palestinian islands in a distinctly Israeli space can be summarized as that of partial Palestinian cultural autonomy. Uninhibited use of Arabic in public places, the kinship idiom, and organized self-help are carefully played out. The acute awareness of the unique but limited nature of this space establishes its own meaning as well as that of the bulk of the surrounding space of Natzerat Illit.

Al-Kūrūm ('The Orchards') is the Arabic name of the all-Palestinian residential area on the steep slope at the extreme northwestern corner of Natzerat Illit (see map 2). It is the fourth spatial subzone.

Some Palestinians refer to Al-Kūrūm by its official Hebrew name, *Hakramim* (Hebrew for orchards or vineyards). The area includes parts that at some point had been cultivated by Palestinians from the neighboring village of Raina. Al-Kūrūm, in fact, is an abbreviation for Kūrūm Raina (the orchards of Raina).

Al-Kūrūm was not included in the municipal territory of Natzerat Illit when the town was first established in the 1950s; it was not included in the town's perimeter until the 1970s, when the municipal boundary of Natzerat Illit was finally determined.[16] Unlike the procedure in the 1950s, when virtually all land annexed to the town was expropriated from its Palestinian owners to become state-owned, this time there were no expropriations, with land remaining the property of its original Palestinian owners. The slope thus became the only part of Natzerat Illit where land is privately owned.[17]

The incorporation of the slope into the municipal boundary brought a change in land use status from rural to urban. The immediate implication was that building permits, normally refused for plots designated as agricultural land, were now available. A new prospect for development surfaced, and a wave of trade in and construction on the land quickly followed. Some Palestinian owners built homes and moved to Al-Kūrūm. Others sold land to friends and relatives, who put the plots to similar use. A hill virtually empty until the 1970s was transformed and has approximately 250 families now living in it or in parts immediately adjacent to it. Many occupy attractive private homes.

The spontaneous emergence of a new Palestinian suburb within a carefully planned and centrally controlled town took the all-Israeli local leadership by surprise. The municipal officeholders were not particularly enthusiastic about investing effort and resources in infrastructure and municipal services for the newly formed, unsupervised, exclusively Palestinian residential area.

Al-Kūrūm whose residency represents approximately a third of the Palestinian population of Natzerat Illit, became a significant, well bounded Palestinian space and one of the most cohesive residential groups in the entire town. Its success and desirability triggered more expansion, with Palestinian families buying houses in an older, all-Israeli suburb of Natzerat Illit that borders the area to the south. This enlarged the territorial continuum of Palestinian presence and ownership.

The key concept used by the more prosperous, suburban residents of Al-Kūrūm to refer to those Palestinians living in the mixed parts of Natzerat Illit is the in–out metaphor. Those of the mixed areas are described as living *dakhil,* Arabic for inside. This use of *dakhil* is not unique to Natzerat Illit. Significantly, it is used by West Bank Palestinians to refer to Israel proper (within the 1967 borders), and in particular to the Palestinian citizens of Israel, labeled *Arab al-dakhil*—those of the inside.[18]

Curiously, the in–out metaphor is present also in Israeli military jargon, where *khadira* (penetration), *knissa lashetakh* (entrance to an operational zone), and related phrases denote presence and action beyond enemy lines. In all three examples, the other's territory, linked to insecurity and discomfort, is described as 'within'; the speakers, in contrast, see themselves on safer ground, outside that territory or on its margin.

Residents of Al-Kūrūm, then, see the main bulk of Natzerat Illit as space to which they—just like Nazarenes or neighboring villagers—are quite external. Their own neighborhood, it must be stressed, is formally within the jurisdiction of Natzerat Illit. But it is by no means space turned Israeli by virtue of state or municipal jurisdiction. It is the territory 'inside' that is perceived as Israeli, leaving Al-Kūrūm in an ambiguous spatial limbo. It is marginal and discriminated against, but nonetheless safer.

This surfaced in January 1989, when the activists of the exclusively Palestinian Independent List considered hiring a place to house their headquarters for the approaching local government election. A basement flat in Al-Kūrūm, was considered. Its location, at the bottom of a steep and slippery slope, was not ideal. Most activists lived in the mixed neighborhoods 'inside,' some distance away, and had no private cars. There is no bus service to Al-Kūrūm, and street lighting is poor and restricted. Work sessions that winter were inevitably going to take place at night, after people had returned from work. These drawbacks notwithstanding, the basement flat was hired anyway. Pragmatic considerations such as access and convenience obviously came second to operating from a place within a space perceived as safe.

External ity is not the only idiom that establishes Al-Kūrūm as Palestinian space. The other is infrastructural discrimination, visually manifested in environmental neglect. Water supply, the sewage system, the presence and maintenance of roads, street lights, nursery schools, and other municipal amenities are all wanting in Al-Kūrūm. Israelis as well as Palestinians in Israel are all aware of the distinction between the landscape of Palestinian communities and that of Israeli settlements. Inequalities in central government budgeting, variations in tax collection, differences in budgetary priorities, and Palestinians' more limited access to the planning process result in public space in Palestinian communities in Israel (villages as well as towns) being considerably less attended to than that of Israeli settlements of similar size. In fact, the disparity goes well beyond the built-up residential areas and covers industrial parks, public amenities, and regional roads. A Palestinian friend once pointed at the poor road we were using on our way to his remote village in Galilee, and exclaimed: "This is an Arab road. Comparing it to that smooth, safe road leading to the new cluster of Jewish settlements over there is like comparing these rugged mountains to Florida."

Not surprisingly, the issue of municipal services and environmental neglect became a major point of friction between the residents of Al-Kūrūm and the residents of the municipal council of Natzerat Illit. The council's explanation for the indisputable disparity between the neighborhood and virtually every other residential area in the town is always linked to the difficult topography, the dispersed nature of development, the low number of households per unit area (which pushes per capita costs higher), and the rapid and unplanned development of the area. The residents, predictably, perceive these explanations as mere excuses, and see the real reason as discrimination against them as Palestinians. This gradually revealed the highly political nature of the problem, and was one of the factors that pushed the Palestinian residents of Al-Kūrūm to seek independent representation on the town's council.

The fifth and final spatial subzone is the interior of buses on the local public transport service of Natzerat Illit.

In the 1920s the British administration granted the 'Afifi family from the village of Safūrya[19] a franchise for public transport in northern Palestine. The franchise included destinations such as Haifa, Damascus, and Jenin, as well as Nazareth and its rural hinterland. One peripheral service the 'Afifis operated connected Nazareth with Ain Mahil, a village situated 8 kilometers east of the town (see map 1). As it happens, the old road from Nazareth to Ain Mahil runs along the ridge where the first residential areas of Natzerat Illit were built in the late 1950s. The new town thus found itself within an area included in a public transport franchise owned by Palestinians.

Pre-state Zionism, with its preoccupation with movement of people over land, placed great emphasis on public transport. Threats to buses, taxies, and lorries were invariably interpreted as anti-Jewish brigandry fueled by indiscriminate hatred of Jews and backed by Palestinian and pan-Arab nationalism.[20]

Later, with the advent of Zionist settlement, the capability of providing transport to and from outlying posts became three-pronged: a logistic necessity, a means of asserting territorial presence, and an issue involving national pride. After the establishment of Israel in 1948, private and cooperative bus companies in various parts of Israel were expected to dissolve and surrender their franchises to the new nationwide bus cooperative Egged. The cooperative, which enjoys a monopoly in subsidized public transport, gradually became identified with Israeli hegemony over space in all parts of the newly founded state, and grew into a recognized and popular part of Israeli national sentiment. Egged's mission, after all, involved the periphery, hardship, and adventure, a pioneering spirit, an ongoing contact with the Palestinian frontier. It is collectively owned by a virtually exclusively Jewish membership, has a *Tiyulim* department for educational exploration tours of hidden sites and landscapes of the newly discovered homeland, and has contributed logistic assistance to all of Israel's armed conflicts to date.

Most pre-1948 regional franchise holders were Jews, who viewed the merger with Egged as their national duty. The 'Afifis, not surprisingly, failed to share this sentiment and the family simply went on supplying its old services in the rural hinterland of Galilee. With few Israeli settlements around, Egged was understandably unperturbed by the competition. Only later, after the establishment of Natzerat Illit, did the question of the lucrative Nazareth–Haifa line and the issue of urban public transportation in newly formed Natzerat Illit present themselves. Tension began to build.

A history of the legal battle that involved 'Afifi, Egged, the municipality of Natzerat Illit, and the Ministry of Transport is beyond the scope of this chapter. The outcome, however, is relevant: the supreme court, acting as a high court of appeals, upheld 'Afifi's rights as granted to him by the old franchise. The franchise was recognized as including the right to operate bus routes over the entire Nazareth region, including the hills where Natzerat Illit is now situated. As a result of this ruling, the Nazareth Bus Company (herewith NBC), of which the 'Afifi family is chief owner, now operates Natzerat Illit's internal services as an integral part of its Nazareth-based metropolitan network. Additionally, while all intercity lines between Natzerat Illit and the rest of Israel are operated by Egged, the cooperative was forced by the supreme court to share the Haifa line, the most frequent and lucrative intercity line serving Natzerat Illit, with G. B. Tours—another company partly owned by the 'Afifis. Egged and G. B. Tours thus share the Haifa line, supplying buses alternately.

NBC buses are the only means of public transport in Natzerat Illit, as well as between Natzerat Illit and Nazareth. All six internal routes serving the various parts of Natzerat Illit either begin or end their journey in downtown Nazareth. Each journey thus has at least one crossing from Nazareth to Natzerat Illit.[21] But while passengers always include Palestinians as well as Israelis, incidents and tensions on board the buses are few and far between. I witnessed none nor heard of any during my eighteen months of fieldwork.

The social space of the buses themselves is clearly Palestinian. Israeli residents refer to the vehicles, as well as to the service generally, as 'the Arab bus' (*ha'otoboos ha'aravi*). The drivers, who are in charge of fares and ticketing, are all Palestinians. As passengers climb in, drivers select either Arabic or Hebrew for the fee-and-change transaction and seldom err. They know many of their Palestinian passengers personally. Those they do not know are nevertheless treated quite amicably, in a manner suitable to relative age and gender.

This is not the case with Israeli passengers, whom drivers hardly seem to acknowledge. Although fairly fluent in Hebrew, drivers tend to be reserved when dealing with a Hebrew speaker. The treatment is cordial, by no means affable. The radio is normally tuned to a station broadcasting in Arabic, usually the Israeli Broadcasting Authority's (IBA) Arab program. Most Israelis are unaware of the differences between IBA's Arab program—often described by Palestinian citizens of Israel as a clumsy apparatus of state propaganda—and stations broadcasting from Syria, Lebanon, or Cyprus. For Israelis, the language seems to be be the crucial point: *radio bearavit* (radio in Arabic) is the generic expression, often used in a derogatory tone.

Palestinian children, generally restrained in the presence of adults, tend to be uncharacteristically boisterous while on NBC buses, especially on return journeys from school in Nazareth in the early afternoon. They radiate a sense of personal and collective security, probably based on the assumption that the danger of public reprimand in the presence of Israeli passengers is slim. Israeli children, on the other hand, tend to be less clamorous than usual when traveling on NBC buses, radiating a certain vulnerability.

But the establishment of NBC bus space as Palestinian becomes apparent most vividly through the idiom of hospitality. I became aware of this following three chance meetings I had with Palestinian acquaintances on board NBC buses. Two of the three were men my age or younger, the third, was a married woman ten years older than me. There was nothing in either of our respective relationships that might imply any social obligations on their parts toward me. We had met before a number of times, and now found ourselves at the same bus stop, waiting for the bus. Significantly, however, on all three occasions, as soon as we got on the bus my Palestinian companions insisted on paying my fare. Moreover, on all three occasions the deals were clinched without consulting me. They came following hushed, staccato dialogues with the driver, which I could hardly hear or follow above the roar of the seasoned engine. This was telling, and in line with another tendency they displayed, namely, to see to the successful completion of my journey. They all made sure I knew the route and had a clear idea of where I had to alight.

My Palestinian friends clearly felt I was their guest aboard the Palestinian-looking, Palestinian-owned, and Palestinian-driven buses. They were quite obviously in the prescribed role of hosts, with the driver in the role of minor member of the household, running errands to ensure the ritual went smoothly.

CONCLUSION

For Palestinians, formal municipal boundaries are evidently less meaningful than cultural constructs, symbols, and metaphors of space. NBC buses and Al-Kūrūm, clearly regarded as 'Palestinian' through the metaphors of hospitality and externality, are clearly set apart from the three remaining sub-zones of Natzerat Illit. In fact, they appear to be construed as extensions of adjacent Palestinian Nazareth.

Palestinians, who construe the main bulk of Natzerat Illit as primarily Israeli, associate it with a number of cognitive and behaviorial limitations. The mixed parts of town are, as far as Palestinians are concerned, generally safe for individuals, but perilous for all assertions of Palestinian collectivity. They are inherently discontinuous, and more or less penetrable as the case may be. As spheres of social action they engender some aspects of 'Arabness' as legitimate: the family, child care, home recreation, consumerism. Purely or predominantly Palestinian islands within this bulk legitimize an expanded but not unlimited gallery of assertions such as meaningful activities in residents' committees and explicit, often visible interfamilial ties.

The in–out boundary between Al-Kūrūm and the rest of Natzerat Illit emerges as both subjective and conjunctural. It is, I argue, inextricably linked to the overall stance of Israel's Palestinian citizens vis-à-vis the state and its exclusive, virtually impenetrable Israeli core. If, as Smith (1981) persuasively argues, actors perceive the development of terrestrial space to represent the changes that 'the people' undergo, then the in–out idiom is a clear sign of the place the Palestinian citizens of Israel assign to themselves, or are resigned to: marginal outsiders, living on the fringes of a well-defined core.

Al-Kūrūm is conceptualized by Palestinians as a visual symbol of the gap between the nominal equality and the actual discrimination they experience as Israeli citizens. Their endless negotiation with the municipality over development, amenities, and basic services becomes a repetitive reenactment of their basic argument in local politics: that by paying taxes—fulfilling their civic duties—citizens should be entitled to the same amenities and services as all others, regardless of affiliation. The Palestinians perceive this neglect of public spaces and facilities as a standing testimony to the failure of the authorities to stand up to their own implicit duties and commitments. The clear physical boundary between tended and deserted public space thus becomes the confines of civil equality.

Israeli actors, looking outward from the core, see residential exclusivity and the redeeming modernizing impact of Zionism as simply engendering a demarcation between two types of territory. Palestinians, watching from the fringes, see the differences in terms of deprivation and inequality. Environmental neglect thus becomes a natural continuation of the initial injustice— the transfer of land from Palestinian to Israeli ownership. This, I argue, is the paradigmatic Palestinian view of the frontier in Israel.

The insistence of Palestinians on playing hosts on board NBC buses is telling. Palestinians, in Natzerat Illit as elsewhere, are enthusiastic hosts. The role is invested with pride, honor, and a sense of power over the recipient. But while hospitality in the private domain is similar whatever the territory, its application to an essentially public social space is intriguing.[22]

Here again, the conduct displayed by Palestinians in the Palestinian-within-Israeli territory echoes the phenomenon of Palestinian pride and hospitality toward Israelis visiting their communities in Israel at large. Political differences and latent resentments are put aside on such occasions, and the etiquette of hospitality comes to the fore. Rather than a social norm dictated by mere custom, hospitality is performed and displayed as a sign of strength, a mental note of dominance and ownership. In a political context whereby ownership and spacial dominance are inherently disputed, hospitality and its rites become a last defense in the subtle battle for security of the national realm, a means by which to tackle the paradox of being a displaced host in one's own homeland.

ACKNOWLEDGMENTS

This chapter is based on fieldwork conducted in Natzerat Illit in 1988–89 as part of a Ph.D. program at Cambridge University. I am indebted to the

Merchant Taylor Fund (Pembroke College), The William Wyse Fund (Trinity College), The Avi Hayishuv Fellowship, and to two anonymous benefactors for financial assistance that made the completion of the project possible. I have benefited from the time and insight of Ernest Gellner, Paul Sant Cassia, Declan Quigley, Eyal Ben-Ari, Yoram Bilu, and the writing seminar at the Department of Social Anthropology (1989–90), to all of whom I am indebted.

NOTES

1. Liebman and Don-Yehiya (1983:3–4) and Shokeid (1988) indicate the symbolic importance of rurality and agriculture for Zionism.

2. The Palestinian citizens of Israel—approximately 785,000, excluding residents of East Jerusalem (figures issued by Israel's Central Bureau of Statistics, May 1992)—are often referred to as Israeli Arabs, Israel's Arabs, or the Arab citizens of Israel. Elsewhere (Haaretz 10.5.1992) I specify the reasons why I believe 'Palestinian citizens of Israel' is a more appropriate label.

3. Palestinism is used herewith as shorthand for the Palestinian national movement. Derived from Palestine, the western version of the Arabic *Falastin,* it essentially denotes the popular contemporary movement whose aim is to establish a state for Palestinians on an unspecified part of the land it labels Palestine. In this respect it is analgous to Zionisn—the Jewish national movement that aimed to create, and now aims to maintain, a state for Jews on the very same territory, which it calls Zion (after the biblical *Tsiyon*).

4. My spelling and pronunciation of the town's name, 'Natzerat Illit,' is a transliteration of its official Hebrew name. *Natzerat* is the official Hebrew appellation of the neighboring old Palestinian town *E-Nasera,* known in English as Nazareth; *Illit* is 'upper.' It should be noted, however, that Israeli maps, signposts, and documents in English carry the town's name in a variety of forms, including *Upper Nazareth, Nazareth Illit,* and *Natzeret Illit.* Writers in English use various forms, too, most frequent of which is *Upper Nazareth*—a term hardly ever uttered in daily use.

The Israeli residents of Natzerat Illit are horrified whenever they encounter the erroneous suggestion that their town and adjacent Nazareth are one and the same. Curiously, however, many of them refer to their town as simply *Natzeret,* the folk term most often used by Israelis for old Nazareth. In recent years they tend to use *Natzeret Illit* more often.

The Palestinian inhabitants of the area, including those residing in Natzerat Illit, use other appellations for the town. One most frequently used is Al-Shikūn—'the housing estate.' *Nassera el 'Ulya*—'Upper Nazareth'—is also used sometimes, as is *Natzeret Illit.*

5. The Israeli Communist Party (*Maki*) had various fronts and coalitions over the years, including the New Communist List *Rakah* and, since the 1980s, the Democratic List for Peace and Equality (DFP), known in Arabic as the *Jabha* (front).

6. Labor has controlled municipal institutions and gained best results in the Parliamentary elections ever since the town was established. The margin in favor of Labor has been reduced since the ascent of right-wing Likud to central power in 1977. My impressionistic assessment, however, is that Labor supporters in Natzerat Illit tend to align themselves with the right wing of the party, whose stand vis-à-vis the Palestinians is similar to that of Likud.

7. This is the case to date. The second half of 1990 saw the arrival in Natzerat Illit of approximately ten-thousand Jewish immigrants from the Soviet Union, which brought about a 40 percent increase in the number of Israeli residents.

8. 71.8 percent of the Palestinian adults who lived in Natzerat Illit in 1989 were natives of Nazareth (170 out of 237 valid cases in my survey of 247 Palestinian households in the town in early 1989).

9. The section in my survey of 1989 regarding ownership of residence reflected 75.7 percent owner-occupation, 20.6 percent rentals, and 1.6 percent key-money lease arrangements (242 valid cases).

10. Shipler (1987:281) quotes a statement by a Palestinian woman from Natzerat Illit that emphasizes the link between Palestinian presence in the town and the history of land expropriation. I have run across a similar view on one or two occasions. Such statements, however, are few and far between and do not represent a common awareness among the Palestinian residents.

11. The new political body was officially named 'The List for Peace and Co-existence,' and is herewith referred to as the Independent List. Unofficially associated with the Communist Party, in 1989 the Independent List succeeded in recruiting approximately 65 percent of the local Palestinian vote. The leader of the List became the first Palestinian ever to be elected to the municipal council.

12. An exception within the community center's complex is the swimming pool, where a number of Palestinian early morning swimmers, most of them residents of Nazareth, were regulars in 1988 and 1989.

13. Each of the two areas do in fact have about half a dozen Palestinian families as residents. Most Natzerat Illit Israelis, including residents of the areas in question, seem to be unaware of this, and the general understanding in the town is that the two neighborhoods are still exclusively Jewish.

14. Operating under the law of communal property, these voluntary committees, which manage the joint estate, are in effect the only formal manifestation of the residential compound. Palestinians I knew who participated in such meetings and decisions tended to play as minor a role as they possibly

could—a level of performance that seemed to suit their Israeli neighbors' expectations.

15. The 1988 voters' roll (State of Israel 1988b) indicates that only thirty-five Palestinian families in Natzerat Illit had more than twenty-five listed voters. Out of the thirty-five, only thirteen families had the majority of members living in residential clusters—all of which were located in Kūrūm Raina. No such cluster was to be found in the mixed residential quarters. See also Bar-Gal 1986:58–60.

16. Municipal boundaries in Israel are determined by the Boundaries Committee (*Vaadat Gevulot*) of the Ministry of the Interior in Jerusalem. The initiative to incorporate the northern slope into the municipal jurisdiction of Natzerat Illit in the 1970s was part of a wider move aimed at creating a buffer zone between the residential area of Natzerat Illit and the Palestinian communities bordering the town. The buffer zone was designed to allow future expansion of Natzerat Illit, as well as to arrest potential encroachment of spontaneous Palestinian development from without which, it was feared, could merge the outskirts of the town with those of neighboring Raina, Nazareth, and Àin Mahil. The move created territorial disputes with Palestinian local authorities and private owners, particularly with Àin Mahil to the northeast. The tension reemerged in late 1990 when part of the disputed area, earmarked by Natzerat Illit's municipal planners for housing for newly arrived Jewish immigrants from the Soviet Union, was being prepared for development.

17. Rights in most of the municipal territory of Natzerat Illit (as in more than 90 percent of Israel's landmass) are vested in the Israel Land Administration, an institution that operates as caretaker on behalf of the (international) Jewish National Fund. For operational purposes the Israel Land Administration is affiliated with the Ministry of Agriculture.

18. An alternative appellation is *Arab Tamanye Waarba'in,* the Arabs of forty-eight, meaning those who came under Israeli rule following the 1948 hostilities and the establishment of the State of Israel.

The use of *Arab* instead of *Falastiniyun* (Palestinians) is intriguing. It may reflect the dubious status, in the eyes of Palestinians outside Israel, of the Palestinian citizens of Israel, often regarded in the Arab world as having lost authenticity and moral standing through their ongoing, and seemingly successful, liaison with Israel and Israelis. Alternatively, it could signify an all-encompassing Arab unity against Israel. The Arab world is divided in two—all Arabs who live outside Israel, and those who live inside. A third option is to look at *Arab* in its less politicized context, meaning simply 'people,' sometimes restricted to a residential group (cf. Abu Lughod 1986).

19. The village, some 8 kilometers west of Nazareth, was demolished by the IDF in 1948. Many of its inhabitants initially fled to Lebanon, their land

consequently seized by the state and allocated to a new *Moshav,* Tsipory, in the vicinity. A considerable proportion of ex-Safūriates and their descendants now live in Nazareth, in a part of town called Safūrya.

20. In retrospect, at least some of these assaults could probably be better analyzed as attempts by local Palestinians to protect their rights in conveyance.

21. Since none of the bus lines serve Al-Kūrūm, the issue of crossing over from 'Israeli' to 'Palestinian' turf within Natzerat Illit does not really arise.

22. The conduct on board NBC buses was matched, incidentally, by the conduct of Palestinian acquaintances I sometimes chanced to meet in the streets of Nazareth. There too—but never in the public domain in Natzerat Illit—the rituals of hospitality were automatically invoked, appropriately modified to the makeshift situation of a conversation on the main street of a small town.

REFERENCES

Abu Lughod, Lila 1986 *Veiled Sentiments* Berkeley: University of California Press.

Anderson, Benedict. 1983. *Imagined Communities: Reflections on the Origins and Spread of Nationalism.* London: Verso.

Anzaldua, Gloria. 1987. *Borderlands/La Frontera: The New Mestiza.* San Francisco: Spinsters/Aunt Lute.

Bar-Gal, Yoram. 1986. Penetration and colonization of Arabs in Natzerat Illit—early evidence. In *Residential and Internal Migration Patterns among the Arabs of Israel,* A. Sofer, ed. Haifa: University of Haifa.

Bisharat, George. 1992. Transformation in the political role and social identity of Palestinian refugees in the West Bank. In *Culture, Power, Place: Explorations in Critical Anthropology,* Roger Rouse, James Ferguson, and Akhil Gupta, eds. Boulder, Colo.: Westview.

Dominguez, Virginia. 1989. *People as Subject, People as Object.* Madison: University of Wisconsin Press.

Doron, Yochanan. 1987. *Geographical Aspects of the Relations between Nazareth and Natzerat Illit.* M.A. thesis, University of Haifa.

Garbuz, Y. 1973. Natzerat Illit—socio-economic development. *Shikun Uvniya* 38. (Hebrew)

Ghosh, Amitav. 1989. *The Shadow Lines.* New York: Viking.

Gupta, Akhil, and James Ferguson. 1992. Beyond 'culture': space, identity, and the politics of difference. *Cultural Anthropology* 7(1):6–23.

Jackson, John B. 1984. *Discovering the Vernacular Landscape.* New Haven: Yale University Press.

Kimmerling, Baruch. 1977. Sovereignty, ownership and 'presence' in the Jewish-Arab territorial conflict. The case of Ikrit and Bir'im. *Comparative Political Studies* 10(2).

———. 1983. *Zionism and Territory*. Berkeley: Institute of International Studies.

Liebman, Charles, and E. Don-Yehiya. *Civil Religion in Israel: Traditional Judaism and Political Culture in the Jewish State*. Berkeley: University of California Press.

Malkki, Lisa. 1992. National geographic: the rooting of peoples and the territorialization of national identity among scholars and refugees. *Cultural Anthropology* 7(1):24–44.

Morris, Benny. 1987. *The Birth of the Palestinian Refugee Problem, 1947–1949*. Cambridge: Cambridge University Press.

Rabinowitz, Dan. 1992a. An acre is an acre is an acre? Differentiated attitudes to social space and territory on the Jewish-Arab frontier in Israel. *Urban Anthropology* 21(1):67–89.

———. 1992b. Trust and the attribution of rationality: inverted roles amongst Palestinian Arabs and Jews in Israel. *Man* 27, 3:517–537 (n.s.) 27(3).

———. 1997 *Overlooking Nazareth: the Ethnography of Exclusion in a mixed town in Galilee*. Cambridge: Cambridge University Press.

Rosaldo, Renato. 1987. Politics, patriarchs and laughter. *Cultural Critique* 6:65–86.

———. 1988. Ideology, place, and people without culture. *Cultural Anthropology* 3(1):77–87.

———. 1989. *Culture and Truth: The Remaking of Social Analysis*. Boston: Beacon.

Rosenfeld, Henry. 1988. Nazareth and Upper Nazareth in the political economy of Israel. In *Arab-Jewish Relations in Israel*, J. Hofman, ed. Bristol, Ind.: Wyndham Hall.

Shafir, Gershon. 1989. *Land, Labour, and the Israeli Palestinian Conflict, 1882–1920*. Cambridge: Cambridge University Press.

Shehada, Raja. 1982. *The Third Way*. Tel-Aviv: Adam. (Hebrew)

Shipler, David. 1987. *Arab and Jew*. New York: Penguin.

Shokeid, Moshe. 1988. *Children of Circumstances: Israeli Immigrants in New York*. Ithaca: Cornell University Press.

Smith, Anthony D. 1981. *The Ethnic Revival*. Cambridge: Cambridge University Press.

Spilerman, S., and J. Habib. 1976. Development towns in Israel: the role of community in creating ethnic disparities in labor force characteristics. *American Journal of Sociology* 81(4):781–812.

State of Israel. 1988a. *Statistical Abstract of Israel, 1988.* Jerusalem: Central Bureau of Statistics.

————. 1988b. *Voters' Roll, Natzerat Illit.* Jerusalem: Central Elections Committee (unpublished). (Hebrew)

————. 1990. *Statistical Abstract of Israel, 1990.* Jerusalem: Central Bureau of Statistics.

Suttles, G. S. 1972. *The Social Construction of Communities.* Chicago: University of Chicago Press.

————. 1984. The cumulative texture of local urban culture. *American Journal of Sociology* 90(2):283–304.

Weintraub, D., and V. Kraus. 1982. Spatial differentiation and place of residence: spatial dispersion and composition of population and stratification in Israel. *Megamot* 27(4):367:–81. (Hebrew)

Williams, C. H., and A. D. Smith. 1983. The national construction of social space. *Progress in Human Geography* 7:512–18.

Yitzhaki, Arie. 1982. Nazareth in the war of independence. *Kardom* 19:43–48. (Hebrew)

8

The Double Site of Israel

ZALI GUREVITCH

EDITORS' COMMENTS

This chapter by Zali Gurevitch is entitled "The Double Site of Is-
rael." Gurevitch takes off from a struggle over place—Hamakom.
Yet this is not a struggle between "us" Israelis and others, be they
Palestinians, Arabs, Europeans, or diaspora Jews. It is, rather, a
struggle within "us." Thus, in talking about Hamakom—the
place—he does not explore the significance of specific points in the
Land of Israel but examines the place as it figures in different ver-
sions of Jewish and Israeli identities. He shows that there is some-
thing that is not fixed, not final—perhaps never fixed or final—in
the definition of place in Jewish and Israeli conceptions. Gurevitch
has written a midrash, an interpretation. In the tradition of the
midrash, the study is a way of interrogating, of asking things of
place.

An anthropology written from one's own place is an attempt to approach
the place's blindness. The term 'blindness' signifies more than the inability
to see one's own back or background. It marks a sense of place that can be
felt but not apprehended from within. A perspective is needed in order to
shed light, to find the distance of a spectator, the zone from which a *theoria*
can be formed from and about the place.[1] Such a prescribed zone must be
both in and out of place, so the way to it might start from a distant point in
time where others have searched for an answer, but to a similar question and
in the same place.

The point of reference or beginning in the past is, again, neither fixed nor agreed upon. To determine which point is indeed the point of beginning is in itself a theory rather than pure recollection.[2] In the present chapter two beginnings are suggested as reference points to the theory of the place. One is fairly recent, going back to "the Zionist pioneers" who came to this place about a hundred years ago from the East European Jewish diasporic world. The other point of departure is the ancient story of the place written in the biblical text.

The connection between these two beginnings, three thousand years or more apart from each other, is that the ones who have come to the place at the turn of the twentieth century as to a new and virgin land, have had the full story of the place before ever having set foot in it. They were in their own eyes beginners of something that has already been. The actual events that made the place's recent history have been perceived, from the start, as steeped in a long-told story—a tradition of reading, telling, and praying. Though coming to a place called Palestine, the Jews were, in their own language, coming to a land that had nothing to do with Palestine. The place's name—Israel or Zion—resonates another place, a place that existed in the text, issuing its own *theoria* and attachment.

What I would like to bring out here is not a mere repetition of the story echoed in the name Israel, but to point out in the story what I believe is the sense of the Israeli place, which is introduced in the ancient text and repeated in the recent Zionist version. It is, succinctly, the irreducibility of the story to the place, and hence the unrest, the schism, perhaps, between the Israelis and their native place, namely Israel. That unrest is the blind spot which, though felt, still cries for theory, for understanding and judgment.

The path tracing back to the roots of this unrest, and to the puzzling gap between story and place, leads to the earliest version of the story upon which all other, later stories are based, as a continuation or critique. This is the mythical/historical story found in the first books of the Judaic text, the Bible. Focusing on that "primary" story does not necessarily mean it had a deterministic power of a "mental gene" that permeated the Judaic mind. Rather, my suggestion is that the power of the story lies in its readoption by the various Zionist movements. By readopting the story, the choice of Palestine as the site of the new Jewish settlement was a choice not only of rescue and revolution of the diasporic state, but a choice of return. The story meant returning to the land once called Canaan, or Judea, or Israel, and thus to the site of the biblical scene. The power of the story, then, is in its adoption, not in its inevitability, about which one can hardly say much.

In this chapter, a discussion of contemporary Israel and Judaic history, and of the general notion of place, will finally lead to a reading of the Bible as the book of the place. In that reading I will look for a point of beginning, which, as mentioned above, is simultaneously a recollection, a myth, and a theory. In the reading of the biblical text from a retrospective anthropologist's and modern Israeli view point, I will attempt to expose the Bible's own anthropology of the place, assuming that the text for its writers was also a kind of *theoria,* meant at one and the same time to create the blindness of the place and to shed light upon it.

EXILE AND LOCALITY

The gap between the story and the place is easily detected in a basic distinction between two concepts that are used in the Bible to define the people of Israel. One is mostly used in a derogatory sense, referring to the Jews who are assigned and confined to their place as the native gentiles are: *Am-Haaretz* (literally, the people of the land, natives). The concept implies a notion of distinction from the people of the land, who are always, and from the very beginning, others. That distinction is connected with a sense of distance based on the perspective of the book. Indeed, from a certain point in their self-realization on, Jews have defined their attachment to the land as founded on a second concept—*Am-Hasefer* (literally, the people of the book). These two sources—the land and the book that claims the supremacy and the authority over any notion of the land—form the double site of Jewish identity. The land that draws to its "nativity," to being-in-place on earth, is contrasted by the book, which calls beyond the land itself—to being-in-place in the Place—the abstract, uncanny law of a divinity that transcends the earthly realm of place.

The book is, then, received as the source and resource of the story. There are human voices in the book who come from the place and tell the place's story, utter words of wisdom, song, or prophesy. But there is in the book another voice, a voice that does speak in the book, commands, describes, questions and answers, takes part in a dialogue, but is figured as nonhuman—as the worldly embodiment of a divinity that assumes no visual or tactile image. The story of place told by human voices is "undervoiced" by this divine voice. Every story of the place is referred back to this voice that fills the book, and which occasions the very writing of it as is told in the book itself.

In this distinction within the book, between the human voices that tell the story and the divine voice that occasions the telling of the story and also takes part in that telling, lies the gap between the story and the place. If the choir of human voices is heard as coming from the place, and as resounding the place's manifold tongues, the divine voice is constrastingly and avowedly placeless. It never fully attaches itself to a place, not even to the place that it points out as the topos of its own story. The revelation of the voice (and it is clear that hearing the voice is possible only in a state of revelation) takes place mostly outside the land, in a zone unlocated and not inhabited, in a liminal space dividing and connecting between places but is itself placeless. The voice behind the voices of the story, the declared "source" of the story, comes from somewhere else. In this way, the identity of voice and place is constantly undermined and disjuncted. Consequently, no unity is achieved, and no harmonious centering of voice and place, and, therefore, of identity, can ever be brought into closure.

This restless, double-sited structure of the book of the place, which both places and is itself unplaced, is curiously reflected in the history of the Jewish people—in the wavering of the Jews between place and out of place. Jews have found themselves living repeatedly, and for the most part of their history, outside the land. In the diaspora the book (Bible, Talmud, and commentaries) has become the substitute for Jewish territory, while the promised land has retained a symbolic reality that preserved the actual places in which Jews led their lives for centuries as exiles.[3] Thus, this wavering between place and out of place is not only a history of exiles and returns caused by external forces, but is itself perceived by the Jewish story as a story of contradiction and tension between land and book.

The most recent return from exile and the development of Israeli identity has evoked the wish to end once and for all the exilic state of the Jews and to go native—to return to a primary state of unity between the land and the people, the land and the story of the land. The return to the land was bound to bring Judaism to a reaccomplishment of itself—to reunify book, people, and place.

This unity, however, is not achieved in a simple, harmonious way. With Zionism the old paradox of the place came to life, newly embodied in the Zionist act—calling to rebuke the book that is "Jewish" for the land, yet through this very return to the land to enact the voice of the book. The immigrants who came in the first decades of the century idealized the return to the land as soil, and idolized the pioneers who till the soil with their bare hands. But the passage to secularism through the connection of body and soil also proved to be tricky. Abraham Shlonsky, a Zionist immigrant from Russia, describes this in these words: "We ran away from the excess of one sacredness . . . only to find an excess of another sacredness."[4] The work in the field that was meant as an escape from the book became itself a type of religious accomplishment. The revolution found itself in the same old conceptual world.

The effort to shake off Judaism, and with it the diasporic notions inherent in Zionism in order to become mere locals, has not been realized in the straightforward manner hoped for. The Judaic notion of the place, coupled with the massive presence of Jewish communities all over the world outside Israel, and of religious Jewry declaring itself in various ways non-Israeli within Israel, have all worked against such notions of nativity.

Zionism has not discarded the book but rather tried to base its ideology and culture on a secular and "native" reading of selected parts of it. But by refraining from discarding the book as an alternative source of identity, and with it the Jewish nucleus of the Israeli, the book crops up with the voices of Jews who have been natives of the book, many of whom (who even live in Israel today) still regard the book as their most natural home. *Am-Hasefer* has not forsaken the belief that it can be displaced again, and can keep itself intact as a people outside its native land. *Galut* (diaspora) remains a viable counterpart of Jewish life side by side with Israel.

If *galut* is one deep fear of the Israelis, mere locality (nativity) is another—even if it seems like the ultimate resolution of *galut*. If nativity is fulfilled, it may imply the betrayal of that which has conceived and made meaningful the whole idea of that nativity, the idea of "Israel." As Baruch Kurzweil, an eminent critic of Israeli society phrased it: "Zionism is startled by the real-ization of its own dream."[5] The Israeli discourse of identity is thus inherently connected to the dilemma of place. The ambivalence toward the place, the unresolved core of what it means to be an Israeli, is tied with the Judaic sources of that identity, and to the paradoxical seesaw of the place that is found in the "articles of establishment" of the place—the biblical text.[6]

The tension toward the place within the Israeli "covenant" has its bearing on the Israeli-Palestinian conflict, which centers on the place. The counter-claims of the parties over the territory are based on very different concep-tions of what this place is all about. Behind the politics there is an anthropological or theological perception that is important to understand. From the Israeli perspective, there is a curious repetition in present reality of an ancient theme of settling and conquering the land in which other people—non-Israelite natives such a Philistines, Jebusites, and Canaanites—lived. I would not go so far as to suggest a parallel between now and then, and be-tween Palestinians and Jebusites, but for the Israelis the analogies do exist. To the extent that the Israelis see themselves as the offspring of the Israelites, the local indigenous people (the Palestinians are called "the locals" by Is-raelis) are conceived of as the "others" from the point of view of the book, while the Israelis/Jews are perceived by the Palestinians as "others" from the point of view of natives of the place.

It should also be clear that the place is a site of contradiction not because of the Canaanites or Palestinians. Even when the Israeli-Palestinian problem will be solved by, let us say, dividing the land into two separate "places," the problematic of the Israeli place with itself will remain. The place stands not only between Israelis and their Arab neighbors, but also between Israelis and themselves.

FROM THE PLACE'S MOUTH

Before entering the biblical text I would like to examine place in its "native" version and its relation with voice. I should like to make it clear that although the native's story of place is founded on perspective and distance, a crucial difference exists between the native's story and the Judaic story of place that subverts the settled idea of nativity.

The voice of the native is the multiple voice of the place. The place speaks and sings itself through the mouth(s) of the native. Charles Olson, who is a poet of place (Gloucester, the polis), describes this in his concept of "Muthology." Muthology indicates that logos is "simply words in mouth." It is the combination of muthos (mouth) and logos. The logos of the place is uttered from its mouth, the mouth of (in his example, Herodotus the Logographer) "he who can tell the story right." The mouth that utters the place, that can tell the right story of the place, must be of the place. Only the native is the right storyteller.[7]

The notion of the native as the one who dwells within a told place makes nativity a complex issue, since storytelling in itself needs perspective, distance, and imagination. Walter Benjamin's storyteller is, indeed, the one who comes from afar in space and in time to tell what is very near. The storyteller is a native who comes back to the circle.[8] From Benjamin we learn that the native is confined to his circle not necessarily in that he never leaves, but in that he must return in order to tell the story. The place is ground and background, the first horizon(s), which delineate what horizon is. As voice (story), it is the blindness of a mother tongue. The ear is there much earlier than the mouth. The mouth listens—drinks directly from the mouth. One hears the place speak.

This hearing is founded on the experience of being open as a child to the seeds and rains of the place. The voices that enter the native's ear of the mind form his own distinct voice, which is more than the Chomskyian native capability to speak a language right. The ability to utter a voice at all is tantamount to the ability to tell the story. Mother tongue is but one generic name for the sundry and diverse voices that enter each individual voice, and which makes this individual voice a native-voice, "our voice." Nativity is thus founded on the identification of voice (self) and place (world). It is being-in-place as dwelling—the self and the world cosmologized in the place.

In contemporary anthropology the notion of the native as being one with history and tradition is seen as a distortion of the actuality of people's lives even in what seem like native places.[9] The concept of native and place as representing the blindfoldedness of self-identity is thus reexamined. The unreflective mode of existence is unaccepted, and the assumption that people are one with their places and worlds is challenged. It is argued that all people have a degree of freedom granted by distance and reflexivity. The revised concepts introduce diversity in natives' life-worlds, the poliphony of their voices, and their ability to regard their places from external perspectives.

This critique echoes a fundamental problematic in contemporary sense of place. The highlighting of the free, reflexive, and self-distant spirit of the metropolitan Westerner gives prominence to those features of experience where we shall find otherness rather than oneness. We (late moderns) wish to do away with our incarcerating nativity, and to liberate our thought from anything that seems "given"—a given world, a given language, fixed horizon. Place as given seems more a limitation than a source of growth and expansion. We are always to an extent out of place, both free from and deprived of self-confinement. To quote Derrida (in a recent interview): "I have attempted more and more systematically to find a non-site (non-lieu), or a non-philosophical site, from which to question philosophy . . . so that it can interrogate and reflect upon itself in an original manner. . . . Such a non-site would be irreducible to philosophy.[10] The analogous question concerning place would be to find a non-place that is irreducible to place wherefrom to interrogate place.

The Non-Place stated by contemporary thinkers is not the chaotic non-place—a desert, a black forest, or an endless ocean—that borders on cosmos from outside. It is thought itself, located as it is in the reflexivity of thought, which refuses to anchor itself in anything but itself, in the non-site of thinking.

In this spirit of inquiry the Jewish concept of nativity can be studied as a corpus of ancient/modern anthropological thought that defies the "natural" notion of nativity by apprehending its own place as essentially other. Yet the Judaic notion of place highlights more than the distance necessary for critical thinking, for *theoria,* or for storytelling. The concept of place in the biblical text divides between two sites, that of the voice (and the book that is built about it) and that of the land. That is why the divide is at the foreground of the story, not merely in the condition of its making.

From circa 1000 B.C. to this day, the Jews see themselves as a unique type of natives, who dissociate themselves from ordinary and neighboring notions of nativity. Their book that pointed to the land, repeatedly pointed beyond the land, to itself as to a voice that comes from no-where, from non-place, and itself never settles. The voice in the Bible is irreducible to "our voice" in the native sense (which includes, obviously, the voices of gods of the place). As the following few exemplary moments in the biblical story reveal, the voice of the book, a voice that makes the book a book, is the voice of an Other, who is symbolically encountered out of place, and who resists and defies the very possibility of placement.

THE VOICE OUT OF PLACE

The place, the locus, the topos of the story is a stretch of land where now modern Israel is inhabited—on the eastern shore of the Mediterranean, south of Lebanon, west of the Jordan River, north of the Sinai desert.

The story of the place is portrayed in most of the book of Genesis, in Exodus, and in other books of the biblical anthology. These texts form together the book of the place. Directly or indirectly they unfold the landscape, the history, the heroes, the blessings and curses of the place. The story remains always earthly—the men and the women are regular people, and their place is basically like any other place. Yet the mundane is told as part of a larger framework. The story of the place and the people is played down by the story of the voice.

This general feature can be clearly discerned through the movement of the people toward and away from the place. The ordinary desires associated with people's coming and going are the search for food, for power, for freedom, for a better place to dwell, or for a golden fleece. Yet the structure of the biblical story is serial, suggesting that the circumstantial movement is prefigured as an idea—arrival signifies promise, and departure signifies that place is forever temporary. Departure (immigration, exile) is crucial here, since it reopens the mind to a new arrival, a re-vision of what is closed in upon itself by "dwelling securely in their land."

Over and against the place stands the viable possibility of the world-Aram Naharaim, Goshen (Egypt), Babylon, Europe, New York. Between the place and the world lies the non-place, the desert, wherefrom the voice comes and where the book is given. Three elements thus take part in the myth: the land (the place), the diaspora (another place, or the world), and the desert (the non-place). The world always precedes the place in the earthly (human) level, and the voice (coming from non-place) precedes it in the spiritual realm. The place as the site of nativity is inevitably breached.

The serial movement that opens in the story of Abraham who arrives with his household to an Other land ends up elsewhere—in Egypt, where Jacob and his sons are given a place (Goshen) to dwell (note that the last words of the book of Genesis that tells the story of Canaan are "in Egypt"). There they stay in a state of somnolent detachment for four hundred years until Moses is born and goads them into awakening. But Moses himself never goes into the promised land. The entrance is not completed. An exit remains, and therefore another entrance, with a renewed state of promise.

Even when the land is conquered and settled, it is unsettled from within by prophetic threats of exile aimed at a people that prefers to steep itself in nativity. And again exile indeed occurred and then again a return to Zion from Babylon, and once more destruction and exile. The last eighty generations' long exile partly ended (and this is not anymore a part of the biblical text) a hundred years ago in the Zionist reestablishment of the place.

To go back, now in more detail, to the first irruption of this idea, we should open in Genesis 12, where Abram, on his way to Canaan in his usual wandering with his folk, is encountered by a voice that commands him to leave his place: "Get thee out . . . unto a land that I will shew thee." The land is not an Eldorado of some sort, but the same land he had anyway been on his way to (Genesis 11:31). The voice simply intervenes in the natural course of earthly wandering from place to place, and plucks it out of its ordinary meaning. To reach (and attain) his Place, Abraham must leave his place— "thy country, thy kindred, thy father's house." The notion of place is thereby radically altered. The wandering to Canaan in search of grazing land is transformed into wandering in search of faith. Faith requires a departure from everything that is conceived as natural. Place transforms its native sense to an idea, a place commanded by a voice.

To reinforce this conception, the text insists on the arbitrary choice of the land. The choice, in itself important, is never really explained. The land is not presented as superior to other lands of the earth. It is both a land of milk and honey and a land that eats up its inhabitants. And to Abram it is simply put as "A land that I will shew thee." The land is "given"—a fact, even when it is given as a present to Abraham and later his son and his grandson: "For all the land which thou seest, to thee will I give it, and to thy seed for ever" (Genesis 13:15). Though it is "ours" it remains but another land, and though given, it remains unowned, as later it is declared by the voice: "The land shall not be sold for ever: for the land is mine; for ye are strangers and soujourners with me" (Leviticus 25:23).

The second moment in which this dialectic is revealed is the episode told in Genesis 28, in which Jacob, the grandson of the first comer to the place, the third-generation native, is said to have "*struck* the place." Jacob lighted upon the place (as the word "struck" is translated in the King James Version) when he is on the way out of the place, on the way to the place wherefrom his grandfather came, to take a wife for himself. It gets dark and he decides to stay there for a night's sleep.

In this place, Luz, he puts a stone from "the stones of that place" under his head and in his dream sees "a ladder set up on the earth, and the top of it reached to heaven." The striking of the place is immediately connected with a revelation in which Jacob is promised the place: "The land whereon thou liest, to thee will I give it," as if this arbitrary place that he only lighted upon because the sun was set, and which he is going to depart from in the morning, becomes the very metonymy for the whole promised land. Indeed, in Hebrew, the word "struck" means more than "lighted upon." Jacob, when lighting upon the place, "struck the idea of" and "made contact with" place(ness).

Note that the revelation of the place takes place in the dream, that is, out of mundane reality of the place. The Midrashic interpretation at this point relates explicitly to this idea of out-of-placeness. Regarding the phrase, "He struck the place," Midrash Raba says: "Why is God called Place; because He is the place of the world and the world is not His place." At the very moment of striking the place, Jacob connects through the earthly place with the place that is wholly outside it, in the dream, in the idea, in the voice that gives the place from without.

It does not surprise us, then, that Jacob, who struck the idea of the place, eventually left the place altogether and went with his sons to Egypt, where the big mythic slumber of oblivion began. Truly, it is an initial, naive forgetfulness. The Egyptian exile is not charged with the later sense of exile as punishment for forgetting and denying God. Egypt functions as the world-womb for the growth and birth of the "people." The story brings the people to a new point of origin in the world outside. Only from there, according to the story, can Israel be reborn—not in the place, not as natives, but as strangers, as sojourners who strike the place. At the background of their renewed nativity resides a memory of strangeness. Aram in the north, Egypt in the south, and the desert in the south and east remain the origin-duplex of the myth. The duplicity of the origin denies the place the taken-for-grantedness that characterizes a native place.

The voice reawakens after four hundred years of slavery, of living as oppressed captives in a foreign land, and encounters Moses as it had encountered Abraham before, outside the place, this time in the desert. There Moses sees the burning bush and hears the words of the voice: "Put off thy shoes from off thy feet, for the place whereon thou standest is holy ground" (Exodus 3:5). The place called holy is an arbitrary unrecognized piece of land. Moses lighted upon that place in his wandering with the flock of Jethro, unaware of its holiness. The place of destiny (Canaan) is never called holy in all the Pentateuch. Holiness is reserved for non-place. In non-place the voice names the place.

Indeed, Moses, as the figure of the voice, is held back in non-place. He is never allowed to enter the place: "Yet thou shalt see the land before thee; but thou shalt not go thither unto the land which I give the children of Israel" (Deuteronomy 32:52). The voice must remain in the desert, and is never to be placed, to be embodied in the land as locality—country, kindred, father's house. The place is of the voice and not vice versa. Only the voice must remain holy, not the land. Thus, the voice that delivers the Israelites from slavery to bring them into the promised land, remains in the desert to keep the desert a living essence of the myth.

When standing at the gates of the place, Joshua takes the place of Moses. He enters the land with the book in his hands (as pointed out in the book of Joshua, chap. 1), and transforms the people of the book into the people of the land. But the book and the desert where the book had been given and the voice had been heard are not sublated by this transformation. The desert (see Jeremiah 2:2) is remembered not only as suffering and necessary pangs of collective birth, but as a glorious moment in the relations with God.

The celebration of "dwelling securely in the land" in religious/agricultural holidays symbolically reminds us of this counterpoint of place and non-place. For example, both Passover and Sukkot commemorate the desert and stress wandering rather than settlement. The ritual text of Passover tells the story of deliverance in which the leaving of Egypt and the crossing of the desert are clearly depicted as formative events in the birth of the people, not the land of Canaan. Sukkot is an agricultural rite (thus of the place), yet it commands the family to eat all meals and even reside for a week outside the permanent home in a temporary hut (*sukka*) with a roof made of branches freshly cut from trees to symbolize the possibility of leaving.

The hallmark of this ritual is nonpermanence. The permanent dwellers of the land are required to leave the permanence of their homes and sit in a *sukka* to return symbolically to life in the desert. In this way, in the midst of the tranquillity of nativity and the celebration of the yield of the (owned) land, the desert is commemorated and revived as an antithetical myth of the place. Dwellers of the land must come to grips again with their essential strangeness in the land. The necessity of place is thus counterpointed with a ritual of temporariness and of movement that highlights non-place and the freedom from captivity in place.

CONCLUDING REMARKS

The place can never be owned. There is a tear between the people and the land. In the first place, Abraham is torn from his nativity (Aram) to go the place; then his offspring are torn from their given place (Canaan) into exile (Egypt); and then as people they are torn from their "flesh pots," and in the place itself newly conquered and settled—the tear does not heal, since the very idea of the place defies healing—backgrounded nativity and merging in the place as mere locals is resisted. The book that tells the place's story and constructs the complex conception of "Israel" as a people and a place also resists the place as a totality that harmonizes the relation between humans and their immediate earthly abode. In Judaic thought, the place is human but its meaning is taken from the voice that is out of place and defies placeness. Therefore exile, though posited as punishment, does not entail the destruction of the people or the abandonment of the book.

Indeed, the Jews in the diaspora have found many ways to cope with the place without positing themselves against Judaic notion of place. They have even developed the theme of exile as a desired state. A modern example is Jewish philosopher Franz Rosenzweig: "Even in its land Israel was not a nation like other nations. The third exile could not be the end of the people of Israel, since from its inception the history of the Jews passes from one exile to another, and since the spirit of exile, the essential foreignness to the land, a struggle for higher forms of life against the confinement of the land and the time, is rooted in this history from its beginning."[11] A more recent example is the poetic work of the French-Jewish poet Edmond Jabès, which conveys the idea of exile as a mystical state of consciousness and connects between the book and the desert making them the Judaic place itself: "Le pays des Juifs est un texte sacré. . . . Le jardin est paroles; Le désert, écriture. Dans chaque grain de sable, un signe surprends."[12]

The tear from the place in the place itself is much more complex, and cannot be solved by a mental division between actual place and the book. The dialectic of book and land, and between land and exile, touches reality in its entirety. A wide range of solutions exist in modern Israel, all coping with the same old dilemma of the place.

Those who pretend to be the sole legitimate heirs of the Judaic legacy in modern Israel, that is, the orthodox, themselves seem to differ on the issue of the place. The difference between them is that which meets the eye. The ultraorthodox, on the one hand, sanctify the book and live in a book-cult that is said to disconnect them from the place and preserve a diasporic attitude toward Israel. On the other hand, there is *Gush Emunim*,[13] who sanctify the land to an extent that makes them appear as fetishizers—making the holy soil the realization of the book. However, these two religious groups have one basic thing in common, which is more telling than the seeming difference between them: they ostensibly resolve the tension between book and land by adhering to the book as the one ultimate reality.

The secular-Zionist Israelis stand between the religious book-oriented resolution and another no-tension resolution—that of the "Canaanite" ideological movement that was formed in the 1940s, and marginal as it was politically, had a distinct and influential voice in Israeli culture, literature, and art. The thrust of the Canaanite ideology was to discard Jewishness and its diasporic spirit altogether, and to return to pre-Jewish faith and identity that centers on locality and nativism. The Canaanites rejected any connection to Jewish legacy, and hailed Hebrew identity and its primordial autochtonic relation to the land. In this way, the two diametrically opposed resolutions to the dilemma of place, namely, the Canaanite and the orthodox, resemble each other. They both attempt to rid themselves of the dialectic of book and land—the orthodox by encapsulating the place in the book, and the Canaanite by doing the same, only with the land.

The Israeli "middle" wavers between these two resolutions, between book and land, between being *Am-Hasefer* and being *Am-Haaretz*. Therefore, it is not in itself resolved, but is most explicitly ridden with ambivalence. This state opens up a wide and paradoxical range of attitudes and inspires the ongoing discourse of secular-Zionist Israeli identity. The ambivalence characteristic of this discourse is not necessarily a sign of weakness, or thing to get rid of. It comes from and in fact expresses the deep core of Judaic understanding of what the place is. It draws from the powerful source of the book that tells the story in a way that gives the place as the home in the world, and at once disowns it for fear that the place would become the beginning and the end to identity.

NOTES

1. About the connection among perspective, distance, and *theoria,* see Peg Birmingham, "Local Theory," in *The Question of the Other,* edited by Arleen B. Dallery and Charles E. Scott (Albany: State University of New York Press, 1989), 205–12.

2. Ned Lukacher, *Primal Scenes* (Ithaca: Cornell University Press, 1986).

3. Emanuel Maier, "Torah as Movable Territory " *Annals of the Association of American Geographers* 65(1)(1975):18–23.

4. Abraham Shlonsky, "From Tomato to Symphony," in *Yalkut Eshel* (Tel Aviv: Sifriat Poalim, 1960) 237–41. (Hebrew)

5. Baruch Kurzweil, "On the Young Hebrews" in *Our New Literature —Continuity or Revolution.* Shocken, 1965.

6. For a discussion of the subversive Mosaic tradition in the Bible, which emphasizes wandering and losing the land and its possession as against the royalist Davidic tradition, see Harry Berger, Jr., "The Lie of the Land: Text Beyond Canaan," *Representations* 25 (Winter 1989):119–38. The following quote is from that article, p. 123: "The Old Testament ideologeme . . . sets the tent against the house, nomadism against agriculture, the wilderness against Canaan, wandering and exile against settlement, diaspora against the political integrity of a settled place."

7. Charles Olson, "Poetry and Truth," in *Muthologos,* vol. 2 (Bolinas, Calif.: Four Seasons Foundation, 1977), 7–54.

8. The following quote can also be referred back to the beginning of the present chapter, where the anthropologist is described as the one who approaches his own place as a spectator or a maker of *theoria*: "The intelligence that came from afar, whether the spatial kind from foreign countries or the temporal kind of tradition, possessed an authority which gave it validity, even when it was not subject to verification." Walter Benjamin, "The Story Teller," in *Illuminations* (New York: Schocken 1969), 89.

9. See the whole issue of *Cultural Anthropology* 3 (1)(1988), devoted to the question of place and voice, and specifically the introduction by Arjun Appadurai, "Place and Voice in Anthropological Theory," p. 16–20 in that issue.

10. Jacques Derrida, "Dialogue," in Richard Kearney, *Dialogues with Contemporary Continental Thinkers* (Manchester: Manchester University Press, 1984), 108.

11. Franz Rosenzweig, *Naharaim* (Jerusalem: Mosad Bialik [1919] 1977), 67. (Hebrew)

12. Edmond Jabès, *Le Livre de Questions* (Paris: Gallimard), 1963.

13. "The Bloc of the Faithful"—an extremist religious movement that has spearheaded the settlement in the territories after the 1967 War.

9

A Response from New York
Return of the Repressed?
JONATHAN BOYARIN

The quote from Robert Paine that opens the introduction to this volume suggests a fundamental irony. Paine says that "the people themselves . . . have been deterritorialized through the millennia." He means that they have continued to exist despite the loss of their national homeland. Yet it is ironic that the process of de-diasporization—"the predicament of homecoming," as an earlier set of essays in Israeli ethnography has it (Deshen and Shokeid 1974)—represents simultaneously an attempt to take up an interrupted continuity with ancient Israel, and a break with traditional diaspora Judaism. The process of ingathering, conceived as a return to a shared and collectively possessed land, is not only the fulfillment of a lack. It also involves shedding of habits of thinking, daily practices, and strategies for interaction with non-Jews that have been developed over the course of centuries.

All of these—the collection of the Jews of the world to the Jewish State of Israel; the identification of contemporary Israelis with ancient Israelites; the "modernizing" rejection of traditional Jewish religious and cultural frameworks—represent tendencies, not exhaustive or totalizing dictates. Each signals a key area of difference and struggle over the realization of Jewish identity at the end of the twentieth century.

Paine goes on to write that "they [the Jews] have restored themselves to the primordial territory." This language contains the suggestion—no doubt inadvertent but all the more effective for that—either that Israeli Jews are here acting as the agents and representatives of Jews the world over, or that those Jews who have *not* so restored themselves are in effect no longer counted. The suggestion is belied, of course, by the millions of Jews who choose not to migrate to Israel, and perhaps even more sharply by the hundreds of thousands of Israeli émigrés overseas (Shokeid 1988).

Such language, by which a usually careful and incisive observer such as Paine suggests that the Zionist notion of "the reversal of exile" has already been suggested, effectively complements the "suture" by which contemporary Israelis are seen as the direct inheritors of the ancient Israelites and their kingdoms. Groups promoting sharply contrasting ideologies have all joined in the attempt to use the ancient Israelites as an ideal model for the transformation of diaspora Jews into rooted Israelis. For the romantic agrarian socialists of the Second Aliyah, contemporary Bedouins were a model to be emulated; thus we have photographs of young Russian Jewish immigrants riding horses and wearing flowing robes. For the Temple Mount Faithful who are today still seeking ways to hasten the replacement of the Dome of the Rock with the Third Temple, and for their comrades who study at Yeshivat Ateret Cohanim preparing to assume their priestly duties there, the notion of restoration hangs on theocratic ritual. As different as these dreams and practices are, both are fundamentally dependent on realization in space—whether it be the open desert of the nomad or the specific and sacred space of the Temple Mount.

As to the third theme I suggested just above, the rejection of Jewish diaspora traditions by Zionist pioneers should not be confused with a successful abandonment of centuries of tradition. Jewish symbols, fears, and values continue to inform Israeli society at several levels. One is civic, as in the traffic safety campaign whose slogan is "and you shall drive [behave] near your neighbor as if he were yourself." Another is in the rhetoric that casts the contemporary political enemies of the State of Israel in the role of the eternal anti-Semite. Meanwhile the harangues of the prophets are available to dissident Israeli intellectuals, who sometimes liken the policies of the government to the disastrous chauvinism of ancient Israelite kings.

All this suggests an overarching tension—documented by the various chapters in this volume—between the pulls of Jewish and of Israeli identity. Certainly, the fact of living in a Jewish state affects the politics of identity. Certainly as well, the territorialization of identity is a key strategy in the attempt to turn Jews into Israelis (Boyarin 1992:chap. 7). But we must also remember that Jewish life in the diaspora is affected by the space within which it takes place, and draws on space for the construction of specific and resilient identities. Equally important, as the spring concatenation of Passover, Israeli Memorial Day, Holocaust Remembrance Day, and Independence Day remind us (Sivan 1991), Israeli identity is ultimately nothing without memory. While appeals to collective memory and projects for the elaboration of public memory are common to virtually every national project, the imperative to remember seems unusually strong in Judaism (Yerushalmi 1981; Funckenstein 1989).

These are themes I find most compelling in this volume—the tension, and often the rich interaction, between Israeli Jews and Jews in other global spaces today; the space of Israel as the resource for inventing an unbroken link with the biblical past; and the ambivalent legacy of Jewish memory, a rich yet awkward supplement to the symbolic bounds of the Israeli nation-state.

There is one more crucial theme, however, which is hardly discussed in this volume. In my understanding both of Israeli historical identity and of the dynamics of the Israeli-Palestinian conflict, the dispossession of the pre-1948 Palestinian residents—"the origins of the Palestinian refugee problem" (Morris 1987)—looms large. So fundamental is this history to any discussion of land and space in Israeli identity that it actually does break through, implicitly, in several of the chapter—in Katriel's retelling of oral accounts by socialist-Zionist pioneers; in Ben-David's summary reference to "the hostility of the surrounding Arab countries", in the Handelmans' reference to the structure of Yad Vashem, which implicitly criticizes that institution's message that "the evil [gentiles] are hidden from view", in Rabinowitz's mention that in a certain neighborhood, the Israeli name "Hakramim" neatly occupies the semantic space of the former Arabic "Kūrūm Reina." But even in the one chapter here that talks about Arabs as subjects—not just symbolic or moral problems for Israeli Jews—it would have been quite germane if Rabinowitz had explained to the reader that the Arabs of Nazareth are people who stayed when others left. Surely their sense of minority identity in the Jewish state is conditioned by their contacts with and their awareness of their fellows outside. The editors of the volume note that the chapters discuss a range of "others" with whom Israelis interact and construct their identity, including Moroccan Muslims and European "Greens." Again, to make the point as clearly as I can, I find the Palestinian diaspora to be conspicuously lacking from the list. Who better to listen to, if one's goal is "to problematize the taken-for-granted realities of Israeli space and place"? One of the best ways to do this (as the editors have done) is to recall the Arab place-names that have been supplanted by Israeli names, thus reminding us that every "place . . . is a palimpsest" (de Certeau 1984:109). In these palimpsests memory and territory, space and time come together to form the framework of contentious experience. In lifting, ever so slightly, the veil of memory over the contention for space in Israel/Palestine, the editors and contributors to this volume are not only contributing to the lively examination of space and place in contemporary anthropology (Appadurai 1988; Ferguson and Gupta 1992). They are indeed also participating in a "certain opening," a significant reconsideration of Israeli history. It is in that spirit that I turn to the individual chapters.

André Levy's chapter both marks and furthers the reclamation of particular ethnic heritages on the part of Israeli Jews roughly over the past two decades. It is a clear indication that becoming "Israeli" need not and often does not entail a complete divorce from the country of origin—even when that country is part of the "third world." Levy suggests his own debt to symbolic anthropology by suggesting that Moroccan Jews traveling from Israel to Morocco are less affected by "the structural features of the setting" than by their own frameworks of interpretation. But several of the topics described in Levy's ethnography—starting with the very possibility, on technical, financial, and political grounds, of Moroccan Israelis making such a returning pilgrimage—begs further analysis as part of the circulation of money, persons, and symbols within a regional political economy. What can the presence and reception of Israeli Jewish visitors tell us about the politics of Morocco? How does the particular place of Morocco in the Arab/Islamic world affect the responses by Israelis to such visits? Indeed, Levy's point that "No one . . . claimed that the trip was for relaxation" should lead us to consider the close interaction of structural and emotional determinants of tourism. Such further efforts would also promote the reintegration of Israel into the ethnography of the Middle East and North Africa, by anthropologists within and without Israel.

Obviously, of course, Levy's "Moroccan" Israelis are not just tourists. In a sense, when they go to Morocco they are returning home. The title of an earlier ethnographic account of Moroccan Jews in Israel receives an odd twist, as these travelers experience the predicament of another kind of homecoming. Many points in this encounter with the place of memory seem to demand much more elaboration than Levy has space for. Why, for example, is it that the place of the king seems to remain so stable in Morocco, such that, as Levy writes, "the [Jews'] patron–client relationship with the king remains unchanged" (cf. the extended analysis of Moroccan royal-religious authority in Combs-Schilling 1989)? What does the brief mention of Israeli tourists' encounters with Moroccan prostitutes suggest about the relations among power, ethnicity, domesticity, and gender? How are the Jews who stayed behind in Morocco affected by these contacts with their Israeli "cousin"?

I remain uneasy with the implications that these immigrants are rightfully, successfully, and happily Israelis, not Moroccan. Rather than assuming that "in the past, Jews were largely unconscious during their daily lives of the fears and anxieties to which they were subject in living together with Muslims," or that one informant should be taken at her word when she tells the ethnographer "that she became aware of the fear only after her immigration to Israel," we should be carefully attentive to the situations in which such claims are enunciated, and equally cautious in asserting that unconscious responses exist where they are not manifest.

Harvey Goldberg's chapter forcefully brings home the point that the Land of Israel is not the only "space" of consequence in Jewish life; indeed, its primary focus outside Israel fruitfully pushes at the boundaries of this volume. Goldberg subtly explores the linked issues of multiple national allegiance and gender-based metaphor. His chapter is also innovative in the way it focuses on a single individual for the exploration of space, and not only memory. The eloquent Raffaello, attempting to explain to the ethnographer from Israel how he could remain loyal to a country that had betrayed its Jews, states that "Even if she is a prostitute, she [Libya] is still our mother." Raffaello neatly distinguishes between the sentimental yet powerful ties of memory to the "motherland" and the practical, differently consequential ties of citizenship in the "fatherland" (a distinction that might be borne in mind when considering the Palestinian rhetoric of longing to return to lost homes).

One important determinant of spatial identity for many Jews outside Israel, like Raffaello, is precisely this sense of multiple homelands. Raffaello is attached to Libya, to Italy, and to Israel. Likewise, the Polish Jews in Paris whom I got to know during my doctoral fieldwork (Boyarin 1991) felt attachments to Poland, France, and Israel—all in powerful and ambivalent ways. The same might probably be said of most Jews in the twentieth century who have migrated from their birthplace to a new home other than Israel. The concepts of diaspora is stretched to its limit in these cases, acquiring a painful yet rich ambiguity. Jewish history might be categorized as a series of re-diasporizations, in which the balances among the textual and liturgical homeland (the Land of Israel), the place that grants a particular ethnic Jewish identity (Spain, Morocco, Eastern Europe, India), and the difficult new "home" (Israel, France, the United States) are constantly being negotiated. Because he is acutely conscious of this negotiation, and because he is unembarrassed about his multiple loyalties, Raffaello is an unusually eloquent exponent of the dynamics of Jewish historical identity.

Goldberg helpfully delineates various forms of sacred space (such as the synagogue and the cemetery), suggesting a few of the outlines for a broader comparative study of spatial determinants in Jewish life. While the Land of Israel certainly stands for millennia as *the* sacred space of Jewish life, the domestic and communal spaces in Jewish communities around the world are also marked as separate and special ,whether by religious law, legend, or familial affect (cf. Bahloul 1992, on memories of domestic space among Algerian Jewish families). But even in the situation studied by Goldberg, the very notion of Jewish sacred space always seems to return, albeit metaphorically, to the Land of Israel. Thus, when Raffaello wanted to re-create a trace memorial to the Tripoli Jewish cemetery in Rome, he had some sand brought

from the Libyan shore to be integrated into the monument. Surely this re-
calls the bit of "earth from the Holy Land" that pious Jews like to have
buried with them, when it is impossible to be actually buried in Israel.

The editors' chapter draws on insights from ritual anthropology on one
hand, and from the sociology of administered groups on the other, while remaining free of the abstract theory of the former and the condescension of
the latter. The analysis of proliferating holy sites in Israeli development
towns is a moving examination of the autonomous responses of people subjected to highly centralized social policy. (Given the concerns of this volume,
I would stress the spatial politics implicit in the term "central planning", as
Ben-Ari and Bilu make abundantly clear, the planned development towns
were for those who needed developing, not for the planner.)

Themes in "Saints' Sanctuaries" echo Goldberg's chapter in striking ways,
most notably the focus on the creation of "diasporic" sacred space inside Israel. Thus the way Rabbi David u-Moshe's grave was "transported" through
dream communications to Israel is strikingly reminiscent of the much more
urbane process by which Raffaello planned to create a replica of the Tripoli-
tanian Jewish cemetery. On a different plane of inter-Jewish comparison, the
reestablishment of the "traditional pattern of a community with "its' own
tsaddiq" among North African Jews in Israel might fruitfully be compared
to the appearance of a North American Hasidic leader known as the *Bo-
stoner rebe*—whose followers now include a group living together in a neighborhood of Jerusalem!

The saints were "abandoned" once, but having been "refound" in the development towns, they evidently will not be left again for the foreseeable future. Rather they are used to buttress the new ethnic place of the North
African Jews in Israel. There is thus a striking disjuncture between the outcome of the original tension between leaving Morocco and coming to Israel
on one hand, and the later decision (which Ben-Ari and Bilu see as being me-
diated by the supernatural injunction to create a sanctified space for the
saint) to remain in the immigrant neighborhood rather than disperse again.
Here in the geographical and social margins of Jewish Israel, traditional resources are marshalled to perpetuate alternative "centers" of particular identity grounded in commemoration. This points again to the need for
articulation of the local-symbolic and state-hegemonic levels within which
people contest their relations to each other and to the space they share.

Handelman and Shamgar Handelman exhaustively problematize the
problem of Jewish commemoration. Their studies of Israeli state iconogra-
phy are important contributions to the anthropological study of contemporary nationalism. They ably demonstrate that the sanctification of the land
of the contemporary Israeli state is a *project* ("military memorialism is revi-

talized continuously"), one at least as difficult and critical as the archeological reconstruction of the land's history.

Yet by the very force of the detail with which they document the forms and dilemmas of commemoration in Israeli space, do they not perpetuate—effectively if not intentionally—the effacememt of Palestinian traces in the Israeli landscape? What is the effect of speaking of "contested space" without mentioning who contests it?

Ultimately the Handelmans seem to hold back from analyzing the way in which the struggle for commemoration is embedded in the struggle for symbolic and military possession of the land. This may help explain why their third footnote implies a direct link between "Judaic traditions" and "Zionist usage" concerning death, commemoration and burial—a link which may or may not exist, but would in any case need to be demonstrated. Curiously, the genealogical reference back to "Judaic traditions" is attached to a passage that has emphasized the specific link between military burial and territoriality in modern nationalism per se—which might indeed suggest the further exploration of possible links between biblical notions of sacred land and modern nationalism.

Meticulous as this essay is, it deals almost primarily with the aspect of production of national symbols, and only secondarily with their reception. Anecdotal evidence suggests that military symbols are not always taken with the same intentions as they are produced. Thus, while it may generally be true that "All graves conform to army regulations," at least one Israeli mother has fought long and hard to have the inscription, "Killed in Operation Peace for the Galilee" removed from her son's headstone. She was one of the many Israelis who had been bitterly opposed to the Israeli incursion into Lebanon, and refused to have her son's death sanctified in this shallow way. In this one case at least, "the stories generated by the headstone text" could hardly be said to have "articulated easily with greater national landscapes."

The Handelmans' data suggest several points of possible allusion to traditional Jewish narrative themes. By "possible allusion," of course, I'm fudging a bit myself: whether these hints are received as such by Israelis is hardly for me to say. But the extraordinary power of biblical models in legitimating countless practices of those cultures which hold the Bible as a central and sacred text make even such possible associations worth considering. It seems worth pointing out, for instance, that "the little head cushion" made of stone is reminiscent of the stone pillow on which the patriarch Jacob laid his head when he went wandering—if only to have readers ultimately reject this suggestion. Other allusions are quite explicit, and yet curiously ironic—such as the "pillar of fire" that commemorates, not the Israelite Exodus from

Egypt, but rather the successful *conquest* of the Sinai by Israeli armed forces in 1967.

"Landscapes of Sacrifice" is a striking example of the power of anthropological analysis when it brings together functional and symbolic perspectives. The authors are well aware of the complex interactions between memory and embodiment. Their observation that the absence of the body of the person to be commemorated called for "complex metaphors of substitution" could and should be addressed by students of the poetics of commemoration in a range of cultural settings. The metaphoric reference to a "decapitated" jeep is immediately followed by the example of a memorial that "asks the visitor to enter the body of the plane" of the type from which parachuters jumped to their death. Thus the instruments of war become, not only part of the landscape, not only *aides-memoire,* but material parts of the symbolic body of the nation.

Ben-David's chapter on *tiyul* describes a central moment in the wedding between Israeli Jews and the Land of Israel. Not only the Society for the Protection of Nature in Israel, but thousands of tour buses, jeeps, and rubber inner tubes are vehicles by which Israeli civilians are regularly deployed out and across the land, reenacting their inseparability from it. Yet Ben-David's chapter seems marked by a fundamental ambivalence. Does she assume that the landscape is indeed "natural," or already marked by millennia of settlement? To the extent that the landscape in question is regarded as a part of nature, the role it plays in the Israeli collective imagination may have to do primarily with the problematics of identity in an advanced industrial civilization, "divorced" as it were from the life-giving realities of the environment. To the extent that even this desert has been marked by millennia of human habitation, the Israeli footsteps in the sand help mark it *now* as part of the Israeli national state—a rather different issue.

The editors are justified, I think, in wanting to stress Ben-David's point that the modern opposition between nature and culture is at least as operative in the SPNI hikes as is the opposition between "our land" and "their land." Certainly the particular region in which the main hike she discusses takes place—the Arava, an extreme desert region at the southern end of the country—would lend itself to this interpretation. The Arava has been less than hospitable even to the Bedouin, who are specialists at making do with scattered grazing and less water. Furthermore, the fact that the society for the Preservation of Nature in Israel finds itself at loggerheads not only with the Voice of America but with the Israeli air force effectively argues territorial assertion. Indeed, as far as biblical sanctions or imperatives go, the Arava is *not* "*Eretz Yisrael,*" lying outside the southern bounds of the land. Yet in other parts of the country, groups of Israeli nature lovers troop—respectfully and carefully, to be sure—through Palestinian fields ruled by military occupation (Langfur 1992). And Israeli Palestinians find it ironic that they are forbidden by Israeli conservation laws to collect wild *za'atar,* the thyme they consider their "national spice." Is the nature–culture opposition quite the same in these cases?

Tamar Katriel's "Remaking Place" focuses on the founding myth of the Zionist agricultural pioneers. She takes the notion of place as palimpsest and shows us just how rapidly, in terms of calendar years, layer can be added on to layer. The very notion of a landscape becoming "more and more densely dotted with local-historical museums" suggests that perhaps soon the museums will crowd out the spaces they represent, in a process that the French theorist Baudrillard calls "the precession of simulacra" (Baudrillard 1983). Thus Katriel cites (I'm tempted to write "sites") the suggestive slogan of the museum she analyzes: "The valley is a dream." But, far from indulging in ungrounded postmodern theory-slinging, Katriel's analysis continues to rework the representations of a very local history.

Her theme is postmodern in a very prosaic sense: the process of museumification, that is, of the reflective invention of a codified collective past for the kibbutzim that can be presented as a consumer spectacle, has taken place in a very short time. Europeans might think that the theme park at Colonial Williamsburg reenacts a historical heritage that is ridiculously narrow, only two hundred years old (Gable et al. 1992); but the kibbutz museums enshrine the heritage of a generation whose last representatives are only now passing away.

All these local-history museums reinforce the waning image of the pioneer generation. Of course, these grandparents of contemporary Israelis were not "the first people who came to the land [of Israel]." It is entirely understandable for Israeli adults to speak of the pioneers in those terms, but in fact it is hardly more true than the child's reply, "Oh yes, you mean Adam and Eve." Actually, since *ha'aretz* can mean both "the Land of Israel" and (especially in biblical Hebrew) "the earth," the child's interpretation was culturally accurate, whereas the adult's implication of an "Edenic [and hence previously uninhabited, virgin] quality [to] the place" constituted another iteration of a historical distortion.

Katriel reports a bit of narrative told by one of the elderly museum guides to a group of schoolchildren. By way of helping the children imagine the biblical patriarchs, the narrative turns contemporary Bedouins into models of biblical Jews. Abraham is made to speak Arabic, saying "tefadalu" to the three angels, and granting them stereotypic Arab hospitality. This association has a venerable history, stretching back at least as far as claim by nineteenth-century philologist Ernest Renan that "we may affirm that, concerning the most important things, an Israelite of Samuel's time and a nineteenth-century Bedouin would be able to understand each other" (Renan

1863:464). Both the Bedouin and the Israelite patriarch are removed to a time "impossible" to imagine in linear time. Or perhaps they are situated not so much in a "time-before-time," as Katriel seems to understand the guide's discourse, as a place outside of time—a diorama in a museum.

The conclusion to Katriel's chapter raises a very complex issue. Why is it that, precisely during the years of political ascendancy of the right-wing Likud Party, when Oriental Jews have come to constitute the majority of the Israeli Jewish population, when the kibbutzim have lost their early function as moral and practical mainstays of the state, and the population is over-whelmingly urban—precisely in these years the heritage of the secular so-cialist agricultural pioneers is not simply becoming irrelevant, but instead reconfigured? Does the boom in kibbutz nostalgia neatly signal that the kib-butzim have seen their day, or does it presage a new configuration in which their central place in Israeli public history will be consolidated?

Dan Rabinowitz's study of Natzerat Illit is a sobering look at one of the few parts of contemporary Israel that could conceivably be called "residen-tially integrated." It points out that the often tortuous working out of the re-lation between space and identity occurs not only on the national and symbolic levels, but also on the everyday level of housing, shopping, and commuting to work. Here as well, questions of perspective—those of the ac-tor and those of the analyst, who cannot be neatly separated out when Is-raeli scholars write about Israel—must affect the account of inclusions and exclusions, symbolic power and symbolic slights. Ironically, the one chapter that deals explicitly with the Arab presence in Israel also reminds us that there are no Palestinian Arab scholars included in this volume. Like several of the chapters, Rabinowitz's takes up numerous themes that could fruitfully be explored further. One is the emphasis on public transportation in relation to control of space—which, by way of tying in Rabinowitz's chapter to Ben-David's, also informs us that the Israeli national bus cooperative Egged once "had a *Tiyulim* department for educational exploration tours of hidden sites and landscapes of the newly discovered homeland." Equally suggestive—perhaps because I find it confirmed by my own memories of being warmly received in Israeli Arab villages—is Rabinowitz's point that "hospitality is performed and displayed as a sign of strength, a mental note of dominance and ownership." But this "performance" is clearly a poetic substitute for ac-tual political and economic control (cf. Lavie 1990).

Rabinowitz attributes greater Jewish resistance to the "phenomenon" of collective Arab presence than Arab resistance to Jews largely to the fact that Arabs "are not as trained as their Jewish fellow citizens in interpreting trick-les of individual families in terms of movements with dynamic intensity and collective intent." This may be true, although their cousins in the occupied West Bank are by now very well trained at interpreting the ominous portent of "trickles of individual families" moving into trailers near their villages. The point is that the comparison is presented as a simple cultural contrast, without any overt reference to the differential power available to the "two sides." If Natzerat Illit Arabs talk less about the threat of large numbers of Jews moving in, it may not be because of their own sense of secure identity, but rather because they sense themselves powerless to do anything about it. After all, it is on behalf of the Jewish residents of the town, not the local Arabs, that the Ministry of the Interior took steps aimed at creating a "buffer zone around the built area of Natzerat Illit . . . [thus] arresting potential encroachment of spontaneous Arab development" (n. 9). Rabinowitz finally does refer to "the appropriation of the land where the whole town stands from Arabs to Jews," but only as the articulation of an "alternative view"— in the interests of pluralism, perhaps?

Zali Gurevitch attempts to use theory—"seeing"—as a way to overcome the presumptive blindness of the native. His strategy reflects an intellectual temperament that is closer to Katriel's than to any other author's in this volume. Where Katriel speaks cogently of "the double-layered act of making place," Gurevitch explicitly announces his choice—not arbitrary to be sure—to double the origins of place, referring simultaneously to the culture of Zionism and to the biblical images of the land.

That the two sites Gurevitch has chosen are appropriate ones can be shown through reference back to the "Yankelevitch" character in Katriel's chapter. The Jewish pioneer insists on walking on the land where "the prophet Elijah, and King Solomon and King David and . . . all the prophets" had walked. The Arab, who is represented in the story about Yankelevitch as having lived on the land continuously, *and hence unreflectingly,* doesn't understand why the "crazy Jew" fights progress. Only the Jewish immigrant, filled with the consciousness of the "double site," simultaneously returnee and pioneer, can fully appreciate the land.

Gurevitch presents the Zionist choice of "return" to Palestine—and hence of the double site—in terms of a very strong sense of agency with regard to place, arguing that "The power of the story . . . is in its adoption, not in its inevitability." There is a fine irony here. For Gurevitch, the Zionist project is in some ways derailed by the textually influenced choice of Palestine as the place of the Jewish homeland. The traditional Jewish tension between book and place trips up the Zionist attempts to transcend book-identity through a textless rooting (cf. Berger 1989). The contradictory nature of Israeli identity—torn between book and territory—transcends the conflicts of colonialism.

The most important manifestation of book-consciousness, for Gurevitch, is in the continuing powerful moral call of what he calls "the voice," a prophetic demand that militates against the idolization of any place: "the place is of the voice and not voice and not vice versa." How thoroughly or how long that voice will continue to be heard in the Jewish state is another state, however. There are indications that as the succeeding generations are more and more rooted in the territorial state they become less and less conscious of the notion of divine transcendence. Indeed, one young Israeli soldier serving in Lebanon is reported to have asked a friend whether it was possible to pray to God there.

Gurevitch seems to short-circuit very real differences between different political-theological trends among "Orthodox" Jews in Israel. He claims that the ultraorthodox anti-Zionists ultimately are like the national chauvinists of *Gush Emunim*, in that both adhere "to the book as to the one ultimate reality." I would claim to the contrary that for *Gush Emunim*, the land itself has become the ultimate reality of Judaism, and the demands of the book are subsumed to the need to maintain territorial control (Lustick 1988).

The chapter—and hence the volume—concludes appropriately enough on a powerful note of ambivalence toward "place." There is more to be said about the relations not only between place and voice, but between place and state. Not only the geopolitics of Israeli Jewish existence, but its experiential character as well would be quite different if the Zionist dream had been merely re*place*ment, and not the establishment of a Jewish state. Hegemony—the ability to patrol geographic and ethnic boundaries, the monopoly on legitimized use of violence—seems to go hand in hand with more exclusive claims to space than those exerted by non-statist group identities. Such points henceforth are and should be open to debate. Indeed, the very fact that these ideas are expressed for a broader intellectual readership by an (apparently) "secular" Israeli is of both ethnographic and political interest. The various explorations in this volume—looking still further into the paradox between the book that helped bring Jews to Palestine, and the troubled land that stubbornly refuses to be monolithically remade into a reflection of anyone's ideas—constitute a potential, and potentially hopeful, development in at least one Israeli culture of space.

ACKNOWLEDGMENT

This afterword draws on research which I conducted as a Social Science Research Council/MacArthur Foundation Fellow in International Peace and Security.

REFERENCES

Appadurai, Arjun. 1988. "Introduction: Place and Voice in Anthropological Theory." *Cultural Anthropology* 3(1):16–20.

Bahloul, Joelle. 1992. *La Maison de la memoire: ethnologie d'une demeur judeo-arabe an Algerie.* Paris: Editions Metailie.

Baudrillard, Jean. 1983. *Simulations.* New York: Semiotext(e).

Berger, Harry. 1989. "The Lie of the Land: The Text Beyond Canaan." *Representations* 25:119–38.

Boyarin, Jonathan. 1992. *Storm from Paradise: The Politics of Jewish Memory.* Minneapolis: University of Minnesota Press.

———. 1991. *Polish Jews in Paris: The Ethnography of Memory.* Bloomington: Indiana University Press.

Combs-Schilling, Elaine. 1989. *Sacred Performances: Islam, Sexuality, and Sacrifice.* New York: Columbia University Press.

de Certeau, Michel. 1984. *The Practice of Everyday Life.* New York: Columbia University Press.

Deshen, Shlomo, and Moshe Shokeid. 1974. *The Predicament of Homecoming.* Ithaca: Cornell University Press.

Ferguson, James, and Akhil Gupta (eds.). 1992. "Theme Issue: Space, Identity, and the Politics of Difference." *Cultural Anthropology* 7(1).

Funkenstein, Amos. 1989. "Collective Memory and Historical Consciousness." *History and Memory* 1(1):5–26.

Gable, Eric, Richard Handler, and Anna Lawson. 1992. "On the Uses of Relativism: Fact, Conjecture, and Black and White Histories at Colonial Williamsburg." *American Ethnologist* 19(4):791–805.

Langfur, Stephen. 1992. *Confession from a Jericho Jail.* New York: Grove Weidenfeld.

Lavie, Smadar. 1990. *The Poetics of Military Occupation.* Berkeley: University of California Press.

Lustick, Ian. 1988. *For the Land and the Lord: Jewish Fundamentalism in Israel.* New York: Council on Foreign Relations.

Morris, Benny. 1987. *The Birth of the Palestinian Refugee Problem, 1947–1949.* New York: Cambridge University Press.

Renan, Ernest. 1863. *Historie generale et systeme compare des langues Semitiques.* Paris: Michel Levy Freres.

Shokeid, Moshe. 1988. *Children of Circumstances: Israeli Emigrants in New York.* Ithaca: Cornell University Press.

Sivan, Eyal. 1991. *Izkor.* Documentary feature film.

Yerushalmi, Yosef Haim. 1981. *Zakhor: Jewish History and Jewish Memory.* Seattle: University of Washington Press.

Epilogue
(Three Years Later)
YORAM BILU AND EYAL BEN-ARI

This short epilogue was written almost three years after the other contributions to the volume had been collected. The space of time attesting to the odyssey of this compilation on its way to publication has made us more aware of the extent to which Israeli public discourses on land and territory are historically situated. Along these lines it may be suitable to more generally situate the present collection within the major historical vicissitudes in the narratives and discourses about space and place in Israel.

Clearly, the overarching reference to most Israeli public discourses on place should be the sweeping success of the Zionist movement in realizing its territorial aspirations. No more than five decades after its emergence on the world scene, with some of its first adherents still alive to witness their dream come true, it was able to transform its evocative motto, "a land without people to a people without land," into a political reality. Of course, the gross distortions brought about by the realization of this maxim have become the major sources for the struggles and belligerence that accompanied the actualization of the Zionist dream. This point holds for the periods before and particularly after the establishment of the state of Israel. But beyond the naked political conflict with the Palestinians and the Arab countries, the salience of the territorial prescription in Zionism and the imminent danger that it become a superordinate worldview to the exclusion of other values, have imbued the construction and maintenance of the Jewish Israeli identity with paradoxes and tensions (the reverberations of which are subtly but recurrently represented in this volume, especially in the contributions of Gurevitch and Boyarin).

The Zionist glorification of territory and boundaries should be assessed in the historic context of the rise of the modern nation-state. In this broader

231

context, the secularization of political sentiments and the shift from personal
to territorial allegiances gave rise to the sacralization of territory (Schama
1989). In the Zionist "civil religion" of Israel (Bellah 1967; Liebman and
Don-Yehiye 1983) this sacralization, cultivated already in the first years of
the Jewish pre-state society (*Yishuv*), has been a basic tenet permeating the
lives of Israeli Jews in a myriad of forms and participating in constructing
their social reality.

Thus the mystification of the landscape in artistic creation and through
the archeological and historical reconstruction of ancient Jewish geography,
and the apotheosis of "working the land" have been the twin pillars on
which the territorial ethos of Zionism has rested since the movement's formative years. An elaborate system of socialization practices has been insti-
tuted, beginning in the pre-state Jewish society, to inculcate this ethos
(Almog 1994). Among these practices one may enumerate the emphasis on
nature, geography, and agriculture in the school system syllabus; the exalta-
tion of the hike as a "spiritual journey" (Ben-David in this volume); the
transformation of major religious holidays into nature-related or agricultural festivals (particularly in the kibbutz movement); and the establishment
of national sites—reconstructed archeological excavations, museums (Katriel in this volume), monuments, and cemeteries (Handelman and Shamgar-
Handelman in this volume)—commemorating heroic moments in the history
of the country, and their transformation into "sacred shrines" and centers of
civil pilgrimage.

The unselfconscious attachment to the land that this massive indoctrina-
tion created was tested time and again during the military ordeals that the
Jewish society had to withstand before and after the establishment of Israel.
The national euphoria in the aftermath of the Six-Day War, with the reap-
propriation of the lost mythic and historic centers that figured so promi-
nently in Jewish collective memory, may be viewed as the apex of this
attachment. Dialectically, however, this renewed alliance with the cherished
lieux de memoire (Nora 1984), and the national and mystico-religious revi-
talization that it entailed, also marked a process of disillusionment and demythologization which, from a present-day perspective, might be deemed
the beginning of a paradigmatic shift in "spatial sentiments." While critical
voices against this taken-for-granted, unconditional attachment were always
present in the Israeli political discourse on land, they became louder and
clearer during the 1970s and 1980s, when the Yom Kippur and the Lebanon
wars and the Palestinian uprising (Intifada) gradually eroded the value of
commitment to, and glorification of territory.

Risking an oversimplification, it might be argued that the post-1973 war
years constituted the critical period in which the Zionist ethos (particularly
in its secular-socialist version) began to lose its hegemonic position among

wide segments of Israeli society. Clearly, the revival in Israel of such practices as Maghrebi hagiolatry, discussed in this volume by Ben-Ari and Bilu,
should be counted among the rival ideologies that have gained salience at
that time. These alternative ideologies included a "return" to orthodox Judaism, participation in mystical cults, or turning to esoteric modes of healing (Aviad 1983; Beit-Hallahmi 1992). Against this background, it is not
coincidental that the 1970s also witnessed the emergence of subversive
"counternarratives," which challenged the national myths associated with
some of the most prominent sites in the Zionist civil religion (Aronoff 1989;
Zerubavel 1994). The deconstruction and demythologization of these hegemonic myths, particularly evident in the growing devaluation of the core
narratives of national sites such as Tel-Hai and Masada (see Schwartz et al.
1986; Zerubavel 1994), have persisted through the 1980s and 1990s. In
many ways, these critical voices, and the postmodern *zeitgeist* underlying
them, have informed this compilation.

Excluding Gurevitch's and Boyarin's discussions of the existential paradoxes of Jewish Israeli identity in relation to place and Rabinowitz's case of
Israeli Arabs, the six remaining chapters deal with Jewish constructions of
place in two broad contexts. One set of chapters discusses various spatial
representations of key symbols or key scenarios in Israel's civil religion: the
hike (Ben-David), national death in wars and the Holocaust (the Handelmans), and pioneer settlement (Katriel). The other set deals with the construction and maintenance of "spatial sentiments" among North African
Jews and their descendants (Ben-Ari and Bilu, Goldberg, Levy).

The concern of the first group of chapters with the problematization of
the official discourse on space and place in Israel is reflected in the very selection of the nation's most cherished monuments and shrines as suitable objects for analysis and deconstruction. It is not surprising that topics related
to collective memory and the construction and "sanctification" of space
were not part of the agenda of Israeli social science before the 1980s. Even
if we do not accept that Israel of the 1990s is a "post-Zionist society," the
critical stance of the researchers toward the symbolic inscriptions of the
Zionist ethos on the land, based on skepticism, distancing, detachment, and
a modicum of irony, seems to be constituted by (but also constitutive of) the
demythologization process charted above.

The museumification of pioneer settlements, to take one example, may be
viewed as a present chapter in the ongoing endeavor to glorify heroic projects, so characteristic of Israel in its formative years. But in alerting us to the
hasty and unrefined nature of the construction of the settlement myth, Katriel not only presents the scientific ideal of seeking to objectify and demys-
tify value-laden phenomena, but also represents a broader social *zeitgeist*
promoting a more skeptical and cynical view of the nation's exalted myths

and monuments. Highlighting the lucrative aspect of the project, the museum as business (given the desperate economic situation of many kibbutzim), and the very mummification of a way of life that until recently was unquestionably accepted as an exemplary model for the rest of society, add an ironic twist to the analysis.

Similarly the hike, as cultivated in the Society for the Preservation of Nature in Israel, may be viewed as a current version of the practice of foot trekking and journeys that the *Yishuv* school system and youth movements, and later military circles, transformed into a semireligious experience. While here the continuity is apparent, the present-day hike is suffused with ecological themes that are quite divorced from the classic concerns of the Zionist ideology. Moreover, the current custom of many young Israeli Jews to trek in Asia or South America combines the actualization of this older practice with wider (perhaps global) patterns of travel.

Moving to the Maghrebi group of chapters, an intriguing tension may be discerned between our work on the revival of Moroccan saint veneration in Israeli development towns and the contributions by Levy and Goldberg. While our work was written in the mid-1980s, the other two depict more recent developments, and their comparison sheds light on another aspect of the shifting conceptualizations of space and place in Israeli society. We interpreted the "migration" of Jewish Moroccan *tsaddiqim* to Israeli development towns as a multifaceted process in which past Maghrebi traditions are assertively revived to articulate a set of experiences that bespeak of a growing sense of localism and rootedness in the community. In other words, the centripetal movement that places key cultural figures of the Moroccan past in the Israeli scene brings to completion the transformation of the newcomers from Maghrebi Jews into full-blown Israelis.

Levy makes a similar argument in claiming that in visiting Morocco, Israelis of Moroccan extraction discover how detached they have become from their former heritage and how deeply ingrained they are in Israeli culture and way of life. But the Israeli visitors to Morocco come to their native land as pilgrims no less than as tourists. Their itinerary is partially determined by the "sacred map" of popular saint sanctuaries scattered all over the country. Thus, the danger exists that the phenomenon of migrant saints centripetally following their adherents to the Holy Land will be stopped and even reversed. Israelis in growing numbers will be moving in the centrifugal direction, from the holy centers of Zion to the peripheral diasporic saint sanctuaries. Goldberg's chapter—a case study of a Libyan Jew whose sentiments toward his native country are spatially represented in Rome no less than in Jerusalem—may be viewed as reflecting the same centrifugal process. The mushrooming of journeys of Israeli youth to the central sites of the Jewish Holocaust in Poland, which in recent years have probably become the most important socialization vehicle in the Jewish Israeli civil religion, may also be taken as an indication of the decreasing importance of the "proximal" Israeli-based sites in constructing the Israeli identity. Let us be clear that while we do not envisage a wholesale desertion of sites located in Israel, we are witnesses to a more complex attachment and movement of people to places outside the geopolitical boundaries of this country.

To conclude, maybe it is not too far-fetched to contend that the gradual erosion of the unselfconscious attachment to territories and locations in Israeli public discourse was a prerequisite for the political process of reconciliation and peace that is taking place now among Israel, the Palestinians, and some of the Arab countries.

REFERENCES

Almog, Oz. 1994. *The "Sabras"—A Sociological Profile*. Unpublished Ph.D. dissertation, University of Haifa.

Aronoff, Myron J. 1989. *Israeli Visions and Divisions: Cultural Change and Political Conflict*. New Brunswick, N.J.: Transaction.

Aviad, Janet. 1983. *Return to Judaism*. Chicago: University of Chicago Press.

Beit-Hallahmi, Benjamin. 1992. *Despair and Deliverance: Private Salvation in Contemporary Israel*. Albany: State University of New York Press.

Bellah, Robert N. 1967. Civil Religion in America. *Daedalus* 96:1–21.

Liebman, Charles S., and Eliezer Don-Yehiya. 1983. *Civil Religion in Israel*. Berkeley: University of California Press.

Norra, Pierre. 1984. *Les Lieux de Memoire*, vol. 2, *La Republique*. Paris: Gallimard.

Schama, Simon. 1989. *Citizens*. New York: Knopf.

Schwartz, Barry, Yael Zerubavel, and Bernice Barnett. 1986. The Recovery of Masada: A Study in Collective Memory. *The Sociological Quarterly* 27:147–64.

Zerubavel, Yael. 1994. The Death of Memory and the Memory of Death. *Alpaim* 10:42–67. (Hebrew)

Contributors

Eyal Ben-Ari is associate professor at the Department of Sociology and Anthropology and senior research fellow at the Harry S. Truman Research Institute of the Hebrew University of Jerusalem. He received his Ph.D. from the Department of Social Anthropology of the University of Cambridge and carries out research on Japanese society and culture, the anthropology of organizations and social and cultural aspects of the military. His most recent publications include *Changing Japanese Suburbia* (London: Kegan Paul International) and a forthcoming volume *Body Projects in Japanese Childcare* (London: Curzon).

Orit Ben-David is a doctoral candidate at the Department of Sociology and Anthropology of Tel-Aviv University. Her current research interests involve cultural aspects of organ transplants in Israel. Her MA thesis explored the dynamics of The Society for the Protection of Nature in Israel.

Yoram Bilu holds a joint appointment with the Department of Psychology and the Department of Sociology and Anthropology at the Hebrew University of Jerusalem from which he received his Ph.D. in 1978. His research interests include psychological anthropology, ethnopsychiatry, dreaming and culture, folk-religion in Israel, and Moroccan Jews. His recent publications include *Without Bounds: The Life and Death of Rabbi Ya'acov Wazana* (Jerusalem: Magnes Press, 1993) and "Culture and Mental Health in Israel" (in *Culture and Mental Health, an International Perspective*, I. Al-Issa (ed.), Madison: International Universities Press, 1995).

Jonathan Boyarin lives is New York City. He has written and edited several books, recently including *Thinking in Jewish* and *Palestine and Jewish History*. He currently studies at Yale Law School.

Harvey E. Goldberg is professor in the Department of Sociology and Anthropology at the Hebrew University of Jerusalem. His research concerns ethnicity in Israeli society and the social and cultural history of North African Jewry. His most recent books are *Jewish Life in Muslim Libya: Rivals and Relatives* (Chicago: University of Chicago Press) and an edited volume: *Sephardi and Middle Eastern Jewries: History and Culture in the Modern Era* (Bloomington: Indiana University Press).

Zali Gurevitch is senior lecturer at the Department of Sociology and Anthropology of the Hebrew University of Jerusalem. His studies focus on the anthropology of place and language in Israeli society, and on the phenomenology of conversation, literature and culture. He has published essays in both areas, and is currently completing a book entitled *The Break of Conversation.*

Don Handelman is professor in the Department of Sociology and Anthropology at The Hebrew University of Jerusalem. His research focuses on national symbolism, on myth and ritual in South India, and on theories of play and bureaucracy. He has been a Fellow of the Netherlands Institute For Advanced Study (NIAS), the Swedish Collegium For Advanced Study (SCASSS), and the Institute For Advanced Studies at The Hebrew University, as well as Academy of Finland visiting professor at the University of Helsinki and Distinguished Visiting Scholar at the University of Adelaide. Among his recent publications are, *Models and Mirrors: Towards an Anthropology of Public Events* (Cambridge University Press, 1990) and, coauthored with David Shulman, *God Inside-Out: Siva's Game of Dice* (Oxford University Press, in press).

André Levy is a lecturer at the Department of Behavioral Sciences of Ben-Gurion University. He received his Ph.D. from the Department of Sociology and Anthropology of the Hebrew University in 1996. He is currently involved in research dealing with the historical and cultural origins of saint veneration in Morocco.

Tamar Katriel is associate professor at the University of Haifa, holding a joint appointment at the Department of Communication and the Department of Education. She received her PhD from the Department of Speech Communication at the University of Washington, Seattle, and her research has been concerned with cultural patterns of communication in Israeli and Americn society. She is author of *Talking Straight: 'Dugri' Speech in Israel Sabra Culture* (Cambridge: Cambridge University Press, 1986); *Communal Webs: Communication and Culture in Contemporary Israel* (Albany: SUNY

Press, 1991) and *Performing the Past: An Ethnography of Israeli Settlement Museums* (New Jersey: Erlbaum and Associates, forthcoming).

Dan Rabinowitz, who obtained his Ph.D in social anthropology from the University of Cambridge in 1990, teaches anthropology at the Department of Sociology and Anthropology at the Hebrew University in Jerusalem. His research interests include ethnicity, nationalism, transnationalism, critique of liberalism, Palestinian citizens of Israel, environmental issues and the history of anthropology. His recent work includes *Overlooking Nazareth* (forthcoming in 1996 at the University of Cambridge Press) and *Anthropology and the Palestinians* (forthcoming in 1996 at Hakibbutz Hameukhad and the Centre of Arab Israeli Studies).

The late **Lea Shamgar-Handelman** was associate professor in the Department of Sociology and Anthropology and in the School of Education of The Hebrew University, and a senior researcher in the Institute for the Study of Innovation in Education at The Hebrew University. She received her Ph.D. in Sociology from The Hebrew University. Her research focused on childhood and the state, family organization, and sociologies of death. She had been a Fellow of the Netherlands Institute For Advanced Study (NIAS) and of the Swedish Collegium For Advanced Study (SCASSS), a Fulbright visiting professor at the University of Minnesota and a visiting professor at the University of Helsinki. Among her publications are, *Israeli War Widows: Beyond the Glory of Heroism* (Bergin & Garvey, 1986), *Childhood as a Social Phenomenon: Israel* (European Centre for Social Welfare Policy and Research, 1990), and "Family sociology in a small academic community: family research and theory in Israel," in *Marriage and Family Review* (forthcoming).

Index